Interpretation and Bible
Essays on Truth in Literature

Sean McEvenue

A Michael Glazier Book
THE LITURGICAL PRESS
Collegeville, Minnesota

A Michael Glazier Book published by The Liturgical Press

Cover design by David Manahan, O.S.B. Gospel Book of Schäftlarn: St. Mark, Bayerische Staatsbibliothek, Munich.

1   2   3   4   5   6   7   8   9

Library of Congress Cataloging-in-Publication Data

McEvenue, Sean E.
  Interpretation and Bible : essays on truth in literature /
Sean McEvenue.
    p.   cm.
  "A Michael Glazier book."
  Includes bibliographical references.
  ISBN 0-8146-5036-8
  1. Bible—Hermeneutics. 2. Hermeneutics. 3. Lonergan, Bernard J.
F.—Contributions in doctrine of hermeneutics. I. Title.
BS476.M334 1994
220.6′01—dc20   93-4696
                                                              CIP

Contents

Preface   5

THE AFFIRMATION OF TRUTH IN THE BIBLE
1. "Can You Really Believe the Bible?"   7
2. The Spiritual Authority of the Bible   23
3. A Mandala for Biblical Commentary   40
4. Theological Doctrines and the Old Testament:
   Lonergan's Contribution   47
5. The Bible and Trust in the Future   65

TRUTH IN LITERATURE
6. Truth and Affirmation in Poetry   74
7. Sense About Endings: A Reaction to a Detail   81
8. Northrop Frye, "The Great Code": A Critique   85

EXAMPLES OF INTERPRETATION IN THIS MODE
9. A Commentary on Manna   95
10. The Rise of David Story and the Search for a Story
    to Live By   113
11. The Elohist at Work   123
12. The Basis of Empire: A Study of the
    Succession Narrative   142

PREACHING BASED ON OLD TESTAMENT TEXTS
13. The Authority of Text and the Liturgy   158
14. Uses and Abuses of the Bible in the Liturgy
    and Preaching   168

Author Index   177

Biblical Index   181

Preface

These essays were written over a decade or more as lectures for special occasions. Some were converted into articles for publication. They attempt to exploit the extraordinary clarity which the late Bernard Lonergan has brought to our understanding of interpretation within the general task of theology; and in particular to use his rehabilitation, within cognitional theory, of that crucial human act whereby we affirm truth. Lonergan's own writings did not focus on the specific questions of biblical interpretation. In extending Lonergan's thought to this field, my own thought has been stimulated and clarified through encounter with the thought of the late Albert Outler through debate and problem solving with my colleagues on the editorial team, and with members of the Governing Board, of a forthcoming International Catholic Bible Commentary, centered in Dallas, to be published in English by The Liturgical Press late in the 1990s.

The original publishers of the ten essays which first appeared elsewhere are acknowledged in the following list numbered according to their present chapters. I am grateful for their permission to reprint in this volume.

2. The Spiritual Authority of the Bible, in T. Fallon & P. Riley (eds.), *Religion and Culture: Essays in Honour of Bernard Lonergan S.J.* (Albany: State University of New York Press, 1987) 205–219.

3. A Mandala for Biblical Commentary, appeared in Spanish: Mandala para un comentario biblico, *Revista Bíblica* 47 (1992/3) 155–162.

4. Theological Doctrines and the Old Testament: Lonergan's Contribution, in McEvenue and Meyer (eds.), *Lonergan's Hermeneutics, Its Development and Application* (Washington: Catholic University Press, 1989) 133–154.

5. The Bible and Trust in the Future, in J. Gagné (ed.), *The Exploration of the Future in Pastoral Studies* (Quebec: University of Laval Press, 1991) 23–32.

9. A Commentary on Manna, appeared in French: Interprétation scientifique et exégèse d'Exode 16, *Théologiques* 1 (1993) 55–78 (University of Montreal Press).

10. The Rise of David Story and the Search for a Story to Live By, in Matthew Lamb (ed.), *Creativity and Method: Essays in Honor of Bernard Lonergan* (Milwaukee: Marquette University Press, 1980) 185–195.

11. The Elohist at Work, *Zeitschrift für die alttestamentliche Wissenschaft* 96 (1984) 315–332.

12. The Basis of Empire: A Study of the Succession Narrative, *Ex Auditu* 2 (1986) 34–45.

13. The Authority of Text and the Liturgy, in J. G. Nadeau (ed.), *L'interprétation, un défi de l'action pastorale* (Montreal: Fides, 1989) 57–66.

14. Uses and Abuses of the Bible in the Liturgy and Preaching, *Concilium* (1991) 91–99 in the English edition.

Sean McEvenue

Chapter 1

"Can You Really Believe the Bible?"

A Good Book

Most would agree that the Bible is basically a good book, as long as they are not pushed too hard on the topic. According to The Bible Society, it is still a best seller both in the United States and right around the world. And for every person who really bases his or her life on it, one can suppose there are many more who at least imagine they do.

But there are major problems in the book itself. It is so full of factual errors regarding science and history, and contains so many contradictory affirmations, that it is positively embarrassing. Some of the inspired authors would possibly not succeed even in our much maligned high schools. More embarrassing still are its many texts which exult in war, or which imply approval of patriarchal practices or of racist intolerance.

Simple readers of the Bible have to choose between rejecting its authority or rejecting their own intelligence. More sophisticated readers suspend judgement for a while, in the hope that something helpful may occur. . . . But they run into major problems in our culture. Certainly, much of the academic community doubts or denies the possibility of truth of any sort, let alone biblical truth. It used to be common knowledge that history is a lie, but more recently we have learned that even physics is subjective. And it is not only our senses which are deluded, as we were once told, but now we learn that our theories are politically motivated, politically sustained, and politically destroyed. And, one has to admit, the academic community does well in the sense that we daily need to be given a break from dogmatic people, who use information to push us around. Still, total cynicism is not much of a thrill either, except for those academics who in turn use it as a tool for dominating others.

Of course, the sophisticated readers will soon discover that the Bible is not a textbook, but rather an anthology of texts written in diverse literary genres. But what is the truth value, or potential religious authority, of literature? Interpretation theory is so wild today that it even makes it into the columns of ombudspersons in our newspapers. And there is no simple answer or easy model for thinking about it. The major experts in the field introduce their articles and books with disclaimers about the possibility of doing justice to the whole topic, or even of naming all the major authors whose books last year are now to be refuted.

Still, it is always therapeutic to the writer, and sometimes intriguing or even helpful to the reader, to gather some threads and mark out some coherent path through the maze. In what follows an attempt will be made to give a rational basis for reading the biblical texts as a source of religious truth. A first fairly lengthy section will discuss truth and literary texts, such as biblical texts, to show that they can be read as affirmations of sophisticated truth. A second section is a plea for a new kind of publication about the Bible, namely one which is academically rigorous without being either trivial because of historical rigour or frivolous because of literary rigour. A third section will add a word about theological truth.

Religious Truth

The definition of terms which is proposed here will depend very much on the cognitional theory of the late Canadian Jesuit Bernard Lonergan, whose collected works are progressively being published by the University of Toronto Press.[1] Lonergan's approach begins with an invitation to being attentive to one's personal inner experience of thinking as the primary data for investigating cognition. In a second step, the conclusions of such self-study are compared by Lonergan to examples of successful thinking found in the intellectual disciplines of Western culture, and systematically organized in a set of mutually defining terms and relations. This essay will not presuppose familiarity with Lonergan's work, but rather it will attempt to use his insights and terminology in a way which evokes common experience.

By truth, then, I mean an authentic affirmation of reality. Within that definition, the word "authentic" means that the affirmation is based on one's experience attentively observed, and intelligently understood, and reflected upon with all the critical resources one possesses out of a concern to deal with reality as it is. Secondly, within that definition, the word "reality" means whatever is intended in experience, whatever is attended to, wondered about, inquired about, reasoned about, whatever is eventually affirmed to be thus and so, whatever is loved and desired and decided about. Of course we sometimes care about our purely subjective states, without objectifying them. But at other times we care about what is not ourselves. When we really care, and progressively mature to care more and more about what is not ourselves, then the sense of reality and the discipline about attending to reality authentically in order to know it and care for it emerges clearly in our consciousness.

If we agree to understand truth as "an authentic affirmation of reality" in the sense I have indicated, then religious truth will be defined: an authentic affirmation about ultimate reality.

The question to which Part I of this essay is addressed is the following: is literature about truth? Or, to put it more explicitly, does literature make any affirmations about reality? For example, did George Sand's novels explore the experience of human relationships and the values of the French Revolution, or did they explore only the possibilities of language and expression? Is Monty Python about cleverness and pictures, or does it preach something about how we should deal with our culture? Is art in general really for art's sake, as they say, or is it concerned with reality? This is a pivotal point in cultural philosophy, and a crucial point in biblical hermeneutics. For if you will agree that the genres of writing in virtually all biblical texts are literary genres, rather than theoretical genres, or scientific, or historical in a critical modern sense, then we cannot escape the question about the relation of this literature to truth and reality. Does biblical literature make authentic affirmations about ultimate reality?

Certainly the late Northrop Frye does not think so. In his view, caught as he is within a Kantian universe of discourse, it is very important to affirm again and again that literature does not deal with reality in any way beyond providing an alternative to it. In *The Great Code*, for example, he insists very much on a distinction between centrifugal and centripetal meaning. Scientific genres of writing will be centrifugal, in his view, because the meaning has objective realities as its immediate referent. But literary genres of writing will be centripetal because the meaning is primarily enclosed within the work, and each word, sentence, or paragraph has as primary referent other words, sentences and paragraphs within the work.[2] Ultimately, for Northrop Frye, who is pleased to cite a famous passage of Augustine, the Old Testament means only the New, and the New Testament merely interprets the Old.[3]

If this position is interpreted as merely a reaffirmation of the ideas we all learned from F. R. Leavis and the "new critics," namely that in interpreting a literary text terms and parts are all defined primarily by their relations one to another, and that the understanding of the text must begin by understanding the unified conceptualization within the text, then we all could agree. But, on the other hand, if this position is to be interpreted in the sense that the literary piece as a whole does not mean any reality outside of literature, then I find it simply incredible. In this hypothesis (and it does seem to be Frye's hypothesis), how can we escape the conclusion that *Gulliver's Travels* is to be read as a diverting fairytale and nothing more, or that *Don Quixote* is to be understood merely as a humorous tale of adventure, or that *Who's Afraid of Virginia Wolfe* is a powerfully told but otherwise meaningless account of a domestic squabble?

In many places in his writings, Northrop Frye develops the idea that culture is a move away from primitive reality, a domestication of reality. Because we are born into a culture, and specifically because we know through language, we can no longer be primitives, and can no longer encounter reality as it is in itself, namely, chaotic and wild. Humanity has a pleasure dome decreed, and has built a sheltered universe within which it can live.[4] Within this view of culture, one can well understand that literature should be interpreted centripetally, namely, as contributing to the domestic reality which we have formed to substitute for whatever may exist outside of human control. And all the works of literature are related to all others in the great order of words.[5]

I am not sure what Frye makes of science as one expression of culture. I would argue that research is an enemy to Frye's ordered domestic universe, as we have seen in the case of atomic research. Those who are bitten by research go right to the points of chaos in order to understand the reality which we not understand, not only with the idea of domesticating chaos, but also with the idea of blasting out of our ordered worldviews. Some do heavily funded research in great laboratories, but most humans quietly do private research, important personal research within the sphere of their vital awareness, heading toward the unknown, becoming what they never were before.

And I am not sure what Frye thinks about God. But certainly, insofar as humans address God as transcendent, and not merely as a humanly constructed idol, then once again humans use all their creative powers to institute specifically centripetal symbols, and to write literary texts which lead the mind beyond domestic reality toward the limitless, the infinite. My reading of the Bible finds that it is constantly dealing with God as transcending all limits, as wild and out of control. I would argue that biblical literature is constantly centrifugal and anti-domestic: its power consists precisely in its openness and desire for the unlimited, the unknown, the mysterious, the wild freedom of all-powerful love. In other words, biblical literature is precisely about religious truth. But we shall see this by degree. It will be helpful to begin with a short example of nonreligious literature.

I think that the first poem I ever understood as a poem was Carl Sandburg's "Fog," which was presented to us in third-year high school. As I remember it, it reads as follows:

> The fog comes
> on little cat feet.

It sits looking
over harbor and city
on silent haunches
and then moves on.

What does that poem mean? It does not mean that fog is like a cat. If it meant anything as silly as that it would surely never have been approved by the prestigious Ontario Ministry of Education! It is not a beautiful set of words either—one does not curl up with pleasure in its images and rhythms and sounds. In fact, it is a poem which makes one a little uneasy, a little uncomfortable. I think the poem is about fog. About real fog. And I do not think it domesticates fog—rather the comparison to a cat alienates the fog further—it makes one sharply aware of the fact that fog has an existence which is independent of us, and which is somehow mysterious and sovereign in itself as a cat is mysterious and sovereign. . . . And this sovereign briefly "looks over" our harbor, and our city, and then moves on. It is a bit like Sandburg's "grass" which he depicts in another poem as covering up all the corpses on the battlefields of history: "I am the grass. I cover all."

I would say that I think I understand this poem, and that it is about fog as a revelation that nature is greater than civilization. But I would not say that the poem says nature is greater than civilization. Rather the poem says precisely "The fog creeps in on little cat's feet . . ." and so on. It says a very precise and serious thing about reality, and what it says cannot be adequately conceptualized in any other words than the poet's words. Now I cannot prove these assertions. Each person has to examine very sensitively how he or she reads. I can only urge that I cannot imagine why anyone would bother to read "Fog," or write it, if it is understood in any other way.

The point is that literature is concerned with real life. It is true that many people think of literature as trivial, and escapist, and such people really should dismiss literature. However, those who support and respect literature, those who in effect turn "texts" into "literature," do not have this view. I would argue that those who have been at pains to select these few lines of Carl Sandburg, while rejecting thousands of other texts, and those who have preserved them, and printed and taught them, have done so, not because they found an escapist pleasure in the aesthetic form of this little poem, but rather because they read it as essentially centrifugal, as expressing an authentic, penetrating, and important affirmation about reality. Of course, some literature may provide a mode of escaping a certain reality in favor of an imaginary universe, and some readers may cherish literature because they can read it in this sense. In fact literature as drug may make a lot of money. But I submit that ultimately civilization supports literature because of its contribution to our involvement in reality.

To make the same point in another example: *Driving Miss Daisy* is a movie which tells a story about an elderly, prickly, and slightly infirm Jewish lady and a black chauffeur living in Georgia in the fifties and sixties. It is witty and kindly throughout. I would point to one line of development that emerges through the various incidents. As the film begins Miss Daisy miscalculates and backs her car over an embankment. Her son hires a chauffeur for her, but she is too proud to admit her need for one. When he is imposed on her, she prefers to walk downtown independently rather than accept to be driven by someone else. Years later, as the film ends, Miss Daisy is in an old ladies' home and, although she suppresses any break in the appearance of severe dignity which characterises her, we still know that she is delighted to have that now aged chauffeur come over to visit her on Thanksgiving Day. He sits and talks to her, and eventually shares a dessert with her. In the closing moment she allows him to take the spoon from her shaky hand and put some bit of dessert into her mouth.

Does this movie belong only to an order of words? Or does it say something about reality? Is it merely witty and clever? Does it take us out of ourselves into an artificial world? When I saw it, it moved everybody to tears to the point that many had trouble leaving the theatre when the lights went on. Were they all sentimental dreamers, lost in a sophisticated unreality? Or was something affirmed in the movie, something perhaps inexpressible in other media or in abstract statements, something about human nature where it is wild and undomesticated, something about real life which therefore could touch all our lives? I would argue that if the movie is merely sentimental, then it will be forgotten; whereas if it authentically affirms reality it will gradually be recognized as a classic. The meaning of an authentic movie is essentially centrifugal: it is about reality and truth.

Just what does it affirm about reality? Of course, the affirmation cannot be paraphrased, as a sea of literary critical publication has eloquently told us.[6] However, we can ask further questions: What kind of truth is affirmed in artistic works? What precise inner experience is at the core of literary affirmation?

Artistic or literary expression affirms a form of truth which is subjective. It is subjective, not in the sense that it is not about a reality which others also can possess in common with the artist, but in the sense that it intends, not to exclude, but to include a personal, and often original, perspective and evaluation. It is an affirmation about real life as the poet has come to perceive it should be understood and undertaken. It is about reality with inscribed clues and additional dimensions of meaning. An artistic or literary expression presents a way of human being in the real world. This way of being is merely expressed when the work is done, but it is positively affirmed or enjoined when the work is bought, or performed, or hung on the wall.

Literary works then make a subjective kind of affirmation. We can go further. I shall argue to three qualities of this truth: first, it is a single unified affirmation; second, it is an affirmation of an elemental truth possessed preconceptually; and third, it is an affirmation about reality in the full sense.

First, then, what is affirmed is a unified insight concerning a complex truth. It is a truth which is comprehensively expressed by the integral work. The very first rule we all learned in literary criticism is that one must consider the complete work, and study each of its elements in relation to all others. Aspects of its meaning can be detached and expressed in various logical or scientific conceptual forms. But we all know how impoverished such expressions are. The artistic work is essentially a unity, and its meaning is distorted and trivialized when one says, for example, that the "whole point" of *David Copperfield* is to condemn social injustice in England, or that Van Gogh's "Potato Eaters" is "essentially" a study of variation in darkness. Such narrow meanings did not require a Charles Dickens or a Van Gogh to create them. It is the whole work, understood as a whole, which expresses an insight which readers and viewers have found to be life-giving.[7]

Secondly, the truth being affirmed in artistic affirmation is not possessed in abstract form. The affirmation must be described as elemental in the sense that its truth is possessed only as incarnate. It is totally imbedded in the sounds or colors or images of the work. Moreover, an elemental affirmation is preconceptual. This can be understood in examples such as the elemental affirmation of a smile, or a cry of pleasure or pain. Such elemental and preconceptual affirmations are not obscure, and they can be understood and described, but they cannot be fully articulated in concepts or fully expressed in any other medium of expression than the human face or voice, or imitations of these. Similarly, the artist does not tell us what we would know if we saw what he or she sees, but rather she brings before us precisely what she does see and wants us to see because this seeing is meaningful. Similarly, the poet does not communicate an idea by assembling a variety of clues about it. Rather, one assembles sounds and images and notions and narrative, and plays with them until they finally express what one has been trying to grasp, that is, until they finally enable one to express preconceptually, elementally, what one has already understood in a heretofore mute insight. The reader, in turn, grapples with this artistic product, its elements and logic and omissions and contrasts until a unified understanding occurs. Thus, the work incarnates as elemental meaning the artist's insight, and provides an object in which the reader can share that insight.

A key word here is "insight." The poet or artist has an insight, which he or she expresses, not in logical systems, but in artistic forms in which each element relates to all the others. The viewer or reader who then experiences this incarnate expression can be led to experience its originating insight as well. Everybody has the experience from time to time of struggling with and finally "understanding" an artistic work. One sees the whole as a whole, in a single insight. One has succeeded in retracing in reverse direction the mental process of the artist, and in this way one shares the artist's insight.

Artistic or literary insight, though usually complex and subtle is not essentially different from other kinds of insight. If you will indulge me, I would like briefly to consider an example of a simple and crude kind of insight, namely, an insight in geometry. For example, if you are presented with crossed lines:

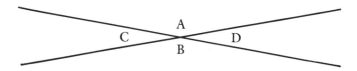

you will know that angles A and B will always be equal no matter how the lines are arranged, and similarly angles C and D will always be equal. You are quite sure of it even though, unless you remember your high-school geometry, you could not immediately formulate it as a law. It is a preconceptual insight. Formulating it as a law is a step away from the preconceptual and toward conceptualization: "when straight lines intersect the opposite angles are equal." Many would use the word "intuitive" here, to describe the kind of knowing which has occurred, but "preconceptual" is less burdened with misleading semantic history. To move toward full conceptualization, one has only to consider that straight lines are 180 degree angles, and therefore:

$$A + D = 180$$
$$B + D = 180$$
$$\text{Therefore } A = B.$$

With that formulation one has understood conceptually a truth which one understood preconceptually right from the beginning.

My point is that an insight is at the core of an artistic or literary work, just as it is at the core of a geometric argument. Unlike the geometric insight, it cannot be expressed in any terms except the artistic elements, incarnate elements, preconceptual elements. If you ask an interpreter what it means, an interpreter can talk about it but cannot express that insight in any other language. Can you imagine trying to tell someone what the Taj Mahal means, or what the song *Old Man River* means? The only answer which can be given will be to bring you to the Taj Mahal, or play the music. If the interpreter chooses to describe the work, or to paraphrase it, or say that "the whole point" is something or other, that may make some sense, and it may lead readers in the right directions, but it will in no sense say the same thing as the piece in question. An accurate description of "La Marseillaise," or its faithful presentation as a musical score on pieces of paper, will simply not convey the meaning which is conveyed when the music is played.

Thirdly, the truth which is being affirmed in artistic works is a truth in the full sense, that is, it is an affirmation about reality. Just as the insight about opposite angles was within a mathematical convention of thought, and yet was developed by Euclid as geometry in order to measure farmlands, and just as the affirmation in that theorem about opposite angles is an affirmation about reality once it is published or taught, so artistic insights are conceived with literary or musical or artistic conventions, and yet once they are published they become affirmations about reality. They are affirmations which include subjective elements along with objective or centrifugal reference. They are affirmations about a way of being in the world, and we tend to accept them or reject them, to love them or hate them, not primarily because of their technical merits as art, but mostly in so far as we accept or reject the way of being which they affirm.

The intrusive nature of elemental affirmation in art is, obviously, very important when one thinks of biblical literature. So I should like to reflect on a further example of insight, and of its move toward conceptualization and of the affirmation it makes. This example is from visual art.

Think of being asked to draw a picture of a man, a woman, and a house. You fiddle a while with your pencil, and eventually you know what kind of thing you want to do, and eventually you find a place to start. For the sake of argument, let us suppose that you have enough technical ability to be able to present a finished picture which more or less satisfies you. It looks as you think it should.

What does it mean? Well it means the whole thing, and it is not to be understood in a unified fashion except by considering the whole thing, without omitting any detail. You might add, or erase, some lines. And then you might be more satisfied than before; or else you might say that these changes were a mistake. The picture is either more or less true to what you intend it to be.

One might be tempted to say that it does not affirm anything. But just consider the questions one can ask of your picture. One could ask about the degree of materialism you affirm in your drawing. Have you drawn a hasty stick-man and woman, but carefully rendered all the details of a beautiful house, with a Mercedes in the driveway? Or have you drawn the clothes in loving detail, leaving the contours of the human bodies, and their facial lines, slightly out of focus? If so, you have affirmed something about the importance of humans versus possessions. Thirty years ago we used to laugh at Marxist literary theory, but now that the economic theory of Marx seems to be on the way out Marxist literary theory seems to be ever more on the way in. There must be something in it![8]

Or one might ask a question about the relative importance you accorded the man or the woman in your picture. Did you make the man stand tall, with imperial gesture, and elegant clothing, while depicting the woman as slight, and plain, and maybe washing the windows? Which one appears to own the house or the car in your picture? Does the man look toward the viewer or some distant horizon, while the woman looks to the man? Surely a lot of affirmation about reality is carried in such details. Feminist criticism has begun to teach us a lot about the affirmations concerning reality which are imbedded in artistic and literary works.

Or a third question might focus on your interest in erotic aspects of life. Does your drawing leave the house in vague outline while focusing on the most sensual contours of the two bodies? Does it depict secondary sexual characteristics in detail? Does it place the bodies in suggestive relation one to the other?

Your drawing has made affirmations about all these and other values. You are startled, and possibly you are embarrassed, when someone points them out. When you were drawing, such thoughts were very far from your mind. You were thinking about the problems of drawing a good picture, not about social values. And yet you can hardly deny that your picture says the kind of things indicated above. You have to recognize that your picture reveals and affirms yourself, and something about your values and your life-choices, your "meaning." Your drawing was commanded by an insight, and you did express this insight by depicting the elements in these ways. Of course Jacques Derrida will deny that there was anything in your consciousness before you began to draw, or paint, or write.[9] But if you try the activity yourself, and if you reflect on your experience: if you ask how you know that this or that is right or wrong in your choice of lines or colors or words or images, then you will have to conclude that Derrida has simply missed something here. True, you did not have the finished product conceived in advance, but still you had an insight which enabled you to move toward expression, and to choose and change elements through a series of artistic trials and decisions. The original insight was a unity, and it is expressed in this unified artistic work as a unity. The picture now affirms this insight. The implications of this insight and this affirmation, which can be conceptualized in terms of materialism, feminism, sexuality, and so forth, were implicitly affirmed about reality by your artistic product.

In reference to biblical literature, these kinds of questions can be asked. However, they are not specifically religious questions, and hence do not immediately fall within the area in which the Bible has played a normative role. The third section of this paper will return to this topic, and consider specifically religious and theological questions which can be addressed to biblical texts.

II. Interpretation

We spend a lot of time telling each other what we meant, or what someone else meant, or what artistic expressions such as movies or plays mean. Academics call this "interpretation," and they get pretty formal about its rules, or at least pretty excited about conflicting theories. The scholarly community, the Academy, is concerned with controlled discourse, and disciplined affirmation. And the educated public has come to expect that kind of writing when serious topics are being discussed.

The Academy is happy to describe accurately, with whatever methodologies it has, the religious behaviors of groups of people, or to tie down specific historical facts, or to analyze structures of thought, and so forth. But the Bible makes affirmations about the ineffable, about the mysterious, about the infinite and the unknowable. What rules of interpretation can the Academy adopt when dealing with such a literature? The pressure is immense on biblical scholars toward easy forms of scholarly respectability, for example by working away at "objective" tasks such as textual criticism, or at questions of dating, or geography, or comparative philology. And all this can be helpful. Similarly, the student of Carl Sandburg can opt for objective questions like: where was the poet living when he wrote "Fog"? What harbor and city was he thinking of? Chicago? San Francisco? New York? And the fact is that for about two centuries most academic publication about biblical literature has headed in those directions. Some have taken on the mantle of ancient Near Eastern studies, or archaeology. Others have preferred more literary studies, and there are numerous activities which are respectable because they are "objective": for example, there is always the endless discussion about sources, the attempt to define literary forms, and the various projects of structure studies or of deconstruction.

Taking another tack, some try to retain a religious relevance by writing "biblical theology," as it is mistakenly called, and they produce histories of ideas about God in successive biblical periods. But this is based on the illusion we have discussed above, namely, that biblical texts, even though they are literary, can be paraphrased and rendered as ideas. The resulting history of ideas turns out, naturally, to be a history of inadequate ideas, ideas which subsequent eras have gone beyond, ideas which are useful only insofar as they provide models of thought within which one can derive ever more precise concepts for understanding texts. And such study is valid, because these models of thought were in fact constructs within which biblical authors wrote, deep structures or surface structures which shaped the text. But none of this has the weight of truth. The author originally made an artistic affirmation by using these models and many other elements of meaning and style and image and sound to make a religious statement. Respectable scholarship which stops at the history of ideas is poking around in a blind corner of what the Bible itself was all about, and is all about. Such work is as useful, but not more directly religious, than that of scholars who establish the exact location of Capernaum, or determine the monetary value of a Hittite coin.

There is an alternative approach. Some classical biblical scholars have always taken it, and recently a quantity of biblical publication follows in this line.[10] Biblical scholars can turn away from the respectable models of history, or philology, or archaeology, or geography, or philosophy, and turn to another respectable model, namely, literary scholarship which adopts all of these but subordinates them to its own purpose. The purpose of literary scholars is to recover the simple meaning of the text. They are not ashamed at this accomplishment, and do not apologize for it.

The publications of literary critics sometimes strike scientists or social scientists or historians as wild, undisciplined, confused, uncool. They are often not written according to the model of "objective" scholarship which other disciplines and their adherents have been trained to expect. Still, their brilliance is often irresistible. Competent literary scholars are simply wonderful in performing the task of making a text sing once again. They succeed in experiencing, and pointing to, the otherwise ineffable meaning of great literary texts. And their work is considered respectable in the academic community—at least by academics who are prepared to recognize any discipline outside their own as respectable! They do not need to tell you that a text means this or that, or that the "whole point" of a story or poem can be summed up in some paraphrase. They don't try to write a history of ideas in English literature, or set out to write a theology based on the canon of English literature as contained, for example, in Norton's anthology. And when the best literary scholars go into textual criticism, or historical questions, or into the history of ideas, they follow the demanding methods of those disciplines, subordinating it all to the task of recovering the simple, elemental, meaning of the literary texts.

There is a further difficulty, however, for biblical scholars. Many academics will object that biblical texts contain faith at the heart of the insight which the texts affirm in preconceptual forms, and they will argue that faith is not something to be taught in the University. Moreover, fait is not something which every competent reader, or professor, will necessarily have.

It is both important and easy to discuss that objection. Much of English poetry is an affirmation of faith. One has only to think of Milton, for example, or Blake. Such authors simply cannot be fully understood by a reader whose psyche has not been opened up to this dimension. Any more than Wordsworth can be fully understood by a reader who has no sense of nature. I suspect that all teachers of literature experience their limitations with regard to understanding certain authors—and good teachers must teach these authors at a distance, using stratagems to avoid getting in the way of the students.

If, then, an academic presentation of *Paradise Lost* may deal with faith, how can one deny the same to an academic presentation of *Genesis*? In completely uncovering the meaning of *Genesis* for students, one is doing precisely the same thing as in competently uncovering the meaning of most literature. Similarly, I would venture to say that most biblical scholars experience an inability to understand the meaning of certain biblical texts, and are constrained either to avoid teaching them or else to teach them at a distance. Their faith experience is not such as to allow them to experience the meaning of that particular author. It may be hard to admit this, as it is a professional failure, and possibly a human failure. Too bad. Such is human limitation.

III. Bible and Religion/Theology

If one studies the Bible out of an interest in the history of religious thought, or the history of the ancient Near East, one may not need a literary approach such as I have been trying to describe. However, those whose biblical studies derive from religious and theological concerns may be more interested. It is in theological inquiry that religious truth becomes the formal object.

There is no need for present purposes of getting into a labyrinth of hermeneutical debate about the truth claims of methods in theology. We can think simply in terms of the classical anselmian definition of theology: "faith in search of understanding." This is a definition to which I think all can assent. And the point here is that theology in Western tradition has been developed in terms of truth, in terms of propositional truth, in terms of truth which is not preconceptual, but which is carefully conceptualized with defined terms and transparent logics. How many angels can dance on the head of a pin?

How, then, does one move from religious truth as affirmed in preconceptual insights to conceptualized theology as affirmed in doctrines?

Of course, not only theology has doctrines. As I have indicated above, one can ask any kind of question of artistic or literary works, and the answers to such questions will be expressed in affirmations or doctrines. For example, a musicologist might ask whether or not music was important in the culture of ancient Israel. Or a political scientist might ask what differences one might detect between the three Isaiahs in reference to the powers of a monarch. Or a feminist might ask what attitude towards unmarried women is implicit in the Song of Songs. The answers to these questions would be interesting, and they might enable us to read the biblical text with ever increased precision. They would reveal affirmations which are implied within the religious affirmation of those texts. However, none of these questions is immediately theological, and none of their answers (i.e., affirmations) would be considered normative in Christian religion or theology.

Now theology is not religion. Both deal with God, but theology in our culture is expressed in a very sophisticated form of discourse. A theological question is a question about God addressed ultimately to biblical revelation. However, the answer will not be couched in terms of what the Bible might say, or in the language and literary genres of the Bible. The Bible was written in a pre-doctrinal culture. In current culture, serious questions are formed in philosophically precise language, and are answered within philosophically complete systems. Religious truth in the Bible cannot be found in that manner of thinking. The fact is that theological questions have been asked within Western tradition which forms all of our thoughts whether or not we are believers. It is a tradition which begins with the Bible but continued through an evolution in which philosophically accurate modes of thought have translated biblical (and other) meaning into systematic meaning, have translated elemental preconceptual meaning into conceptualized meaning. The readers of the Atlantic are inescapably theoretical and scientific thinkers, or at least post-theoretical and post-scientific thinkers. All our questions and answers about truth are post-biblical.

But the immediate response to the biblical text is not a theological question looking for a doctrinal answer. Rather, it is a religious openness in search of foundational rather than doctrinal answers. Such answers are in the area of conversion, and of spirituality, rather than of truth in the narrow sense. Religious questions and answers can respect literary genres. For example, one might ask: in what realm of meaning does a specific biblical text expect revelation to occur, or in what realm of meaning does a biblical text expect God to intervene as Savior? The answer to such a question will demand a stance of faith, and a specific expectancy about involvement with God. For religious believers, this answer will be normative, and may demand changes in their way of living (i.e., a religious response) often called a conversion.

Intellectually, however, the religious answer will probably imply further questions which are theological, and which do demand doctrinal answers.

Let us take an example. If we recall the literary image of God ordering the universe which is presented in Genesis 1—separating light from darkness, earth from water, species from species, and organizing days and seasons—we can see that a specific realm of revelation and intervention is implied. The text elementally expects revelation to occur in the contemplation of the universe. This revelation consists of that cosmic order which was divinely introduced into original chaos. And within that order humans were given a unique role as image of God and master of the cosmos.

This text expects revelation to occur in a specific realm, and not in others. For example, it does not deal with the realm of domestic human love as does the Song of Songs, or the realm of human sin as does the story of Adam and Eve, or in the realm of war and political activity as does the Succession Narrative when David was king. Rather, it operates in a more philosophic realm, contemplating the universe. It moves in the wisdom tradition.

Moreover, this text contains a specific expectancy about our involvement with God, namely, that as image of God we act as God did. The text explicitly instructs humans to rule over the cosmos in establishing order in nature, and in making everything fruitful. In terms of conversion, or spirituality, this text demands of the contemporary reader an undertaking of ecological responsibility. And one who is led by the Bible will feel drawn to follow this directive.

Subsequent to the religious response to the text in terms of conversion, there then can occur a second phase in which specifically theological questions arise, and doctrinal answers are needed. In fact innumerable, specific doctrinal questions have arisen out of this conversion. There are moral questions: for example, how should one balance the immediate welfare of one's family on the one hand and the well-being of future generations on the other? Or ecclesiological questions occur: for example, how should we define the role of the clergy versus that of the laity in ecological responsibility? Or eschatological questions have been asked, such as defining the relation between ecology and the end time: is nature evolving toward a technology-helped perfection a la Teilhard de Chardin? Is life after death to be lived in a spiritual state only, or will ecology play a role? Or one might renew a familiar doctrinal question by trying to link the doctrine of original sin with this conversion to ecological responsibility: is original sin a condition of the individual human psyche? or of political systems? or is it to be understood specifically in relation to all of nature?

Such theological questions are asked because they arise as a real need to know. They arise for people who have been converted in response to a religious affirmation of the Bible, and whose lives now are formed by this conversion and in a real way constricted by it. They arise ultimately out of the experience of Genesis 1, proximately out of a learned personal stance of expectancy about divine action, circumstantially out of the need to make coherent choices in one's personal life. They will be answered by appealing to all the resources of thought at our disposal, and the answers will be conceptualized in scientifically and philosophically precise language.

Can you really believe the Bible? In the sense I have attempted to establish in this essay, most of us really do believe in the Bible and live it out in varying degrees. And this is not only true in pop culture, but also valid within the principles of truth as defined by the Academy.

Notes

1. I refer principally to the two following books, one of which has been reissued by the University of Toronto Press: *Insight: A Study of Human Understanding* (1957; rpt. *Collected Works of Bernard Lonergan*, vol. 3, Toronto: University of Toronto Press, 1992); *Method in Theology* (London: Darton, Longman and Todd, 1972), especially chapter 3.

2. Cf. Northrop Frye, *The Great Code: The Bible and Literature* (Toronto: Academic Press, 1982), especially chapter 3 "Metaphor," and particularly 61–62, and 76–77.

3. Cf. *The Great Code: The Bible and Literature*, 79.

4. Cf., for example, his understanding of Wisdom Literature, not as an invitation to puzzle about the mysteries in nature, but rather in terms of law, the imposition of the past, and changing nature into culture, in *The Great Code*, 121–125. The same idea is extensively developed in his earlier book, *The Well-Tempered Critic* (Bloomington and London: Indiana University Press, 1963).

5. This is a unifying theme in Frye's most widely read work, *The Anatomy of Criticism: Four Essays* (New Jersey: Princeton University Press, 1957).

6. For a most compelling demonstration of this truth, cf. Cleanth Brooks, *The Well Wrought Urn: Studies in the Structure of Poetry* (New York: Harcourt Brace Jovanovich, 1947).

7. The practice of rationalistic reduction of myth is well described by Julian Pitt-Rivers, *The Fate of Shechem or the Politics of Sex: Essays in the Anthropology of the Mediterranean* (Cambridge, Mass: Cambridge University Press, 1977) 132: "Under Malinowski's influence it came to be accepted that myth serves the function of fixing certain values in the minds of people and acts thus as a charter which validates the social structure. This view has much in common with Durkheim's view of religion and like it, it is not so much wrong as inadequate to explain more than one aspect of the phenomenon. This it does moreover in a rather unmethodical way since it provides no clear rules of interpretation. Whatever connections come to mind will do by way of explanation." Pitt-Rivers' critique is correct, but still his own lengthy study of Genesis in this book proceeds to reduce the meaning to one almost exclusive focus, the validation of marriage laws. Is God irrelevant in Genesis? I would argue, however, that a doctrinal theology of Genesis is no less ridiculous than this.

8. Cf. Terry Eagleton, *The Ideology of the Aesthetic* (Oxford: Basil, Blackwell, 1990).

9. Cf. Jacques Derrida, *L'écriture et la différence* (Paris: éditions du Seuil, 1967) 15–17.

10. The recent voices of Robert Alter, Northrop Frye, Frank Kermode, Meir Sternberg and other prominent literary scholars respond to a chorus of prominent biblical scholars such as Hermann Gunkel and Luis Alonso-Schokel and their innumerable disciples.

Chapter 2

The Spiritual Authority of the Bible

The Bible is undoubtedly a collection of literary texts, and as a book it is certainly a classic. Rather it is *the* classic. However, in the Church and within theology, there has been an added character to the Bible, namely, its authority. Whatever one's precise doctrine about "revelation," "inspiration,"or "Word of God," Jewish and Christian readers of the Bible recognize in it a normativity of a kind which they do not recognize in any other book. Insofar as currently popular ideas about "reading the Bible as literature" might imply abandoning this recognition, then such reading will neither be religious nor theological.

I believe it is worth the trouble to be specific about one key difference in the approach. A literary reading of Milton, or a production of a Shakespearean play, aims at stimulating the listener. It is an artistic act, expressive of meaning in some full sense. The text is one element in that meaning, and it is chosen because of its powers. It may not matter whether the resulting meaning for the listener is related to what Milton or Shakespeare historically intended. What does matter is the degree of stimulation afforded the listener. If a given reader or actor can read the text in a number of ways, and evoke a variety of meanings from it, exciting a variety of responses from the listeners, this will be virtuosity. Any suggestion that one meaning is correct and another somehow incorrect, will be universally scoffed at.[1] The text may even be changed for aesthetic reasons. The original meaning of the text, and the original author of the text are deemed irretrievable on the one hand, and irrelevant on the other.[2] The text may have power, but not authority over either reader or listener. We do not submit to limits of meaning in literature nor are we measured by it. We may learn from it, enjoy it, respect it. We are not ruled by it. This distinction was recognized long ago when, for example, Ezekiel is listened to as a troubador rather than as a prophet (Ezek 33:31-32).

Such an approach to the Bible will not be acceptable to the theologian or to the religious reader. One goes to the Bible in order to learn something true. One is prepared for a conversion, for a demand to change one's life, for a radical challenge. One recognizes the authority of a past moment, in which somehow history, and a human author, and a divine intervention combined to change reality and meaning in a normative manner. One desires, not merely to enjoy this text, but rather to relive, or to participate in, the new reality to which it testifies.

A comparison with legal texts may be helpful here. Biblical texts in a context of ecclesiastical theology are like constitutions or pacts or contracts in a courtroom context, in that they possess a historical authority. These texts are normative and constitutive of a social reality which results from them. Their original meaning was freighted with the authority of the writer, whether the writer was understood to be God, or Moses, or a king or prophet, or a government, or a conqueror. Therefore, the author's intention, however uncertain the exact identity of the actual writer, is the normative meaning. Any subsequent misreading of such texts, no matter how creative or useful, are subject to refutation by appeal to the literal sense of the original. Judges and lawyers know as much about historical-critical method as do exegetes.

I. The Problem

It must be admitted, however, that over the past thirty years biblical scholarship has spent much of its time in exile from the context of ecclesiastical theology. Rather, it has been in servitude to comparative philology, or to archeology, or to ancient Near-Eastern history.[3] At present it risks a new slavery in departments of literary studies.[4] And even within the context of theology the sovereign role of Scripture has been undermined by the inconsistent and even abusive methodologies of theologians.[5] Sometimes its authority has been simply denied.[6] Something is wrong with biblical exegesis! Clearly it needs to rediscover itself. Otherwise the Bible itself may be reduced to the level of popular culture, while theology spins off into space without historical root.

Limitations of "Original Meaning"

The triumph of modern biblical scholarship has been to recover the original context and meanings of biblical texts. It comes, then, as an unwelcome shock to note that throughout the history of Judaism and Christianity the original contexts and meanings of the Bible have *not* been normative! The original *texts* have been revered, but the original *meanings* have been overlooked.

The very idea of distinguishing between an original meaning and a convenient contemporary reinterpretation seems to have had no weight at all before the nineteenth century. Within the Old Testament context, or the Biblical context, or the patristic context, or medieval exegesis, or the Renaissance reform scholars, or, in other words, within the historical period in which the body of Jewish and Christian belief was explicitly formed on the basis of biblical faith, critical historical awareness was almost entirely absent.[7] And most recently, both the great biblical scholar Brevard Childs and the great literary scholar Northrop Frye have proposed a form of return to the innocence of old which followed Augustine in finding the New Testament foreshadowed in the Old, and the Old Testament revealed in the New.[8]

It may be helpful to recall one concrete example. Psalm 8:4-6 is cited as an authority in Hebrews 2:6-9. Psalm 8:4-6 had recalled Genesis 1 in order to reflect on the wonder of humankind which was created in the image and likeness of God, an idea which the psalm expresses by saying that man is made "little less than God." The Epistle to the Hebrews cites an inadequate Greek translation of Psalm 8, misunderstands the words "son of man" to mean an individual, disregards the clear intention of the Psalmist to discuss humankind in general, and applies the text to Jesus who, as the text runs, "for a little while" was made less than angels in order to be exalted afterwards. The inspired author of the Epistle to the Hebrews explicitly cites a familiar text *verbatim* in a sense which it originally could not have had, in order to make a point about Jesus.[9]

What matters here is not to note something about the superiority of modern exegesis; rather, quite the contrary, it is to point out that the original meaning was not normative in this case. And this case exemplifies the rule rather than the exception. For us, for contemporary scholars, for sophisticated theology, the original meaning has become important, and even intellectually preemptive. But we must recognize that, where the Bible has been normative, the original text was normative, while the original meaning was not. We must recall just how normative that original text has been. Certainly, the Jewish communities preserved their books with incredible fidelity: from editors of Old Testament books who juxtaposed contradictory sources without harmonizing them, through the masoretes who counted words to make sure none was omitted, and right up to the modern Israelis who amid the turmoil of war in 1948 send an expedition to Aleppo to seize a codex preserved in a monastery there. This tradition finds dramatic expression in Jesus' insistence that not a jot or tittle of the sacred text might be taken away (Matthew 5:18; Luke 16:16-17), and in the citation of Deuteronomy 4:2 in Revelation 22:18-19. As for the Christian communities, despite Paul's warning that "the letter killeth while the Spirit giveth life," our scholarly editions of the Vulgate, the Septuagint, the Samaritan Pentateuch, the Hebrew Bible, and the New Testament, carry on monastic traditions of dedicated copyists, and continue the earlier work of establishing and fixing the Christian canon. The material text surely is normative.

Still, the material text was preserved precisely because of its meaning. It must follow that some meaning of the original text has been authoritative. If not the articulated content, then what content? And we must not take refuge in the shapelessness of the sea of tradition or in the illusion of a total truth in the canon as a whole.[10] For, if the articulated content of the original biblical text has not been normative then subsequent misinterpretations or misunderstandings of that text, which are found in later biblical authors or editors, have not been any more normative.

The Authority of Scripture in General

What then is the authority of Scripture? The question sounds simple, demanding a straight answer. But the word "authority" here covers an uncharted area of culture. The Bible is written largely in the form of stories, poems, laws, and exhortations. Biblical scholarship has come a long way towards a definition of the literary forms found in the Bible, but critical theory has only recently addressed the question of the relation between art and culture, literature and civilization. And this precisely is the larger question within which the authority of Scripture must be examined, both historically as to what it has been, and theoretially as to what it should be.

It may be useful to see this question in the words of a prominent contemporary literary critic, namely Jonathan Culler:

> There are many tasks that confront criticism, many things we need to advance our understanding of literature, but one thing we do not need is more interpretations of literary works. . . . We have no convincing account of the role or function of literature in society or social consciousness. We have only fragmentary or anecdotal histories of literature as an institution: we need a fuller exploration of its historical relation to the other forms of discourse through which the world is organized and human activities are given meaning. We need a more sophisticated and apposite account of the role of literature in the psychological economies of both writers and readers; in particular we ought to understand much more than we do about the effect of *fictional* discourses . . . What is the status and what is the role of fictions, or, to pose the same kind of problem in another way, what are the relations (the historical, the psychic, the social relationships) between the real and the fictive? What are the ways of moving between life and art? What operations or figures articulate this movement? Have we in fact progressed beyond Freud's simple distinction between the figures of condensation and displacement? Finally, or perhaps in sum, we need a typology of discourse and a theory of the relations (both mimetic and nonmimetic) between literature and the other modes of discourse which make up the text of intersubjective experience.[11]

Of course, the Bible cannot be described as fiction. And, as literature, it is unique. Still, in asking about its authority we must recognize this larger cultural context.

Now the Bible's authority is not that of the letter of the law. Nor is the Bible a collection of dogmas, or even doctrines. We must ask, then, what precise aspect of biblical meaning exercises authority? We have ruled out original articulated meaning and later expressed intrabiblical interpretations, because these never have been normative. Must we then turn to unarticulated, implicit, or subliminal messages in Scripture, and to effects of which the reader is unaware? Has the authority of Scripture been applied, not to what Scripture said, but rather to what the texts do to the reader without our adverting to its influence? Should we look to affects rather than ideas? to conversion rather than truths? The answer must be "yes," in some degree, no matter how painful such an admission may be to scholars trained for exact definitions, and for objective data.[12]

In sketching this answer we shall proceed in two steps. First, we shall attempt to show that what the text does to us is determined by an unnamed, unarticulated, and very elusive *"speaker"* who addresses us from the text, and controls our response, and in effect exercises subliminal authority. Second, we shall point to one kind of unarticulated message of that speaker, which will be present in each text, and which will be both normative and important theologially. This kind of message we shall call *"spirituality."*

II. Exegetical Answer: The Speaker

The Subliminal Effects of the Speaker in Literature

In speaking of meaning it is helpful to distinguish two poles: meaning as it occurs in the text, which is derived from the author and what lies behind him, and meaning as it occurs in the reader. The title of this section begins with the reader, speaking of the effects of literature.

It must be further noted that the word "subliminal" in this discussion does not mean unconscious. Rather, it intends to designate a range of awareness stretching from merely potential awareness on the one hand, all the way to full but implicit awareness on the other. Awareness may be considered implicit when verbal articulation is lacking. Take, for example, a simple sentence such as "Victory at last." The reader is conscious of an articulated meaning, and could easily define each of its terms. However, if the sentence "Victory at last" is understood to be spoken by a belligerent clown like Jackie Gleason or Popeye, then there results further nuances of meaning which are harder to define: an expectancy of reversal in Popeye's good fortune, for example, and a feeling of humorous bombast. The reader is aware of these "effects" of the sentence, but no words name them and the reader will not advert to them explicitly unless asked about them. They remain implicit or subliminal. Now if the sentence "Victory at last" is placed in the mouth of Hitler, the reader will experience immediate anger, or rage, or perhaps terror, or else a bitter awareness of irony. These effects will be harder to define and will easily remain subliminal. And if it is to be General MacArthur who says "Victory at last" as he alights in Tokyo, the effects in a post-Vietnam reader will be a still more elusive combination of triumph and irony, a combination which may defy articulation.[13] Or, finally, if in a novel a father or mother figure is made to say "Victory at last," some readers might even require the aid of psycho-analysis to articulate the literary effects they experience. An analogous range of subliminal awareness would exist in the author who chooses words and places them in contexts.

Traditional exegesis has always accepted some responsibility for the nuances, or colorings, or levels of meaning provided by the text, and experienced as subliminal effects of this kind. Form criticism, in more recent times, has added further dimensions by drawing attention to the literary forms, and to their appropriate contexts or "*Sitz-im-Leben.*" The speaker of a text is not a personage named in a text, but rather it is the voice of the text itself; a voice which addresses the reader and elicits a particular response; a voice which, however elusive, must remain identical with itself and coherent if the text is to retain its unity. The speaker's tone of voice is shaped by the literary forms given it, and by the social context in which it is understood to be speaking.

The "*speaker*" of a text must be understood to have several phases. The first phase, or most immediate to the reader, will be the *literary form* of the text in question. The form will be considered a phase of the speaker because if, for example, the form is a limerick or a joke, then the speaker assumes a certain tone of voice, a certain *persona* or stance. This is never thematized in the text, and yet picking up this tone, or "getting the joke," is essential to understanding the text. The second phase of the speaker may be a *personage* like Popeye, who is represented as speaking certain sentences. A third phase of the speaker will be the *unnamed narrator*, a most elusive figure who assures the unity of an action, who knows the times and places of a narrative and who distributes to its various personages the information each will have. The unnamed narrator must remain utterly coherent if the story is to be unified and imaginatively credible. The unnamed narrator may be identical with the speaker if the text is only a story. Otherwise the speaker will contain the unnamed narrator, while establishing a separate identity by adding a framework of some kind, or a comment, or even just a title. Finally, the fourth phase of the speaker will be the *historical author* whose historical reality may or may not be very evident and very important.

Let us see the four phases in a single example, namely the sentence "Let there be light" in Genesis 1:3. Phase one of the speaker is the peculiar tone of a literary form consisting of seven patterned days of creation. Phase two of the speaker is the personage, God. Phase three is the unnamed narrator who is neither man nor God, but who is reassuringly present at the moment of creation and throughout the Priestly narrative. Phase four appears to be a sixth-century exiled Jew, experiencing chaos and despair, and still finding reasons to hope in the future of Israel. All of these phases merge in the one voice of the text which addresses us, and which produces literary effects. These effects usually remain subliminal.

If a Jew or Christian reads this text as authoritative, he or she will be subliminally moved by the voice of the speaker in ways which one would not easily define. Now it is quite possible that an obtuse reader would not experience much of the subliminal effects, or that a perverse reader would experience totally inappropriate subliminal effects. However, distortion in the reader does not affect the subliminal meaning in the text itself. The subliminal meaning of "Let there be light" is not a doctrine of creation, much less an explanation of the origin of light; rather, it is a personal sharing of the Priestly Writer's faith in God's limitless power to illuminate the dark.

Before the age of printing, the unnamed narrator was the dominant phase of the speaker, because texts were not known as texts but rather they were heard as read in public. The voice of the reader (or singer or chanter) would be heard as that of the unnamed narrator. What limitless authority might be felt in that situation!

In view of the traditional concern among biblical scholars after Gutenberg accurately to situate the historical author on the one hand, and in view of current trends, following Gadamer and Derrida, towards giving to the text a life independent of historical authors on the other, a special word about the historical author may be necessary.

It is the historical author who unites all the phases of the "speaker" into one voice. Clearly, the author creates and maintains the unnamed narrator (phase three) as a unifying control over the text. If, for example, a current movie presents a war in the present tense, and yet casts it in the sixteenth century, then the viewer will participate with the unnamed narrator as though its perils were real and the issue uncertain, all the while keeping an aesthetic distance with the current author who lives long after the danger is past. In this way, the voice of the unnamed narrator is retained, and yet radically modified by the voice of the historical author. Similarly, the author modifies the voice of any personage (phase two) in the text. If, for example, an iconoclast like Bunuel has God say "Let there be light" in one of his films, God's voice will be radically different from the voice in Genesis 1:3. And, finally, in using literary forms (phase one) an historical author will inevitably modify them, at least subtly, either by emphasizing some aspect of the form over the other, or by placing the form in a larger context, or by applying the form to some content for which it has not hitherto seemed appropriate.[14] Such subtle changes constitute the originality of the author, require his/her brilliance, and above all lead the reader to perceive the author's perspective and focus. When the reader experiences this fourth phase of the speaker, and hears the text in this voice, only then does he fully experience the subliminal effects of the text.

At stake here is not merely aesthetic completeness, but also theological truth. For even if the fourth phase of the speaker remains subliminal, still current philosophy and theology have created a space for subliminal meaning in the realm of truth. I refer here to Bernard Lonergan and to Joseph Blenkinsopp.

Bernard Lonergan's publication in 1972 of the book *Method in Theology* marked the end of a pseudo-objective, or empiricist, approach to theology.[15] He says little specifically about the Bible, but a great deal about reading texts. According to Lonergan, the theologian must read the tradition on any given question, that is, the authors who have treated it, including the Biblical authors, the Fathers, and so forth. In this research, the theologian must not only understand these authors, but also take a stand by agreeing or disagreeing with them. Lonergan treats this process in a chapter which is not entitled "Controversy" as one might expect, but rather "Dialectic." According to Lonergan, one's decision to agree or disagree will not be based only on the validity or invalidity of the arguments, but rather on the validity or invalidity of the authors. The focus is not on the logic of a position, or on the data or scholarship adduced for it, but rather on what Lonergan calls the "conversion" of the author, a conversion in three parts: "intellectual conversion," "moral conversion" and "religious conversion." Of course, logic and data will also be scrutinized in themselves and for clues as to "conversion." The approach is distinctly *ad hominem*. These conversions will never be thematized in the author's texts, but will remain implicit. To use our word, they will be subliminal. And yet upon them will depend a theologian's conclusion about the truth of doctrines.[16]

The Bible is a special case, in that it teaches little doctrine, and is concerned rather with stories, or poetry, or exhortation. Joseph Blenkinsopp uses the word "prophecy" to designate what is common to all biblical writers.[17] He points out the contradictions in the articulated meanings of the Old Testament. For example, he writes: "What these writings attest to is rather a plurality of 'religions' or religious viewpoints, generally quite diverse and sometimes mutually exclusive."[18] But he finds all the texts in the canon share a single authority which he describes as follows:

The conclusion to which these considerations lead is that the canon is prophetic insofar as the claim to authority which underlies it in one way or another is the claim to a hearing actually stated by the prophets. This claim arises out of personal experience, often of an extraordinary nature, but always within the context of a community sharing a memory and therefore mediating a common tradition. It also tends toward the formation of a new community which embodies the prophetic claim. To speak of the Bible as "the word of God" is to affirm or imply its authoritative and prophetic character. It is this which made it possible for the author of the Epistle to the Hebrews, for example, to refer to all previous revelations as God speaking to the fathers through the prophets (Heb 1:1), and we have seen that the rabbis were in essential agreement.[19]

What precisely does Blenkinsopp understand this authority to be, an authority found in historical writers, law collectors, wisdom writers and prophets alike? This is his answer: "Unlike the priests and scribes, the prophets were not provided with their audience by virtue of a legitimate and acknowledged office. They had to establish their own credentials and stake their own claims by virtue of whatever *self-authenticating* character their words possessed."[20]

In these reflections Blenkinsopp is dealing with community and with canon. Still his position is worth noting for its implications regarding subliminal meaning. For Blenkinsopp the truth, or revelation, of Scripture does not lie in its articulated religious teachings, which may be contradictory at times, but rather in the authenticity of its authors, an authenticity which the community is able to recognize. For Blenkinsopp, the historical author for the Bible as a whole is a collective prophet, or in our terminology a divine "speaker" personally experienced in equal fashion by a series of historical authors, and authentically expressed in their texts.

It is clear that both the author and the reader create and hear the text within a community and in complex relationships with the community. This dimension of the human person, and of meaning, must remain constantly in view in reflections such as these, even though it cannot be articulated at every point of the discussion. Social dimensions complete, but do not alter, the psychological dimension which is the focus of the present analysis.

Concern for the "historical author" is like respect for philosophy. Some may claim the historical author is irrelevant to the meaning of a text, just as others repudiate the very possibility of philosophical doctrines. But this is to choose to be blind. We all have a philosophical doctrine which controls our thinking, whether we advert to it or not.

Similarly, in reading a text, we all project into it a historical author who controls our reading. Fundamentalists project a nineteenth-century historian.

Christian Marxists tend to project a twentieth-century reformer. Exegetes look very sensitively for traces of the real historical author, in order to break out of contemporary idolatries and to recover the meaning of the text.[21]

III. Theological Answer: Spiritual Teaching

The Teachings of the Biblical Texts

So much for the elusive and subliminal. Is it possible to arrive at articulated theology? Is it possible to suggest a methodologically precise exegetical approach, which will discern and name those subliminal meanings of Scripture which have been normative in Judaism and Christianity, or which should be normative? The rest of this book will attempt to define one approach of this kind.

There will be three major steps in this approach. First, one must begin with existing historical-critical methodology. There can be no shortcut in this regard. One must begin exegetically by discerning the articulated meanings, defining them accurately in their historical contexts. This is the only known method for reading out of oneself and into the text, an asceticism all the more necessary as one is reading for spiritual meanings, where our interior inauthenticities drive us unawares to misunderstand and misinterpret.

A second step will consist of naming the speaker in all its four phases, and of articulating as clearly as possible the subliminal meaning of the text. Traditional exegesis has done some of this work, but it may be helpful to distinguish now the first step from the second, at least in order to assure that due place is given to the second.

A third step will consist, not of understanding the speaker further, but rather of asking a theological question of the speaker. Note that we ask the speaker, not the text, since we have seen that the text's articulated content has never been normative. Note, second, that not all questions will be fruitful, as the speaker may not have addressed some of them at all. However, one can indicate at least one theological question which will always be fruitful: *in what realm of experience does God reveal himself?* or in other words, *in what realm of activity is God salvific?*

The answers to these questions are implicit in all biblical texts, and have been subliminally read by Jews and Christians through the centuries. These answers most certainly have been normative in the evolution of Western society. There are two questions, but they are in continuity with each other because revelation and salvation relate to each other as knowledge of God and the data for that knowledge.

The various answers given to these questions by the different biblical speakers constitute various biblical spiritualities. A final section of this analysis will define terms, and apply our method to a specific text, namely, Exodus 15.

The Spiritual Teaching of a Specific Text

Before beginning, two terms need to be defined: the notion of "realm" and the notion of "spirituality."

By *realm* is meant a group of activities, symbols, and meanings which is coherent within itself, complete, and distinct from other similar groups. For example, music is a distinct realm of human activity and experience. Science is another. Sports is another. Each has its own objectives, its own jargon and conventions of expression, and its own material support system.

The notion of *spirituality* is that which is found in phrases such as "Jesuit spirituality" or "Carmelite spirituality" or "Hasidic spirituality," and it involves a specific approach to prayer along with a specific style of life, or an asceticism.

It will be helpful to distinguish between the spirituality in itself and the asceticism which depends on it. We may define spirituality as a *foundational stance of expectancy regarding divine revelation or divine intervention*. Asceticism then will be understood to mean the self-discipline, or a set of practices, which are adopted because of one's spirituality. (For example, if one's spirituality leads one to expect revelation or salvation only at the moment of death, then one's asceticism might exclude involvement in family or in politics.)

Spirituality will be *foundational* in that it relates to ultimate value and proceeds from the deepest foundation of one's potentially conscious self. Being foundational it will govern all dependent operations.[22] It will be a *stance* rather than a doctrine or truth, in that it may or may not become the object of explicit intellectual appropriation, even though it will always command intellectual activities. It is a stance of *expectancy* in that its object is finally transcendent, never definitively possessed, and always in this life to be readdressed in ongoing experience.

Spiritualities will be differentiated then by the "realms" in which God is expected to reveal himself or to intervene. These realms may be diverse, even widely diverse. For example, war is one realm in which God might intervene or appear. If one has a foundational stance of expectancy that God will intervene in war, then a military asceticism will be reasonable. Mental prayer, or mystic union, is a quite different realm, defining a spirituality which might lead to the asceticism of monastic life. Israel's holy war spirituality, as we shall see in Exodus 15, expects God to intervene before the battle by melting the heart of the enemy. In Islam, on the other hand, if there is a holy war or *jihad*, then the decisive intervention of Allah will be at the moment of death when the faithful soldier is carried off to his reward. An entirely different asceticism is demanded in each case: in Israel one must practice passivity during the battle, and religious ritual after it; in Islam, one must exercise suicidal courage, throwing oneself heroically into danger.

We shall attempt to apply this approach, or method, to a relatively short text, by way of example. For the first step, namely, historical-critical information about the meaning of the text, we will simply rely on existing scholarship. In this case, Exodus 15:1-21, we shall rely on a recent study of this text by Frank Cross, Jr.[23]

We may begin then with the first phase of the speaker, the literary form. The text presents a narrative of the celebrations of a victory song in honor of a god of war. The song of the prophetess Deborah in Judges 5 is perhaps the closest parallel. First, the text of the song itself is heard being sung in a cultic setting, where Moses and the people recall the annihilation of Pharaoh's army at the Reed Sea, and then the gathering of Yahweh's people on the mountain of God.[24] There then follows in prose a sort of corrective commentary (vv. 19-21), in which is recalled first the tradition that the miracle at the Reed Sea consisted not only of the annihilation of the Egyptians, but also of the wondrous saving of Israel; and second the original setting of this celebration, namely, a special cultic act involving only women. This allows for the repetition of the first couplet of the song, forming an inclusion.

The song is carried by three images of archetypal power. The first half of the song (vv. 1-12) presents Yahweh as a god of war, an Ares or a Wotan, giving him a shrill war cry, *ga oh ga ah* (v. 1), and praising him as a "man of war" (v. 3). Also in the first part of the song God's radical power is imaged as power over primal water. Water is normally an image of rebirth or of a chaos which God turns to order, an element in which a man or woman floats softly to the surface and to the light. Here, because of Yahweh's right hand, the Egyptians sink like stone in the water (v. 5, and again in v. 8), the water turns into a ravenous underworld (v. 12), and Yahweh mobilizes the water to fight actively against the Egyptians (v. 8). In the second half of the song (vv. 13-18) a third archetypal image carries the meaning: while other people watch in amazement, Yahweh brings his own people over the Jordan (v. 16), and establishes them on his holy mountain (vv. 17-18).[25]

The second phase of the speaker, the personages, softens these effects. Moses and the people first, and then Miriam with her drum and her women recall the past in song. We are not directly present to the events themselves, but only to their celebration. Moses and the people are figures who are assimilated to roles in the Jerusalem Temple liturgy, roles played possibly by the king and a group of singers. Miriam as the "prophetess" and her companions sing the opening verse, whose meaning is here interpreted by the whole song which we have just read. They do not gloat over the victory as does Deborah in Judges 5, but rather they ask for Yahweh's continued protection of Israel as in the days of the Reed Sea. This role is akin to the intercessory prophetic role characteristic of the Ephraimite tradition.[26]

In the third phase of the speaker, the unnamed narrator, we are given even more distance from the violence of the song itself. The narrator has just terminated his account of the events at the Reed Sea. He now proceeds to a creative reflection about them, using a familiar song, and linking together the crossing of the Sea with hitherto separate traditions, namely, the entry into the promised land and the gathering of God's people on a holy mountain. With this consideration the narrator concludes the Exodus story and gives it a very distinctive, composite meaning. (In the ensuing chapters, the narrator turns to other themes and traditions, i.e., the desert stories and the Sinai pericope.) By choosing to recall two very different cultic settings for the song, the narrator achieves a substantial aesthetic distance.

Finally we must consider the fourth phase of the speaker, the historical author. If we take this to be the Pentateuchal editor-author, and place him or her with Israel in exile, apparently removed from God's holy mountain forever, then the text moves up into a very ethereal realm indeed. It becomes a remote memory, an eschatological hope, with mythical meaning and archetypal power. If we take the historical author to be the architects of the Christian Bible, then even greater distance is achieved.

What *spirituality* is carried by the text? In what realm is God expected to appear? Certainly, the realm will be situated where there is a final conflict between God and God's enemies, and where at the same time God is drawing his people to himself in a sacral sphere. Obviously, the Last Judgment is a realm which realizes this scenario perfectly. There are other possibilities as well. If one focuses on the Pentateuchal editor-author, then one might think of a concrete Zionist hope: God will intervene when the Jews are restored to Jerusalem. However, the distancing of the text from historical reality could justify less sharply defined expectancies: God will be expected to intervene to save any Jewish community facing persecution, or to save his Church at odds with any secular power, and so on.

The Christian community developed a lot of war imagery around Christ and his enemy Satan. A classical text for this is, for example, Ignatius Loyola's meditation on "The Two Standards," in the "second week" of his *Spiritual Exercises*. This text portrays the "chief of all enemies" in the Babylonian plain, seated on a fiery throne, surrounded with smoke, horrible and terrifying to behold, summoning his followers to war under his banner. And on the other side it presents "Christ, our Lord" in a delightful field near Jerusalem, humble, most attractive in appearance, friendly, and sending his own on an opposed mission under his banner. In meditating on these images, one making the *Exercises* is invited to apply them to any concrete circumstances of his or her own life and times.

What *asceticism* will be demanded by this spirituality? The Christian image of the meek and lowly Christ in these contexts teaches that warring under his banner involves the way of the Cross and demands humility, poverty and self-denial. At first glance this seems at odds with the god of war depicted in Exodus 15: as though Exodus 15 asked the reader to be warlike as our heavenly protector is warlike! The fact is, however, that Exodus 15 asks no such thing. Rather, it portrays God's people as passive in the war, as exulting in God's power without having or needing any of their own. What is demanded of the reader is trust in God's power, a practice of cultic celebration, fidelity to the community which God has formed on his mountain. This is the asceticism of the lamb, or the trusting and pious faithful. And it is interesting to see how the later Christian tradition, while rearranging the original images, retains the normative subliminal meaning, that is, the original spirituality and asceticism.

This spirituality, like other biblical spiritualities, may be invoked with powerful effect by any spiritual or political leader whose people read the Bible. Recently, Ronald Reagan, President of the United States, invoked the spirituality of Exodus 15 when he depicted the Soviet Union as "the dark empire." One is easily led to think of the cosmic power of an atomic war, of the enemies of God being destroyed, and of America as God's holy mountain with God's chosen people gathered there. We are drawn to wave the flag, trust the government, leave the power to God alone. The Bible contains alternative, and opposed, spiritualities which may equally be invoked by someone else. It is a task for biblical scholars to describe the various spiritual teachings of the Bible, in order to make them all available, and in this way to restore biblical truth.

Notes

1. For a useful survey of current critical theory, cf. Frank Lentricchia, *After the New Criticism* (Chicago: University of Chicago Press, 1980); and Elmer Borklund, *Contemporary Literary Critics* (London: St. James Press, and New York: St. Martin's Press, 1977). An exception to this attitude is E. D. Hirsch, *Validity in Interpretation* (New Haven and London: Yale University Press, 1960). Lentricchia characterizes Hirsch's view as "the hermeneutic of innocence"!

2. The idea that poets do not understand their own meaning goes back at least to Plato's *Republic*, bk. X. Over the past fifty years, because of the towering influence of F. R. Leavis, and the so-called "New Criticism," it has become less and less fashionable to be concerned about the historical context and the historical author. Only the "Geneva School" of "critics of consciousness," led by George Poulet, resisted this tide. H.-G. Gadamer's influential work, *Warheit und Methode* (Tübingen: Mohr-Siebeck, 1960), with its insistence on the independ-

ent life of the text itself after the moment of its publication, gave sharper focus to these perspectives.

3. Cf. Brevard Childs, *Biblical Theology in Crisis* (Philadelphia: Westminster Press, 1979) 97–98.

4. The growth of the idea of treating the Bible as literature has perhaps reached a climax in the publication of Northrop Frye's *The Great Code: The Bible and Literature* (Toronto: Academic Press, 1982). Frye creates a new discipline, dealing with imagery without historical ("centrifugal" is his term) context or reference.

5. Cf. David Kelsey, *The Uses of Scripture in Recent Theology* (Philadelphia: Fortress Press, 1975).

6. Cf. Bernard Lonergan, *Method in Theology* (London: Darton, Longman and Todd, 1972) 276. Lonergan presents a challenge which, if not met, will entail a rejection of the authority of Scripture. This study is an attempt to meet that challenge. His challenge is close to that of Brevard Childs, in that he points out the chasm between historical-critical exegesis and theology.

7. For an excellent demonstration of this fact, cf. Brevard Childs, *The Book of Exodus: A Critical Theological Commentary* (Philadelphia: Westminster Press, 1974). In treating each pericope, Childs provides a series of what he calls "contexts" or later interpretations, which diverge astoundingly from each other and from the original meaning. For another striking demonstration, cf. Gerald T. Sheppard, *Wisdom as a Hermeneutical Construct: A Study in the Sapientializing of the Old Testament* (BZAW 151) (Berlin and New York: Walter de Gruyer, 1980). An excellent study of this fact is to be found in Hans Frei, *The Eclipse of Biblical Narrative* (New Haven and London: Yale University Press, 1974).

8. Cf. Brevard Childs *Theology in Crisis,* especially 107–122, where Childs retains an acute sense of historical context, and proposes mutual illumination of the Old by the New, of the New by the Old, through a dialectic process. Cf. also N. Frye, *The Great Code, passim,* especially 78.

9. This striking example is worked out in detail in Brevard Childs, *Theology in Crisis,* 151–163. Such use of Scripture by later biblical authors, which is not interpretation but rather re-interpretation, was the rule and not the exception. The range is limitless: for example, editorial gloss effecting a change in meaning, as in Genesis 22 where the Elohist's searing tale about trusting God radically is shifted to trust in the merits of Abraham, by the editorial addition of vv. 15-18; didactic comment in the light of synthesizing categories such as "faith" in Hebrews 11 or "wisdom" in Sirach 44–50; daring *non-sequitur* as in Deuteronomy 4:10-24; the rewriting of an old story to carry a new *tendenz* as in Deuteronomy 1:19-46 (which rewrites Numbers 13–14 to emphasize the guilt of the people); the editorial formation of a new synthesis out of older, sometimes unrelated materials, as in the Pentateuch, the Deuteronomistic History, the book of Jeremiah, etc.; a radical re-editing of an earlier complex to create a different message, as in Chronicles; and finally a kaleidoscope of interpretative modes evidenced in Qumran and the New Testament. For the New Testament, Childs presents a representative bibliography in *Biblical Theology in Crisis,* footnote 16, 241. For Qumran and the "intertestamental" period, cf. for example Maurya P. Horgan, *Pesharim: Qumran Interpretation of Biblical Books* (CBQ Monograph Series 8) (Washington: The Catholic Biblical Association of America, 1979), especially Part II, 229-259, with its useful bibliography.

10. For a fuller refutation of the possibility of using the canon as a whole for context, cf. S. McEvenue "The Old Testament, Scripture or Theology," *Interpretation* 35 (1981), especially 236-239.

11. Jonathan Culler, *The Pursuit of Signs: Semiotics, Literature, Deconstruction* (Ithaca, N.Y.: Cornell University Press, 1981) 6.

12. The position which I shall propose is far from isolated, though it must be carefully distinguished from others which share a single trait. For example, the deconstructionist Geoffrey

Hartman, in the Preface of a collection of essays entitled *Deconstruction and Criticism* (New York: Continuum Publishing Co., 1979), vii, heads in the same direction but with very different intent. Northrop Frye develops a literary understanding of Scripture based on archetypal images which at times may not be at all evident to the reader. This position was brilliantly presented in *Anatomy of Criticism: Four Essays* (New Jersey: Princeton University Press, 1957) and then again in a more doctrinaire fashion in *The Great Code*. Finally, "structuralist" reading of Scripture, whether focused on surface or on deep structures, deals with subliminal meaning and effects of the text. Cf. Robert Polzin, *Biblical Structuralism: Method and Subjectivity in the Study of Ancient Texts* (Philadelphia: Fortress Press, 1977), with its useful bibliography. The possibility, method, and limits of a structuralist poetics have been laid out with welcome clarity by Jonathan Culler, *Structuralist Poetics, Structuralism, Linguistics and the Study of Literature* (London: Routledge and Kegan Paul, 1975).

13. It may be precisely the need to give expression to such subtle and complex knowledge which leads some authors to write fiction and poetry, rather than descriptive or scientific prose. Cf. Cleanth Brooks, "The Heresy of Paraphrase," in *The Well Wrought Urn* (New York: Harcourt Brace Jovanovitch, 1975) for a compelling demonstration of the impossibility of saying what a poem means in any other words.

14. The work of Claus Westermann, for example in his commentary on *Isaiah 40–66* (Philadelphia: Westminster Press, 1969), has made extensive use of this kind of observation.

15. This work applied to theological ideas most of which he had worked out in his earlier book, *Insight: An Essay in Human Understanding* (New York: Philosophical Library, 1958), written in the same city and published one year before Frye's *Anatomy*.

16. Cf. Bernard Lonergan, *Method in Theology*, 235–266.

17. Cf. Joseph Blenkinsopp, *Prophecy and Canon: A Contribution to the Study of Jewish Origins* (Notre Dame: University of Notre Dame Press, 1977).

18. Cf. ibid., 6.

19. Cf. ibid., 147.

20. Cf. ibid., 144.

21. It may be helpful to adduce evidence that historical authors themselves *intend* the subliminal meaning, rather than the articulated ones, and that the method proposed here is not drawn only from the idiosyncratic needs of a biblical scholar. Doris Lessing, in a novel first published in 1962 entitled *The Golden Notebook*, puts the following analysis on the lips of a novelist named Anne: "The novel is 'about' a colour problem. I said nothing in it that wasn't true. But the emotion it came out of was something frightening, the unhealthy, feverish illicit excitement of wartime, a lying nostalgia, a longing for license, for freedom, for the jungle, for formlessness. It is so clear to me that I cannot read that novel without feeling ashamed, as if I were in a street naked. Yet no one else seems to see it. Not one of the reviewers saw it. . . . And it would be that emotion which would make those fifty books novels and not reportage." (Bantam paperback edition, 63.) What Lessing calls "emotion" is clearly a foundational stance which remained subliminal for the "reviewers," but which for the author was the real meaning. An exegesis which overlooked the *Sitz-im-Leben* of the historical author, namely, war in Europe, would radically miss the point, reducing the novel to reportage! The fourth phase of the speaker gives the essential clue. If that clue were missing, still a very perceptive reading might correctly identify the stance, and even identify the historical context of the author, namely, reestablish the clue.

22. The notions of "realm" and of "foundation" are drawn from Bernard Lonergan, *Method in Theology, passim*, but especially 272 and 267–269.

23. F. M. Cross, "The Song of the Sea," in *Canaanite Myth and Hebrew Epic: Essays in the History of the Religion of Israel* (Cambridge, Mass: Harvard University Press, 1973) 121–144. This study seems to compel assent. For further discussion and bibliography, cf. Brevard Childs, commentary on Exodus cited in note 7 above, 240–248.

24. For details of the form cf. F. Cross, "The Song of the Sea."

25. For an elaboration of this image, and a study of its origins, cf. Richard J. Clifford, *The Cosmic Mountain in Canaan and the Old Testament* (Cambridge, Mass: Harvard University Press, 1972).

26. Cf. the discussion of the "Ephraimite Tradition" in Robert R. Wilson, *Prophecy and Society in Ancient Israel* (Philadelphia: Fortress Press, 1980), indicted in the index under the entry "Intercession."

Chapter 3

A Mandala for Biblical Commentary

The paths of philosophy and theology repeatedly cross in the wilderness, often with fruitful outcomes. Over the past thirty years we have seen a massive encounter between hermeneutical theory and biblical interpretation. One has only to think, for example, of the explosive impact of Jacques Derrida, both in Europe and in America, during the 1980s.

This paper will not provide an overview of the maze of literary critical theory, or spin a thread to lead one safely through it. Rather, it will provide a framework for reflection, with a view to enabling exegetes systematically to search out a few principles of interpretation (biblical commentary) which have been illuminated through this debate, and which clarify the objectives of commentary.[1]

The principles of interpretation may be grouped in terms of four major relations: the complex or relations between elements within the work; the relation to its author (historic context); the relation to its readers; and the relation to its object, that is, its subject matter.

a) Relations internal to the work

Under this heading are included the principles of "composition criticism," and of what used to be called "the new criticism," a discipline which totally dominated all academic interpretation of literature from early in this century until very recently. It rightly built on the notion that the meaning of a text is expressed by the interrelation of its elements (words, sentences, images, etc.), and that the precise meanings of all the elements of a text are determined, not primarily from the linguistic, literary, and historical contexts which surround the text, but rather from the interrelation of these elements within the text itself. Reading should begin by recognizing these interrelations. Hence, the importance of identifying the exact beginning and ending of the text, and of reading it first as a whole. The text is to be first studied for the meaning it has developed within itself: its narrative or rhetorical structures, its logics and breaks in logic, the coherence and incoherence of its imagery, the relations between meaning and image, between truth and emotion, its genre, its horizon, and finally its precise and idiosyncratic use of language and of literary forms. One must first discover the meaning which is actually carried by these precise words in this precise order, by all of these parts in this whole artistic unity.

For the purposes of a Bible commentary, the biblical "book" should be recognized as the primary literary unit. This will entail the evocation of an implied speaker and of an implied reader who together make of the book an artistic unity. In narrative books the implied speaker is often easily imagined, whereas in other books such as Proverbs, for example, and especially Psalms, the implied speaker is a more subtle figure.

When applied to Old Testament, this method sometimes has to face special problems in making the all-important first step of determining the exact extent of "the text" to be interpreted. For example, the beginnings and endings of poetic units in prophetic books are often not clear at all, and the "sources" and redactional units in historical books are endlessly disputed.

b) Relation of a book to its author (historic context)

Under this heading are included the principles of the "historical-critical method," which was refined principally in Germany as a discipline growing out of the Enlightenment. This method has been much maligned in recent times, but its contribution remains indispensable. This method focuses on the importance of contexts: textual context and historical context. The textual context consists of those texts which the author knew (and which therefore preceded him/her in time), and particularly those texts which the author depended upon, or referred to, in writing. The historical context consists of the events in the author's life, or in the ongoing life of the communities in which the author finds meaning, which were in the author's mind as he/she wrote, and which in some ways motivated or shaped the writing, or provided the subject matter upon which the author intended to write.

In referring to "author" here, there is no intent to evoke an authorial mind or intention beyond that which is expressed or implied by the text. Each text has an "implied author," as most would agree. However, there was also a real author, and it is through that often unknown person that the text is anchored in existential concern, and in specific history. The author spoken of here is not to be thought of as the private historical person whose identity and thoughts we may know from other sources. Rather it is the published historical person as author, that is, the author as expressed in the text.

The historical-critical method also extends to the redaction history, establishing the contexts of the various sources, and of the various redactions, of a book as it headed toward its final form.

It is true that the meaning of a text is not exhausted by meanings defined through this discipline, any more than the meaning of a law is exhausted by the intent of the original law-giver, or the meaning of a national anthem by the political horizon of its writer. However, it is also true that until this originating meaning has been grasped the reader may very well not have understood the text at all. Without the control of this discipline, one risks reading into the text meanings which simply are not there, and missing entirely the inspired meanings which are there. Granted the difficulty of this method on the one hand, and the insidious pressure both of sloth and of bias on the other, biblical commentary must take very special care to maintain this discipline.

Finally, it is important to note that the biblical authors wrote out of religious faith, hope and charity. It is for this quality of their work that tradition has retained their books, including them in a canon. Therefore, historical-critical method has not achieved its purpose until it has ascertained, through the myriad methods at its disposal, precisely what religious affirmation is made in the text.

c) Relation of a book to its reader

Literary scholars have tended to exploit this avenue of interpretation more actively in recent years.[2] One facet of this approach shows that a text implies, not only a writer, but also a reader, that is, a reader with certain qualifications such that the reading will be competent. For example, it implies a reader who knows the language in which it is written (or who is member of a community which is able to translate that text), a reader who is familiar, perhaps, with certain geographical references, familiar with certain historical events, and so forth. It implies a reader with a certain kind of curiosity, and with a certain type of literary expectation. In the case of enduring classics like the Bible, this relation will be to diverse readerships over centuries. All of this pertains to the meaning of the text. Commentary must provide the information and perspective which a specific group of readers may otherwise lack, so that they may become competent as readers of biblical texts.

In the specific case of the biblical text, the implied reader is really a community, and a community which is prepared to apply the text to its contemporary experience of life with God even to the point of reorganizing, editing and adding to the text. Thus the Pentateuch, for example, makes no effort to disguise its use of different sources, its editing, and its self-correction over the centuries. Only in the very last text added to the Pentateuch is there an indication that all of this must now come to an end (Deut

4:2; cf. Rev 22:18-19). This implies a reader with a very special orientation.

The reader implied by the biblical text desires authentic relationship with God. Over the centuries, such a reader will have different characteristics and expectations in different places and cultures. Certain points in the history of reading a text are more significant than others, especially the moments when canonical wholes are established such as the Pentateuch, or the book of Isaiah, or the Old Testament canon, or the dividing of Luke to form the four Gospels over against the Epistles. Most universal and important of all moments of reading is that creative period when the Christian canon was formed during the first four centuries C.E. The implied reader of that period could finally understand biblical revelation as a whole, and this is what a Christian Bible reader wants to experience.

Of course the canon remained partially open. In the sixteenth century the Council of Trent formally recognized one form of canon, but some important aspects of the canon seem still to be under discussion even today. For example, there is no consensus about the Massoretic versus the Septuagint order of Old Testament books, or the order of chapters in Jeremiah, or the division of the Psalms, not to mention the thousands of textual variants, and so forth. All of these canonical decisions, as they are made, will affect the meaning of the biblical text.

This aspect of interpretation, sometimes called "canonical criticism," is not an artificial academic method. Rather, it is a meaning which is intended by the text of the Bible insofar as the traces of growth in the text imply something about the reader and the reading, and therefore imply something about the intended meaning.

The biblical texts imply a reader who has in effect read the whole biblical text several times, over many years, and centuries, and this aspect of its meaning must control something of the contents of a commentary. A commentary cannot provide for every imaginable obstacle to competent reading. However, a catholic commentary will provide for each biblical book the important information and perspectives which the whole biblical community over the centuries has brought to the reading.

The Fathers of the Church, who first formed and edited the Bible as a whole book and were its first expert readers, have also written the first commentaries on the texts understood as parts of the whole Bible. This patristic reading, when the canon was first complete, represents a meaning intended by scripture which must be recovered, modified in the light of contemporary critical understanding, and preserved in commentary today.

d) Relation of a book to its subject matter

One reads texts the better to understand the objects (or subject matters) of which they speak. Conversely, the better one knows what a text speaks of the better one will be able to understand the text. Thus, a modern reader who is conversant with current knowledge of radiation and of its effects on human cells may understand a text of Mme. Curie more fully than she herself could in her day, and commentary on what she wrote will illuminate her text with today's knowledge. Similarly, today's reader of Amos, for example, may have acquired conceptual information about God which goes far beyond that of Amos, through later revelation and through doctrinal development and catechesis. In that sense, today's reader of Amos may understand Amos' text better than its author.

However, when the subject matter is a person, and particularly when it is God, the relation of text to object is more complex. The subject matter of biblical literature is partly historical reality (and the discussion of historicity is endless), and partly mystery, namely, God known indirectly and spoken of through metaphor. Moreover, our knowledge of God, as of other persons or of values, is a psychic reality which transcends conceptualization and reasoned judgement. Knowledge of God includes also what is often termed holiness or authenticity, namely, conversion, love, gift of God (grace), and the extension of these into various sorts of psychic states and moral choices and life decisions and ways of being. In this sense, a reader of Amos will not be expected "to know" as much about God as Amos did. That is why we have returned to the biblical texts for thousands of years.

Obviously, a biblical commentary for today's reader must take account of the theological or catechetical formation of that reader, and use that background in pointing the reader to the knowledge of God which Amos enjoyed.

Within this broad philosophical horizon, we will focus upon two hermeneutical points about the relation of the book to its subject matter: first, the subject matter of biblical texts is the incarnate Word of God; and second, the texts of the Bible are written in a literary mode.

First, biblical texts speak about a truth which will be fully known only in the future. This must be conceived with some precision.

It is frequently said that the Old Testament is fulfilled in the New. This is profoundly true, but it must be noted that this way of speaking is easily misunderstood as suggesting some simple inter-textual relationship such as that between plane geometry and solid geometry. Whereas an earlier text and a later text may both relate to God in exactly the same way, they cannot relate to each other in the same way. A radical asymmetry must be recognized between the relation of an early text to a later one and the reverse relation. Whereas later texts often refer directly and consciously to earlier ones in some sense of fulfillment—and exegesis must point this out wherever it occurs—it is important to note that earlier texts can never refer directly and consciously to later ones.

Moreover, texts do not fulfill texts, though they may intend events which more fully reveal what an earlier text has partially understood. What is true, but ill-expressed in the term fulfillment, is that all texts of the Bible intend, not so much each other, but rather the reality of the Word of God, and that God's Word was gradually revealed through history until it was fully revealed (fulfilled) in the person of Jesus Christ at the time of the New Testament. Even this full revelation in Jesus will be completed for humanity only in the *parousia* at the end of time. All texts of the Bible attempt to speak, from the horizon of their time, of a reality which will be completely revealed only in the end time. Thus, the subject matter of a biblical text is always something which will be better known in the future, either in a later biblical event, or in the historical Jesus, or in the risen Christ.

Second, biblical texts speak of truths which transcend objective categories. Biblical texts are literary in nature (i.e., written with artistic form and subtlety), but not with either philosophic or scientific logic, precision and limitation. There is a wide range of genres between early and later Hebrew poetry, through Hebrew and Greek narrative and rhetorical prose forms, to the post-philosophic genre of the Wisdom of Solomon. But all biblical texts are essentially literary in nature. Thus their subject matter, or truth, will be the sort of truth which is appropriate to literature, and that is why the Second Vatican Council spoke of "salvific truth," and most writers speak of the "message," rather than of the "doctrine," of a given text. In contrast with this, the doctrinal tradition of the Church is philosophic rather than literary. It is based on Scripture; but it exists and develops in a different mode of thought.

If one would write about God as known by faith, then literary genres are particularly appropriate, because literature is a way of writing in which the subjective stance of the writer shapes and controls an inquiry to which the resulting poem, or story, or speech, or letter is a unique answer. The "truth" of literary answers is immediately tested by criteria of form and language, but over time it is measured in terms of authenticity of the subjective stance of the author. The genesis of faith is similar. Faith shares with other knowledge the character of being the answer to inquiry; but it differs from other knowledge in that the inquiry in this case is directly motivated, not by sense data only, and not by ordinary human desire, but by that unlimited love which is infused by grace. The experience of unlimited love (charity) motivates inquiry through questions which would never otherwise be asked, and answers to these questions are the content of faith.[3]

In contrast to this, philosophical and scientific inquiry strives to work "objectively" in a sense which deliberately excludes an agenda based on such a subjective basis. In recent decades, deconstruction has successfully shown the controlling nature of "politics" in all academic writing, thus weakening the wall between that and literature. It remains true, however, that literature relates subjectively to objects, whereas academic writing strives to relate objects only to each other.

One major principle of contemporary literary criticism is that a certain kind of paraphrase of a literary work is taboo. What is aimed at here is that kind of paraphrase which attempts to transpose literary truth into univocal, systematic, universal categories, whether these be philosophical, or ethical, or theological, or psychological, or historical. A typical paraphrase is, for example, to say that "the whole point" of a scene or story is this or that, thus reducing a complex meaning to a narrow thesis. Literary affirmation is always unique, and is often very subtly conceived through ellipse and allusion and juxtaposition and sound and image in such a way that it cannot be expressed in any other words than those of the unique poem, or story, or exhortation, and so forth. To reproduce it in systematic and objective categories and statements is to escape its power, and miss its wonder, and lose its meaning.

According to this principle, when discussing the meaning of a literary statement (i.e., a unit larger than individual words or phrases or sentences), commentators do well to be very cautious whenever they are tempted to write the phrase "that means," and more so the phrase "that meant." Such statements are too often, not only simplifying and reductive, but also destructive of the literary, and literal, meaning. Biblical texts affirm different ways of being open to, or experiencing, the unlimited Word of God, and point the reader to that precise knowledge. Commentary should never presume to carry that burden itself. It should enable the reader to hear, once again, the song which rose in the heart of the biblical writer. It should place the reader in the best location to hear and see. And it should stop there.

Notes

1. The principles articulated in this paper may be seen worked out concretely in chapter 9 in this volume, "A Commentary on Manna," pp. 95–112.

2. Cf. Jane P. Tompkins (ed.), *Reader Response Criticism: From Formalism to Post-Structuralism* (Baltimore: John Hopkins University Press, 1980).

3. Cf. Bernard Lonergan, *Method in Theology* (London: Darton, Longman and Todd, 1972) 115–118, 237–243.

Chapter 4

Theological Doctrines and the Old Testament: Lonergan's Contribution

I. Introduction

This paper deals not with "interpretation" of Scripture but rather with the relation between correctly interpreted Scripture and contemporary theology.

The word "theology" can sometimes be used loosely to designate any form of God-talk. And there have been many forms: myths, legends, sacred histories, songs and poems, liturgies, pilgrimages, religious wars, exhortations, architecture and art, theodicies, polemical tracts, histories of thought, theses, tractates, dogmas, visions, and so forth. However, the word can also be given a more narrow definition, and in the context of this paper a narrow definition will be helpful.

In Western society, theology developed as a discourse controlled by logic and coherence, alongside other forms of God-talk. It may have developed as a technique for narrowing and resolving disputes between religious factions,[1] or it may simply have been one concomitant of a more complex picture of evolution in Western modes of thought.[2] The goal of theology was not so much edification of the faithful[3] as it was that repose of intellect which we call truth, and which has been differently understood as the centuries have passed. The criterion in theology was not artistic excellence, or popular appeal, but rather its derivation from revelation,[4] following appropriate critical scholarship, logic, and methodical demonstration. It is propositional in nature.

Lonergan defines "theology" as a mediator "between a cultural matrix and the significance and role of religion in that matrix."[5] He includes under the category "theology" far more than our definition will allow: in this paper "theology" will signify only theological truths, that is, what Lonergan calls "Doctrines" and "Systems."

Lonergan rejects the possibility of any simple, direct link between theology as we know it and biblical texts: "Scholarship builds an impenetrable wall between systematic theology and its historical sources. . . ." And he claims that exegesis will have to work within a more sophisticated hermeneutic if it is to serve theology: "this development invites philosophy and theology to migrate from a basis in theory to a basis in interiority."[6]

The fact is that, apart from work in relatively recent departments of Near Eastern Studies, biblical exegesis has always intended to serve theology. As a result, it has been influenced by the form of propositional truth employed in theology. Those of us who teach the Old Testament are well aware of the passion some students have to either find or refute historical truths in biblical texts. Scholars have at times been equally passionate in finding or refuting theological truths in the Old Testament. As recently as 1956, P. van Imschoot constructed a theology of the Old Testament, based on remarkably wide scholarship, whose principle of organization was a logical list of topics, and whose aim was to define a set of relatively fixed beliefs under these topics, on the basis of texts cited from various contexts and diverse centuries.[7] For example, he spends seven pages at the end of chapter 2 in the second volume, and much erudition, to establish that there is no evidence that the Jews practiced ancestor worship. Such a question does not arise out of reading the Old Testament, but out of *a priori* concerns.

Van Imschoot was relatively good. I remember a professor, who is best left nameless, spending two lecture hours trying to show that Jesus meant transubstantiation when He said "This is my body." He argued, on the basis of an astonishing list of citations drawn from Greek and Hellenistic philosophers, that by that time the Greek word *estin* ("is") designated substance.

With greater concern for historical horizons, Walter Eichrodt constructed an encompassing systematic theology of the Old Testament based on the concept of "covenant."[8]

Now all of that has become patently unacceptable. Lonergan is right in speaking of "an impenetrable wall." Von Rad's *Theology of the Old Testament* took a far more sophisticated route.[9] He presented a picture of thought and institutions in evolution. He defined no fixed doctrines of the Old Testament, and yet managed to give his study an aura of theological truth by an adroit use of existential vocabulary. It is an extraordinary achievement of historical scholarship, and subtlety of interpretation, and yet it seems to be seldom quoted anymore.[10] Von Rad's recurring technique was to pinpoint the central intent of texts by showing how the author had moved beyond his or her antecedent sources or traditions. This technique describes a line of development in doctrine to which we are heir, without fixing any doctrines by which we are bound.

After Von Rad, most theologies of the Old Testament have felt the need to adopt a new approach.[11] But the search for propositional truths in the

Old Testament continues in other forms of research. First, there is the recurrent *topos* of concepts and "themes" in the Old Testament.[12] Second, there have been studies of the "kerygma" of certain Old Testament authors.[13] And third, in some writers "Form Criticism" can tempt one to think of "basic form" as an inspired doctrine.

We shall begin by articulating the obvious, namely, that the truth of literature is not propositional and cannot be paraphrased. We shall then take an example of a theme study, a kerygma study, and a form study, and show how each yields a proposition which is unworthy of the text, poor theology in itself, and liable to distract us from what we should discover, by a migration "from a basis in theory to a basis in interiority" as truly normative in the text.[14] Finally, we shall show how Lonergan has provided keys to a more fruitful way of moving from a normative literature to normative truths.

II. Doctrines Versus Literature

It is clear, in Lonerganian terms, that the Bible is not written in either a theoretic or scientific mode of thought. It does not define terms, or use them univocally, or proceed according to rigid systems of logic, or by way of controlled experiment. The norms which govern writers of the Bible are norms of tradition, commonsense truth, literary form, aesthetic satisfaction, rhetorical effectiveness, and so forth. The Bible, then, must be classed as literature in a broad sense. Whereas, at one end of the range of literary forms, some passages of the Bible can be classed as pure lyrical poetry, it must be noted that, at the other extreme, probably no chronological note in the Bible, or historical account, or doctrinal discussion, reaches fully beyond the limits of literature to become systematic or scientific in a modern sense. Even if biblical texts are used in the service of establishing theological doctrines, they themselves never are doctrinal. Biblical texts of all stripes share in that marriage of thought and image, truth and emotion, description and metaphor which characterizes literature in general, and which is perhaps most easily studied in lyric poetry.

The best study I can name of the war between propositional truth and poetic discourse is that of the well-known American literary critic Cleanth Brooks in his book *The Well Wrought Urn*.[15] In successive chapters he studies ten major literary works from Donne to Yeats, and then offers a concluding synthesis in a final chapter entitled "The Heresy of Paraphrase." This is followed by a lengthy supportive appendix. His position is expressed in a nutshell as follows:

> And to point out what has been suggested in earlier chapters and brought to a head in this one, namely, that one can never measure a poem against

the scientific or philosophical yardstick for the reason that the poem, when laid along the yardstick, is never the "full poem" but an abstraction from the poem. . . . The essential structure of a poem (as distinguished from the rational or logical structure of the "statement" which we abstract from it) resembles that of architecture or painting: it is a pattern of resolved stresses . . . (it) resembles that of a ballet or musical composition. It is a pattern of resolutions and balances and harmonizations developed through a temporal scheme.[16]

For Brooks, any paraphrase of meaning does not express the inner structure of a literary work, but rather is a scaffolding built outside it in order to deal effectively with its parts.[17] The literary works studied by Cleanth Brooks each requires lengthy analysis. To illustrate our point it may be sufficient to point to a simple and familiar poem: Walter De la Mare's "The Listeners." How can one paraphrase this poem? What does it mean? What is the author trying to tell us? What is the point? the message? the kerygma?

> "Is there anybody there?" said the Traveller,
>   Knocking on the moonlit door;
> . . . But no one descended to the Traveller;
>   No head from the leaf-fringed sill
> Leaned over and looked into his grey eyes,
>   Where he stood perplexed and still.

Louis Untermeyer suggests three kinds of interpretation: it can be read as "the record of an actual quest"; or as "a fable of man's eternal attempt to answer life's riddle"; or "as a courageous challenge to terror."[18] These suggestions, at least if taken up by an interpreter of less sophistication, could lead to ridiculous reductions of meaning. Everything in the poem leads us away from the belief that it is merely an "actual quest," that is, an enhanced account of the poet's visit to an old house. The capital letter on "Traveller" refuses such an interpretation from the beginning. And the reality attributed to the phantom listeners, over against the reality of the Traveller, with "his grey eyes," makes such an interpretation impossible:

> But only a host of phantom listeners
>   That dwelt in the lone house then
> Stood listening in the quiet of the moonlight
>   To that voice from the world of men[.]

Secondly, it can hardly be dealt with as an attempt to answer what Untermeyer calls a "riddle." Such a description might fit a poem like Eliot's "The Love Song of J. Alfred Prufrock." In "The Listeners" there is no puzzle, and no inquiry about an answer to a question. There is only an inquiry about presence.

Finally, there is hardly a question of "terror." The phantom listeners are not unfriendly, and the Traveller desires to encounter them.

Clearly, no prose paraphrase, at least along the lines suggested by Louis Untermeyer, could be close to the heart of this simple poem. And yet the reader has to feel that the poem has a message of some kind:

> For he suddenly smote on the door, even
>   Louder, and lifted his head:—
> "Tell them I came and no one answered,
>   That I kept my word," he said.

Lonergan's discussion of interpretation envisages no reduction; and his move from interpretation to doctrine does not occur through any intervening reduction to paraphrase. It occurs principally through dialectic, where the reader accepts or rejects a text, not directly on the basis of its propositional meaning, but rather on the evidence for intellectual, ethical, and religious conversion in the author. It is a question of the state of conversion in the reader, a foundational stance, encountering the foundations of the author through the text, and coming to terms with the author on this interpersonal ground. One accepts the author, or the poem, rather than the "meaning" of the poem. This approach, of course, flies in the face of all the discredited rhetoric about "objectivity," and offers a legitimate mode of understanding the inclusion of values in the arena of truth.[19]

Without attempting to discuss Walter De la Mare, and conversion, on the basis of such a short text, it may be helpful to indicate one point of his foundational stance as author, which is useful for discerning the "message" of this poem. The whole genius of the poem is focused on the point of contact between a concrete world and a spirit world. A "Traveller" attempts to make precisely this contact. If the reader accepts this poem, he or she must accept the value, or potential for meaning, of this realm of experience. The reader is drawn to this realm, and made to feel that it is important to be there. That is not, strictly speaking, the message of the poem, which is a narrative without a message. But it is the subliminal message of the author.

It is important to recognize that this message is subliminal. It is not in any sense a paraphrase of the poem. It is expressed through the poem, but not directly by the poem. It is not the intent of the author, but the author's starting point, a starting point to which the author may not advert. In writing a poem, the author affirms this starting point, or foundational stance. In reading a poem, we interpret the words and intended meaning, but we also encounter and engage the author's subliminal affirmation.

To return to Cleanth Brooks:

> To repeat, most of our difficulties in criticism are rooted in the heresy of paraphrase. If we allow ourselves to be misled by it, we distort the relation of the poem to its "truth," we raise the problem of belief in a vicious and crippling form, we split the poem between its "form" and its "content"—we bring the statement to be conveyed into an unreal competition with science or philosophy or theology. In short, we put our question about the poem in a form calculated to produce the battles of the last twenty-five years over the "use of poetry."[20]

> [Conventional terms] are positively misleading in their implication that the poem constitutes a "statement" of some sort, the statement being true or false, and expressed more or less clearly or eloquently or beautifully; for it is from this formula that most of the common heresies about poetry derive. The formula begins by introducing a dualism which thenceforward is rarely overcome. . . . [I]t leaves the critic lodged upon one or the other of the horns of a dilemma: the critic is forced to judge the poem by its political or scientific or philosophical truth; or, he is forced to judge the poem by its form as conceived externally and detached from human experience.[21]

After Lonergan's contribution to the theory of interpretation, we are no longer caught on this dilemma. In the operation of interpretation, we need never separate message from form. In a subsequent level of dialectic, we may operate from a theological foundation, including faith and conversion, and then we may accept or reject a work on these grounds. Or we may operate on a different foundation (one to be defined by literary critics), and on these grounds, with their appropriate conversions, we may accept or reject the work as literature. In any case, paraphrase has no role to play. One's interpretation of a work does not focus separately on its "statement," or on its "form"; rather it reveals its inmost structure, the harmony of complex relations, a meaning which could not be expressed except by all the words of the text itself. One's final evaluation of a work will involve accepting or rejecting the foundational values of its author.

III. Themes as Doctrines

I should like to begin with an example of theme drawn from a book entitled *The Theme of the Pentateuch*, written by David Clines.[22] This is in no way a criticism of the book, nor of its author, who displays remarkable sophistication in literary theory as well as erudition in classical literature. It is the refinement of this presentation which makes it an excellent candidate for reflection on method.

Clines is very circumspect in defining theme, and devotes all of chapter 2 to this task. He defines theme progressively as follows: "The theme of a narrative work may first be regarded as a conceptualization of its

plot . . ." (17). ". . . the central or dominating idea in a literary work
. . . the abstract concept which is made concrete through its representation in person, action, and image in the work" (18). "A statement of the theme offers, in abbreviated form, an account of why the material of the work is there, and of why it is presented in the order and shape in which it is" (18). "[T]he statement of theme can serve an historical-critical purpose, of laying bare what the author intended to convey to his audience . . ." (19). The discovery of theme, then, in Clines' view, is the discerning of the author's intention to teach a doctrine. However, he refuses to be trapped in the subjectivity of the author; he explains that it is this subjectivity only as manifest objectively in the work. "To state the theme of a work is to say what it means that the work is as it is" (21). Moreover, later on, in chapter 10, he refuses to discuss the "purpose" of his "theme," preferring rather to discuss its "function," since the former term suggests that we know and care more than we do about the intention of the author, whereas the latter focuses on its effects on the readers (97).

Clines proposes the following definition as the theme of the Pentateuch:

> The theme of the Pentateuch is the partial fulfillment—which implies also the partial non-fulfillment—of the promise to or blessing of the patriarchs. The promise or blessing is both the divine initiative in a world where human initiatives always lead to disaster, and a reaffirmation of the primal divine intentions for man. The promise has three elements: posterity, divine-human relationship, and land (29).

As an interpretative tool this proposal is clearly a useful statement to keep in mind when approaching any pericope in the Pentateuch. Moreover, Clines shows in subsequent chapters that his proposal is fully justified in the text of the Pentateuch. Finally, it is a doctrine which the author of the Pentateuch surely would ascribe to, and which provides many handles for theologians to seize upon for discussion. The doctrine can be expressed, with less circumspection but greater clarity, as follows: God has promised, and begun to grant, nationhood, true religion, and Palestine to the Jews.

In chapter 10, Clines distinguishes between two functions of this theme: a historical function and a theological function. The historical function refers to what meaning the Pentateuch had for its intended first readers, fifth-century Jews in exile. Clines gives the example of Diaspora Jews understanding Genesis 11, not as an account of the dispersal of races and nations of the world, but rather as an explanation of the exile of Israel (98). Now this is well named a "historical function," but further analysis is clearly needed. Clines does not discuss the shift from its first historical function at the time of the Yahwist writing of Genesis 11 in the ninth century under the great Solomonic empire (when Israel was acutely conscious of the dispersal of nations and cultures) to a second historical function during the Exile. Clines does not ask whether this naive appropriation of meaning is legitimate or not: for example, if exiled Jews could read this way in the fifth century B.C.E., should the Armenians or the Irish apply the text to themselves in this century? By distinguishing between historical function and theological function he implies some illegitimacy to historical function. He would need to explain that it was legitimate in the past, but now things have changed: that is, it was legitimate in a cultural matrix in which awareness of historical differentiation played no role, since theology can be asked only to mediate between one's "cultural matrix and the significance and role of a religion in that matrix." In the ancient world, such naive appropriation of meaning to oneself and one's historical situation was doing theology in the only way it could be done.

When he comes to discuss "theological function," Clines betrays indirectly the poverty of his approach. He recognizes that the theology to be derived from the Bible must retain its historical root, and yet achieve universal applicability. He proposes two ways to do this. The first is a discussion of story as an introduction into another world, and an invitation to react personally to what is revealed in that world (102–111). This is excellent.[23] And it corrects any tendency to use theme as a mode of reductionism in the interpretation of meaning (18). However, it bears no relation whatever to "theme." One does not need Clines' theme in order to derive meaning from the Pentateuch as "world" or as "story." In fact, he himself does not refer to the theme anywhere in this section!

The second way Clines proposes to derive a universal function for the Pentateuch is to focus on the word "promise" in his theme and move to a rich discussion of "hope" as diverse from, and preferable to, "existentialism." This also is excellent. However, it is not derived from his "theme," or even from the explicit teaching of the Pentateuch. The category "hope" does not seem even to exist in biblical Hebrew. Among the patriarchs, Abraham is described as having "faith," but this seems to mean something more like "trust" in a present sense, rather than "hope" with its future orientation. Clines derives "hope" from the category of "promise," and simply drops the word "blessing" in this section. However, in the Pentateuch itself, "blessing" is an activity which is ascribed to God far more often than promising. What Clines does here is legitimate, but he does not seem to be aware of the step he has taken. The step is not helped by thinking of "theme." Clines has in fact left theme behind, and moved into the foundational stance of the author. Hope is a passionate religious stance of the author/editor of the Pentateuch, who, in exile, evoked the remote age of promise and liberation, and who collected all the old laws to depict a wonderful society intended by God.[24] As readers, we are subliminally addressed by this stance, and challenged either to accept or reject hope as a way of living. Despite himself, Clines reads the Pentateuch rightly. The step which Clines takes, without adverting to it, is what Lonergan refers to, in the text cited at the beginning of this paper, as a migration "from a basis in theory to a basis in interiority," that is, an interpretation based on awareness of one's foundational stance in dialectic with the foundational stance of the biblical author.

The theme of the Pentateuch as established by Clines is an interpretative tool and a helpful summary. However, the unique power of the Pentateuch, and its normative role in forming Western culture, has not come either from this theme or from the various "historical functions" to which the history of exegesis can point. The foundational stances of the authors and major editors, precisely because they are subliminal, never explicit in the text, have been powerful persuaders and normative in society. The power of the Pentateuch, and its central teaching, consists in its passionate desire to be with God in establishing, at some future time, a great society of justice and prosperity. Clines' book helps us see and feel this more clearly, but its limits in regard to method make its best parts discontinuous with the rest of the book, and could lead us to overlook what is really important in the text.

IV. Kerygma as Doctrine

The word "kerygma" is often understood to mean preaching. However, in studies which speak of "the kerygma" of a text, the notion tends to narrow to "message," in a sense close to doctrine.

Hans Walter Wolffe's study of "The Kerygma of the Yahwist" in 1964 was so persuasive in itself, and so influential in subsequent Pentateuchal study, that it was not only cited in every relevant bibliography, but also translated for a wider readership in 1966.[25] The study began with the relation between Old and New Testaments in a theological perspective, and proposed that the two can be fruitfully related only by articulating and comparing their respective kerygmata (131–132). It then proceeds to discuss the extent of the J text (Gen 2:4a to Num 25:5), its date of origin (reign of Solomon), and its intent (to proclaim a kerygma distinct from its sources) (133–137). There follows a subtle and convincing analysis of Genesis 12:1–4a which concludes that, within the formula that "I will bless those who bless you, but whoever despises you him will I curse," the Yahwist intends to proclaim primarily a blessing which will come to Abraham and through his descendants to all the nations of the world: "So, then, all the families of the earth can gain a blessing in you" (138–140). This universalistic intent, then, is *the* message of the Yahwistic Tetrateuch. Wolffe claims that all the other pericopes are to be read in the light of this overriding message,[26] "even if they originally intended to say something else, and even if they continue to keep their own *secondary* function."[27] The same message was subsequently picked up in modified form by post-Yahwist writers.[28]

This thesis was singularly enlightening, and it has doubtless formed the backbone of many lectures in introductory courses in many universities.[29] I, for one, have always felt guilty when preparing to give this wonderful lecture, because not only was it too easy but also, it never seemed quite to stick.

First of all, it does not do justice to the Yahwist teaching. The message is a message of the Yahwist, but any suggestion that it is *the* message is clearly reductionist. One must note that the universalist message is expressed in only a half verse (Gen 12:3b). Wolffe's thesis would imply that a reader whose attention was ever so slightly diverted during that half verse could never have understood the Yahwist at all! Moreover, Wolffe lists five texts as bridge passages written specifically by the Yahwist: Genesis 6:5-8; 8:21-22; 12:1-4a; 18:17-18, 22b-23. Of these only chapter 12 carries the universalist message directly, and chapter 18 very indirectly indeed. In fact, after Exodus 12:32, no text even recalls this theme or this vocabulary before the very end of Numbers. The Balaam story cries out to be made into an explicit carrier of the kerygma, but the Yahwist perversely uses the wrong root for curse throughout (*qbb*), and when he does introduce the expected formula (Num 24:9b) he changes the form, and chooses not to make the expected point about cursing or blessing the Moabites.

Wolffe has shown us the real meaning of Genesis 12:1-4a, and this meaning does show up several times in the patriarchal stories and once in Exodus (12:32). It should color our reading of the Yahwist Tetrateuch, and it has influenced subsequent biblical authors. However, it is very far from being "the kerygma of the Yahwist." In his desire to transform this kerygma into a useful theological statement, Wolffe has carefully emphasized the positive blessing and universalistic aspect. He has even taken steps to lead the reader to forget almost entirely the negative clause about cursing those who despise Israel. This refinement, I submit, would leave the lusty Yahwist turning over in his grave, even if it might serve certain Christian preaching needs all too well.

This kerygma of the Yahwist was, of course, important in its day, and powerful today as well. Wolffe finds its final home in the person of Christ as Abraham's descendant, and in the idea that today all nations are blessed in Jesus (158). Another reading might find evidence of the blessing and cursing of nations as a result of their treatment of Jews verified in subsequent world history.[30] One must ask what kind of theology such a message can be? Is it a cautionary saying which one can usefully preach to anti-Semitic believers? That is, a salvific truth? Or is it a prophecy regarding the future role of Israel in world history? That is, historical truth? Or is it a universal theological principle about the unique source of grace in the world? That is, a methodical truth? Or is it a call to universal social responsibility to spread blessing through knowledge of Israel? That is, an ethical truth? The reader must ask, Does he or she really believe this teaching as a doctrine, and if so in what concrete application? Or does the reader not feel, rather, that the supposed "message" is no more than a *Tendenz* within a narrative? Has Wolffe not denatured it by isolating it and elevating it to the point of doctrine? Is this a revealed truth which we must believe?

What is true about the Yahwist is that in Genesis 12:1-4a, and throughout his text, his concern is constantly international. He expects God to act, or revelation/salvation to occur, precisely in the interaction between Israel and other nations.[31] Such an expectancy makes sense during the period of Israel's empire-building under Solomon, and at the same time embodies an implicit challenge to readers of any age, a particularly difficult challenge for those whose religious horizon has remained either narrowly individualistic or otherworldly escapist. Such a reader of the Yahwist will be drawn either to convert or else to reject this whole biblical tradition as distasteful. That is the real power of the Yahwist.

Lonergan's approach to texts, distinguishing as it does between common sense knowledge to be found in the Bible and theoretical or scientific forms of knowledge, and distinguishing between the interpretation of a text and an ensuing dialectic with its author, leads us away from biblical doctrines and toward conversion through reading biblical authors. In contrast to this, Wolffe's focusing on a narrowly defined kerygma may run the risk of distracting the reader with isolated doctrines of dubious value, while allowing the reader to avoid struggling with the Yahwist challenge.

V. Form Criticism as Doctrine

Form criticism, at least in its classical sense with its emphasis on discovering the meaning of a form from its *Sitz-im-Leben* at the oral stages, has much in common with structuralism, in that it hopes to recover unintended meaning—implicit, subliminal meaning. It looks for a meaning which precedes the author, to which the author may only dimly advert, which resides in the social structures of human (and divine) interaction and in the resulting structures of language. It looks for a meaning which is larger and deeper than the author, and which therefore easily lends itself to the category of divine revelation.[32] Whereas theme and kerygma risk being thought of as doctrines which an author chose to teach by means of narratives and songs and so forth, forms and structures may be thought of as doctrines which an author did not choose, but which entered the text either through a collective unconscious or through the author's appropriation of his or her cultural tradition. For the purposes of this paper, and in the interest of clarity and cogency, we shall stick to form criticism, and in fact to one great example of it, in order to make a point. However, I believe that the point is valid as a caution in dealing with most interpretations which would move directly to theology through the use of form-critical or structural methods.

Although in choosing a great scholar for critique the task is made harder because such people never actually fall into their own traps, still there is the decisive advantage in such a choice that shedding critical light on great texts might redirect their influence. Moreover, if Lonergan is shown to have contributed to enhancing work of this quality, then his contribution is truly significant. Claus Westermann's contribution in refining the form-critical work of Hermann Gunkel on the Psalms is surely one of the most helpful form studies in the field of Old Testament interpretation.[33] It studies the primordial role of praise and lament in the prayer and theology of Israel, defining these attitudes and tracing their various expressions in biblical literature. Every page of this book offers helpful observations about forms in the Psalms and their significance. However, it is the first chapter, dealing with "The Categories of the Psalms" which has always seemed most fertile to me. We shall focus on that.

Westermann is dissatisfied with Gunkel's categories of "Hymn" and "Songs of Thanksgiving," as he finds it essential to show that both of these forms proceed from a single attitude of "praise," and that they must be carefully distinguished one from another on the basis of the experience which generates praise (9, 18-19). He shows inadequacies and inconsistencies in Gunkel's discussion of hymns, and he proposes that what Gunkel calls "hymns" would be better understood if named "Descriptive Songs of Praise"; whereas Gunkel's "Songs of Thanksgiving" should be described as "Declarative Songs of Praise." This proposal is chiefly based on a study of the Hebrew root *hodah*, usually mistranslated "to thank."

Westermann offers the following differences between the modern concept of "to thank" with the Hebrew understanding of *hodah* and of other words which carry an intention of praising:

> 1. In praise the one being praised is elevated (*magnificare*); in thanks the one thanked remains in his place.
> 2. In praise I am directed entirely toward the one whom I praise, and this means, of necessity, in that moment a looking away from myself. In thanks I am expressing *my* thanks.

3. Freedom and spontaneity belong to the essence of praise; giving thanks can become a duty.

4. Praise has a forum and always occurs in a group; giving thanks is private, for it need concern no one except the one thanking and the one being thanked.

5. Praise is essentially joyful; giving thanks can take on the character of something required. Praise can never, but thanks must often, be commanded.

6. The most important verbal mark of difference is that thanking occurs in the speaking of the words "thank you" or in shortened form, "thanks"; genuine, spontaneous praise occurs in a sentence in which the one being praised is the subject, "thou hast done," or "thou art . . ." (27–28).

For Westermann the attitude of praise is common to the two psalm forms which Gunkel named hymn and song of thanksgiving. Hence, the usefulness of grouping the two forms together, and naming them by the element they have in common. This element, praise, is not a literary form in a superficial sense, but rather a gift of God: "And the fact that the praise of God cannot be learned is certainly an essential feature of this praise. To a certain degree the form . . . can be taken over and learned, but the simple act of praise . . . would lose its genuineness and its significance if it were borrowed" (23). Thus Westermann's "praise" appears to be close to Lonergan's "religious conversion."

What distinguishes declarative from descriptive praise for Westermann is the *Sitz-im-Leben*. The Song of Miriam and the Song of Deborah are declarative because they are based on a single act of divine intervention, whereas Isaiah 6:3 is descriptive because it deals with God "in the fullness of his being and his dealings with the world" (22). Even if both are sung in a cultic situation, still the originating *Sitz-im-Leben* determines their form and meaning:

> The latter (declarative) very clearly has its location "out there," in the midst of history, yes, while still on the battlefield—in the hour and the place where God has acted. It might be said that both were sung in a service of worship which was held after the battle, but it is obvious that such a service of worship has a different character from that which shines through in Isa 6:3. If these are both called "cultic," then this distinction is erased . . . (23).

Westermann states that the originating *Sitz* for declarative praise is a cultic act after a specific historical experience of salvation; and he implies that the *Sitz* for descriptive praise is a mystic experience of participating in the heavenly court. Rich as these observations are, one immediately runs into snags and doubts. Is the *Sitz* of descriptive praise really the court of heaven, and have we learned it by overhearing the angels singing each to each? Can one assign a *Sitz* for descriptive praise? Questions about the literary genre of Isaiah's vocation narrative (chapter 6), and its insertion into the complex history of Isaian text, leaves one feeling that Westermann is very canny in merely implying, rather than stating, anything about its *Sitz*. It is true that one could not praise God without religious conversion. However, the step between feeling the love of God in one's heart and expressing this as praise of God's holiness may well be a process which one could describe and explain, in oneself, and in Isaiah, and in the editors of the Isaian text. Surely a lot of thinking, not just overhearing, went into the formulation that Yahweh, the Lord of armies, is holy, and the evidence of this is to be seen throughout the land.

Similarly, one is delighted, but not really convinced, by the notion that Miriam gathered her dancers and drums and sang her song right on the field of battle. Certainly the longer, but not *necessarily* later, version of the song which Moses and all Israel are presented as singing in exactly the same situation did not proceed from experience of a single intervention of God in history. The Moses version is drawn from a time when Israel is established in Jerusalem and has built a temple there (Exod 15:13, 17). It is a very complex structure, offering declarative praise to Yahweh for sure, but embodying complex acts of experience, understanding, and judging, as is clear to anyone who has read any commentary on this chapter of Exodus.

The point here is to clarify the real *Sitz-im-Leben* which explains literary forms. The suggestions from Gunkel and Westermann about concrete origins are valuable as parables in order to fix the image. However, they are not history. We must not hope to know where a given form originates, or suppose that one origin explains all subsequent occurrences. Each author who originates or uses a form uses it to express something he or she knows through some process which we, too, may hope to duplicate, that is, the process Lonergan has taught us, including experience, understanding and judgment. One help toward this, for us, is the effort to understand the forms which biblical authors did use, and to reach for the foundations of biblical authors on the basis of our own religious conversion, and of our openness to the authority of biblical teaching.

This history of forms, as practiced by Gunkel, Begrich, Westermann, Wolffe, and others, shows that forms are appropriated differently by succeeding authors. In most of the subsequent chapters in the book under discussion, Westermann goes to great lengths to establish a probable historical schema of development based on showing which form may have derived from which. No importance should be placed on this beyond the clarification of meaning in the form itself. In view of the minute care Westermann gives to this analysis, it seems appropriate to caution that all the biblical texts are equally true, and that the authoritative teaching of none is to be reduced to any supposed basic form.

Form criticism is probably the single most helpful advance in interpretative method in this century of Old Testament study. It can be abused, however, if used reductively in order to get some propositional truth out of a biblical text, or if used dogmatically as though literary forms were timeless truths.

VI. Lonergan's Contribution

Apart from the examples of interpretation and history which Lonergan has left in his study of St. Thomas' texts, and in his tractates on the Trinity and on Christology, and apart from some detailed observations to be found in *Insight* and *Method*,[34] Lonergan has made two massive contributions to the use of the Old Testament in theology. First, he has enabled us to understand the author aright, as a dramatic subject. In particular, as against the bias of most of what one reads, he has established the primacy of judgment in knowing and affirming what is real, and hence the primacy of the author's affirmation of truth (rather than the history of ideas, or the meaning of the text as text) in the interpretation of meaning. His own focus has been in the realm of theoretic and scientific and methodical truth, and as a result he has given biblical scholars little help in discussing the kind of truth which is affirmed through aesthetic forms, that is, literary texts. This first contribution, then, gives us little help in relating the Old Testament to theology.

However, his second massive contribution provides the remedy. He has given us the description of theology in its eight operations. This immediately separates interpretation from doctrines (propositional truths) by four distinct successive operations: history, dialectic, foundations, doctrines. Thus, he has removed all need to produce propositional meaning out of biblical texts by reductive interpretation. Moreover, he invites us to enter a dialectic with biblical texts in order to affirm positions and reverse counterpositions, not on the basis of the theoretical or scientific truth of assertions, but rather on the presence or absence of conversion in their authors. This is the outrageous proclamation of subjectivity, based on Lonergan's understanding of foundations, which has given us an entirely different understanding of what humanistic studies are about. One difficulty has been that biblical authors do not make theoretic or scientific or methodical affirmations. What biblical authors do affirm, however, through their various aesthetic forms, always implicitly or subliminally, is precisely their foundational stance. These implicit, affirmed foundations of the biblical authors have been normative throughout the Jewish and Christian traditions (through the centuries when the explicit affirmations of the text, i.e., the original meanings, were simply lost until recent scholarship became able to restore them). With Lonergan, we enter into dialectic with the foundational stances of biblical authors, in a situation in which they are converted, and we the readers are unconverted, or inadequately converted.

Lonergan's contribution, then, has been first to draw our attention to the biblical authors, and second to enable us to move from the authors to theology. Because of Lonergan, we know that the move to theology proceeds in eight operations. We have no need to look to themes, or to kerygmas, or to literary forms, or for any other propositional truth in the Bible. The Old Testament does not offer theology in this form. Rather, it offers a series of normative foundational stances, demanding various conversions of its readers. It is in this way that the Old Testament has motivated and steered the religious movements called Judaism and Christianity. It is precisely in this way that the Old Testament is a normative criterion of theology.

This contribution to literary theory leaves exegetes indebted to Bernard Lonergan. It clarifies the nature of our work, and suggests a new approach in scholarship which will be more helpful in the theological enterprise.

Notes

1. Much modern scholarship tends to see the evolution of Western culture in terms of struggle between factions. Cf. Morton Smith, *Palestinian Parties and Politics that Shaped the Old Testament* (New York and London: Columbia University Press, 1971); many recent gospel commentaries, such as Raymond Brown, *The Gospel According to John,* 2 vols. (Anchor Bible) (New York: Doubleday 1970).

2. Cf. Frederick E. Crowe, *Theology of the Christian Word: A Study in History* (New York and Toronto: Paulist Press, 1978). The massive body of allegorical interpretation, which begins within the biblical tradition, appears to be the first attempt to bridge between story and theory.

3. This distortion in the role of theology appears to direct the work of Cardinal Ratzinger. Cf. Michael Fahey, "Joseph Ratzinger as Ecclesiologist and Pastor," *Neo Conservatism . . . Social and Religious Phenomenon,* ed. G. Baum (*Concilium* 141), (New York: Seabury Press, 1981) 76–83.

4. For a recent discussion of revelation and the Old Testament, cf. Brevard S. Childs, *Old Testament Theology in a Canonical Context* (London: SCM Press, 1985) 20–27.

5. Cf. Bernard Lonergan, *Method in Theology* (London: Darton, Longman and Todd, 1972) xi.

6. Ibid., 276.

7. P. van Imschoot, *Théologie de l'ancien testament,* 2 vols. (Tournai: Desclée, 1954, 1956).

8. In English translation, W. Eichrodt, *Theology of the Old Testament,* 2 vols. (London and Philadelphia: Westminster Press, 1961, 1962). Cf. further H.-J. Krauss, *Geschichte der historisch-kritischen Erforschung des Alten Testaments von der Reformation bis zur Gegenwart,* 2nd ed. (Neukirchen, Switzerland: Neukirchen-Vluyn, 1965).

9. In English translation, G. von Rad, *Theology of the Old Testament*, 2 vols. (New York and Evanston: Harper and Row, 1962).

10. I suggest that the title is an obstacle: this is really an interpretation of the Old Testament texts presented in historical order. It is not a theology in the sense usually given this word.

11. Cf. for example, Georg Fohrer, *Geschichte der israelitischen Religion* (Berlin: Walter de Gruyter, 1969); Walther Zimmerli, *Grundriss der alttestamentlichen Theologie* (Stuttgart, Berlin, Cologne, Mainz: Kohlhammer, 1972); R. E. Clements, *Old Testament Theology: A Fresh Approach* (London: Marshall Morgan and Scott, 1978); Brevard Childs, cited in note 4 above.

12. Cf., for example, the various theological dictionaries of the Old Testament; J. Guillet, *Thèmes bibliques* (Paris: Aubier, 1954); Albert Gelin, *The Key Concepts of the Old Testament* (New York: Sheed and Ward, 1955); Hans Walter Wolffe, *Anthropology of the Old Testament* (Philadelphia: Fortress Press, 1974); David J. A. Clines, "The Theme of the Pentateuch," *Journal for the Study of the Old Testament, Supplement 10* (Sheffield, Eng.: University of Sheffield, 1978).

13. In the Old Testament, the most influential of these has been Hans Walter Wolffe, "The Kerygma of the Yahwist," *Interpretation* 20 (1966) 131–158. It was originally published in *Evangelische Theologie* 24 (1964) 73–97, and also in his *Gesammelte Studien zum Alten Testament* (Munich: Kaiser Verlag, 1964).

14. The method for this approach is explained and justified in the first two chapters of Sean McEvenue, *Interpreting the Pentateuch* (Collegeville: The Liturgical Press, 1990).

15. Cleanth Brooks, *The Well Wrought Urn: Studies in the Structure of Poetry* (New York and London: Harcourt Brace Jovanovich, 1947, 1975).

16. Ibid., 202–203.

17. Ibid., 199.

18. Louis Untermeyer, *A Concise Treasury of Great Poems English and American*, Pocket Cardinal Edition (Richmond Hill: Simon and Schuster, 1958) 424–425.

19. Reference here is principally to Lonergan's positions outlined in *Method in Theology* (London: Darton, Longman & Todd, 1972). As my use of Lonergan will be restricted to the most general, and well-known, lines of his thought, it seems meaningless to attempt to refer to particular pages.

20. Cleanth Brooks, op. cit., 201–202.

21. Ibid., 196.

22. See note 12 above.

23. Its intent is very close to the approach proposed at length in my discussion mentioned in note 14 above.

24. This has been perceived with particular clarity with regard to the Priestly Document, the text which frames the Pentateuch in its final redaction. Cf. Rudolf Kilian, "Die Priesterschrift, Hoffnung auf Heimkehr," in *Wort und Botschaft, Eine theologische und kritische Einführung in die Probleme des Alten Testaments* (Wurzburg: Echter Verlag, 1976) 226–243.

25. Cf. H. W. Wolffe, cited in note 13 above. For the English translation, which we shall cite here, cf. "The Kerygma of the Yahwist," *Interpretation* (1966) 131–158.

26. Cf. Ibid., 151.

27. Cf. Ibid., 148, emphasis added.

28. Wolffe cites the following: Ps 47, end; Isa 19:23-25; Jer 4:1-2; Zech 8:13, 23; Gal 3:8 (156–157). Earlier he indicates the editorial addition in Exod 22:25ff. One might add further texts in the Joseph story, for example, Genesis 47:13ff. which Noth lists as J, but which Wolffe does not mention at all.

29. The latest mode is to argue to a post-priestly origin of Genesis 12:1–3. Cf. Frank Crüseman, "Die Eigenständigkeit der Urgeschichte, Ein Beitrag zur Diskussion des 'Jahwisten'," *Die Botschaft und die Boten, Festschrift Hans Walter Wolffe*, eds. J. Jeremias and L. Perlitt (Neukirchen, Switzerland: Neukirchen-Vluyn, 1981) 11–29. It gets harder and harder to prepare intelligible lectures!

30. One could make a case of this kind on the basis of a book such as Edward H. Flannery, *The Anguish of the Jews: Twenty Three Centuries of AntiSemitism* (New York and London: MacMillan, 1965). Flannery himself has a far more sophisticated interpretation.

31. For a presentation of this general expectation of the Yahwist, cf. chapter 2 in this volume, ''The Spiritual Authority of the Bible,'' pp. 23–39. For a fuller account cf. the third chapter of S. McEvenue, *Interpreting the Pentateuch* (Collegeville: The Liturgical Press, 1990).

32. This larger meaning can eaily be understood as a given in psyche, or experience, without being elaborated by understanding, or affirmed by judgement, or confirmed by value. Cf. Charles C. Hefling, ''The Meaning of God Incarnate According to Friedrich Schleiermacher,'' *Lonergan Workshop,* vol. 1 (Atlanta: Scholars Press, 1988) 105–177.

33. The history and nature of form criticism as applied to the Old Testament is much written about. A brief introduction, and initial bibliography, may be found in Gene M. Tucker, *Form Criticism of the Old Testament* (Philadelphia: Fortress Press, 1971). We will study Claus Westermann, *Praise and Lament in the Psalms* (Edinburgh: T. & T. Clark Ltd, 1965). The German text first appeared in 1961. Another major form-critical study by Westermann is his *Basic Forms of Prophetic Speech* (Philadelphia: Westminster Press, 1967), originally published by Kaiser in Munich with the title *Grundformen Prophetischer Rede.*

34. For a survey of Lonergan's specific discussion of interpretation, cf. Quentin Quesnell, ''Pinning Down the Meaning,'' *Lonergan Workshop*, vol. 7 (Atlanta: Scholars Press, 1988) 298–311.

Chapter 5

The Bible and Trust in the Future

This paper will focus on an attitude toward the future taught by the Yahwist author in the Pentateuch, especially as read in Genesis 12:1–13:4. It will be seen to be a valuable attitude, and one not often mentioned in spiritual or pastoral literature. But we must begin first with a brief discussion of a general vocabulary dealing with the future, and second with a brief presentation of the position presupposed in this paper concerning the nature and effects of literary texts.

The Future

We are all convinced about the need of being fully alive to the present, because God as eternal has no relationship with us except a present relationship, and because we have learned from the New Testament that the present is replete with all peril and meaning since the kingdom of God will come like a thief in the night when we least expect it, and because in the passing of our days and nights each present moment is a vital synthesis of all past and future.

On the other hand, in terms of knowledge, and for purposes of pastoral concern, the present moments can be fully understood only through both the past and the future. The past is the object of therapy. The future is the time of vocation.

Our past is what we know, and what we have failed to know correctly. Our past is reality as we have appropriated it, whether in a healthy or neurotic or sinful manner. Hence, it is the object of therapy.

The future is what we hope for or despair of. The future is what we expect from others as related to what we intend to do about it, and vice versa. Therapy should enable us to face the future with all our psychic engines running. Therapy should enable us to know reality correctly, to open our eyes to all of reality, and to experience our God-given ultimate trust (i.e., faith-hope-charity) as significant and dominant within reality. From this stance of full awareness and trust, we are free to accept, or reject, our vocation for the future.

Diverse attitudes toward the future are appropriate for diverse persons and pasts. But, as part of every attitude, trust in God is appropriate for every person and past, and pastoral care is polarized ultimately toward uncovering that divine presence within us, that gift/grace of trust, and bringing it to the surface.

Literature

The nature of literature, including biblical literature, is very much discussed in current academic publication. This is no place to enter the debate. Rather, if I may, I will refer the reader to some publication, and present the hypothesis upon which I work.[1]

A literary text, like other works of art, is essentially subjective, no matter how much the artist or author protests anonymity. Willy nilly the work of art is primarily a self-presentation, an objectification of one's view of reality unified by a chosen horizon. Literary works, song, and representative visual art, more than other artistic forms, present a whole *Weltanschauung,* a complex statement of how things relate to each other, about what matters, about values, about past, present and future. That is why we intuitively either like them or hate them. It is true that without technical quality no work of art will be considered a masterpiece, or will be preserved. But technical quality does not explain great art. We do not love or hate works of art, and we do not accept or reject them, because of technical quality; rather we do so because of their "humanity," because of what they proclaim as values, because of the author's self which is expressed and proclaimed in the work of art. That is why people who find themselves in a certain culture, surrounded by technically superb architecture, films, musical presentations, and so forth, can feel alienated and horrified. They reject the values of the culture, even though perhaps they have never formulated, or heard formulated, any precise definition of those values.

Literature does affirm something. But its affirmation is not a paraphrase of what is artistically presented as the surface of the text. Rather, it is the complex subjective stance of the author which is objectified in the text. And biblical literature is just one specific case of literature in general.

Biblical Literature

No biblical texts are scientific or theoretical in nature. Such literary genres did not exist for biblical writers. All biblical texts are literary. They all use various literary genres in order to present an author's *Weltanschauung,* or fundamental stance before the world. In the case of biblical writers, the fundamental stance will always include a horizon of faith, in which trust in

God is given a specific form. An adequate interpretation of biblical texts will include the discovery of this dimension of the text.

Let us give some examples. The Pentateuch taken as a whole was composed during the Exile, or at least during a period when there was no satisfactory restoration of Israel; the Jews had no political power, and most Jews felt exile to be their horizon. The Pentateuch's author collected and united numerous documents which presented segments of the history of the Jews, from Adam to Moses. It stops at Moses, who, at the time of the Pentateuch, was known as a fabulous person from a remote past—probably seven hundred or eight hundred years before the Pentateuch was composed. That is as remote from the author as King Arthur, or the Magna Charta, is for us. And the Pentateuch story stops precisely where the Jews and Moses were still in the desert, but were on the verge of entering the Land of Canaan to taste prosperity and security, as God had promised. Thus, the artistic message of the Pentateuch was clear, even though never formulated within it in formal sentences. It is therapeutic in that it goes over all the past, inserting elements of faith and hope and charity in innumerable ways. But it also deals with the future, in that this fabulous memory of the past is all united within the author's commanding horizon: an expectation of future entry into the Promised Land. The author's whole stance toward the world is that a radical meaning of life for his people consists of possessing that Land in the future, and of following God's law and celebrating God's liturgy in that Land, Zionism in its most authoritative voice.

This is a specific attitude toward the future: a view which makes political and social activity the sacred place where the reader will meet God.

A very different attitude is to be found in the Apocalypse. It presents a future in which wild images, drawn, according to the Jungians, from our collective unconscious, carry messages about a total upheaval in history and the breakthrough of a new divinely created reality. Once again the message is not written in any formal sentences. But the author's inner world is presented, and we are invited to accept that as revelation. This is an attitude to the future very different from the Pentateuch. It is a view which abandons linear logic, and historical factuality, and belief in social evolution, or personal responsibility. It is a view in which the reader cannot have any effect, but must wait with trust until God does everything. Therapists might think of this as a neurotic view, but there are real circumstances in some lives where a nervous breakdown is an appropriate reaction (hence the images which have broken through the barriers between conscious and unconscious), and where the real past/present cannot lead to any solution until a totally new reality intervenes.

A third example could be found in the book of Job. This universally admired literary work presents the problem of evil with a power never equalled. There is a denouement of sorts, but the problem of evil is never solved. One can read through all the commentaries, and suspend disbelief before the tortured efforts which have been made to explain how this book solves the problem of evil. Commentators have felt obliged to twist things, insofar as they have thought of biblical books as theology rather than as literature, and insofar as they have not understood the wisdom genre. Similarly, although the book of Proverbs describes its contents as "riddles" in 1:6, commentators have persisted in trying to tell us what they mean, as though they were theological or ethical statements. Job, like Proverbs, is not an answer. It is an invitation to think. It is written by an author for whom the universe is a divine riddle, puzzle, mystery, with divine meanings hidden in it. One is invited to puzzle, to think again and again, (or in our current culture to do "research") in order to discover WISDOM, in the form of insights about reality which have been hidden there for us by God himself. The answer is never given; rather, the questioning itself becomes a religious act. Thus, as wisdom literature, the book of Job inculcates the attitude toward the future which we ascribe today to scientists. More specifically, it is an invitation to abandon facile explanations of suffering, and to examine evil with all the intellectual energies which hope can release. This is very different from the Pentateuch, which is more for politicians, or from the Apocalypse, which is more for helpless victims.

The Yahwist

Despite alternative theories argued by recent scholars, I remain convinced that the Yahwist was a scholarly collector and charming storyteller who wrote the first comprehensive "history" of Israel in Jerusalem, at the time of Solomon or shortly afterwards.[2] He is familiar to all as the author of the story of the fall of Adam and Eve in Genesis 2 and 3. A dominant characteristic of his writing, and an important analytical tool when trying to understand his texts, is what is called its etiological intent. That is, in telling his stories about the past, he is constantly trying to explain the present. He is not trying to impose new understandings, or new obligations. Rather, he is trying to take things which everybody knew and accepted in his day, and say something of how they came about, and, often, of how God was involved in their coming about.

Simple etiologies are found in stories which terminate in naming a well, for example, thus explaining the origin of a name by which the well is still known in his day (cf., for example, Gen 16:14; 21:31; 32:30). The last text explains also the origin of a custom, namely, that Jews in the author's day didn't eat the sinew of the hip because the angel touched Jacob in that place (Gen 32:32). More important etiologies explain how local gods came to be called "Yahweh" (cf., for example, Gen 14:22; 21:33).

But, more than this, it is probable that the burden of the Yahwist writing was etiological in a very broad horizon, in that it was intended to show that the main natural and cultural experiences which Jews took for granted in Solomon's empire (including the possession of the land, the prosperity of Israel, the power of the king, the liturgical calendar) were all due to interventions of God in the remote past. Without attempting to look at the whole Yahwist text, I would like to single out one specific kind of broad etiology which is peculiar to the Yahwist, and which occurs in several incidents.

In the story of the fall of mankind (Gen 2:4b–3), a major point being made is that the mystery and scandal of human suffering was not originally intended by God. The subservience of women to men in Solomon's empire, and the unnatural agony connected with the joy of childbirth, the fact that men had to submit to onerous royal corvees in order to support their families, the horror of the snake which slides on the ground, and the fact of death in human life, all of this was not originally intended by God. God made us without any of this. But then humans sinned, and ruined God's plans by coming to know both good and evil. Then God tried to limit the evil effects of this change in human nature by banishing us from Paradise, and by instituting these terrible things.

Similarly, the system of vendetta practised in Solomon's empire, as the only way to reduce violence in a society without institutions of police and adequate courts, was a horrible fact of life. God did not want it originally. But after Cain killed Abel in Genesis 4, God instituted it as the only way to save Cain's life.

Similarly, the difference in language, which the Jews experienced as an insoluble problem and real limitation of power in the great days of Solomon's empire, was not originally desired by God. But God instituted it when he discovered the danger of human pride in the incident of the tower of Babel in Genesis 11.

Similarly, the "Yahwist decalogue," a code which obliged Jews to avoid intermarriage with Canaanites, and male Jews to leave home three times a year to participate in the Jerusalem cult, was not originally desired by God. It was imposed as a remedy only when God learned about their propensity to idolatry in the incident of the golden calf in Exodus 32-34.

In all of these incidents, natural experience and cultural practices which were terribly unpleasant, are considered. In each case, the reason for it was provided by a human sin, on the occasion of which God realized that his creation was in need of repair. In each case, God sanctions the unpleasantness, in that God instituted it as a remedy for greater evil. The author's view of things invites the reader to accept these evils, place the blame for them upon human perversity, and recognize them as remedies imposed by a caring God.

All of this is etiology. All of it is therapy, curing the past as described above. All of it should enable the reader/believer to accept the evils which accompany human life, and to face the future with *trust* in God. A more specific form is given to this trust in Genesis 12:1–13:4, which in the Yahwist text is programmatic: just as Genesis 2–11 set out the programme for all mankind, so Genesis 12 sets out the programme specifically for the children of Abraham.

Genesis 12:1–13:4

This unit has three parts, as can most easily be recognized by noting that verses 13:3-4 repeat the exact same content as 12:8-9. These verses form a marked inclusion around the third part of the unit, 12:10–13:2, dealing with the famous "story of the patriarch's wife." The second part of the unit, 12:4-7, narrates Abram's migration from Haran to Canaan, and God's promise of the land. The first part, 12:1-3, provides the basic teaching which is then applied in the second and third parts.

Genesis 12:1-3 is a vocation for Abram and the family of Abram. As we shall see immediately, it can only be read as a divine invitation to the Jews to explore the unknown, trusting in God's care. They are invited to leave all that is familiar ("your country, your kindred, and your father's house"), and to go abroad to a place they did not know, to a place which they would know only when God showed them. If they obey this vocation, they will become great, and God will use them to bless all the world. God will care for them by caring for nations that care for the Jews, and by cursing nations that curse the Jews.

Genesis 12:4-7, the second part of the unit, presents Abram as following his vocation straight away, and having his obedience immediately rewarded by being promised the whole land of Canaan, even though at that time the Canaanites still dwelt there. So God has now shown him the place, and begun the process of making his descendants great and blessing the world through them.

Genesis 12:10–13:2, the third part, is the first of many Yahwist stories dealing with Israel's relations with other nations, and it is the first application of the teaching of 12:1-3 about these international relations. The story presents Abram as totally amoral, in that he lies about his wife and cares nothing for her honor. Morals are not what the Yahwist is about in any of his numerous stories. His view of reality focuses on the activity of God, rather than the virtues of humans, and specifically the activity of God in the realm of international politics. This story is about Israel and Egypt, not about marital fidelity.

Originally, the story was probably about marital fidelity, and it was probably told originally, not about Abraham and Egypt, but rather about Isaac and Abimelech, king of the Philistines, as we can see from the other versions of the same story which are found in Genesis 20 and Genesis 26:1-16. But the Yahwist has taken it over, and retold it here in his programmatic chapter, as a paradigm of Israel's vocation. He has transferred the story from Isaac to Abram so that it might better signify the Jews as a whole nation, and he has transferred from Philistines to Egypt in order to invoke, not the details of Exodus, although one must note the mention of "famine" in verse 10 and of "plagues" in verse 17, but rather the whole archetype of Egypt in Israel's imagination.

So the first nation Israel encounters, after Abram has followed his vocation, is Egypt. And, in effect, Egypt curses Israel by abducting Sarah. The beauty of Sarah is very central in this story (verses 11, 14, 15, 17), and it is an aspect of wives and of Israel which is not focused on in the rest of the Pentateuch. It is Israel's very desirability which endangers it, and leads it into slavery. So Pharaoh makes a mistake. However, God, true to his promise in 12:3, immediately curses Pharaoh by sending plagues.

The result of the whole adventure is positive. Abram has solved his initial problem of famine in Canaan by travelling to Egypt. Abram now leaves Egypt "very rich in cattle, in silver and in gold," and returns to call upon Yahweh at his altar between Bethel and Ai.

As usual in the Yahwist stories, we are presented with a simple and yet very subtle reality. Ambiguity in the human effects of beauty, or of all human excellence, is shown in the fact that Sarah's beauty wins the favor of the Egyptians but in the course of time threatens the future of Israel and the life of Egypt. Ambiguity in the human effects of wealth is shown in the symbol of Egypt, which is wealthy enough to feed Abram and to enrich him, but which dishonors him. Abram must leave Egypt because of these ambiguities and their effects, just as later Israel will be saved by Yahweh, who defines himself repeatedly as the god who brought Israel up from Egypt, from the house of slavery.

One must be struck by the fact that the Yahwist, who wrote the very simple rule of thumb in 12:3 ("I will bless those who bless you, and him who curses you I will curse"), should create such story as this to show this rule of thumb in action for the first time. The rule may be simple, but its application in life is very complex indeed.

The Yahwist sees Abram as called by God to go in search of the unknown. When Abram goes, he discovers that the unknown will eventually be Canaan, but that lies in the future. Circumstances, namely, a famine which, like the plagues, are an indirect voice of God, lead Abram on to Egypt which is perilous and partially evil ("then they will kill me, but they will let you live"). Abram prospers in Egypt, and thereby experiences for the first time that God will bless Israel and protect it from all evil, when Israel is involved with other nations!

Implicit in the horizon of this story is the view that the vocation of Abram/Israel is one of international involvement. Readers of this text during the time of Solomon's empire would have seen it as an etiology explaining the incredible international reach of that king. His economic and political control reached from North Africa to Turkey, and down the Euphrates valley. However, Jews in that era may have read it, it remains for all eras an invitation to venture into the unknown, into the mouth of danger, even into the realms where evil seems to prevail. One is invited to trust the Lord, to leave the familiar, and to find both prosperity and God in whatever unknown our path leads us to. (This invitation is very close to Gandalf's invitation to the Hobbit in Tolkien's popular tale.) This trust is not based on one's virtue, but only on one's trust in God. Luther would love this idea!

Conclusion

Of course, the Yahwist text is woven now into the complex frame of the Pentateuch. No doubt the exiled Jew of the Pentateuchal era read this ancient message in a different way: it is a call to courage before the unknown addressed to one who is already living in the unknown, who is alienated and longing to return to Israel. It remains a call to live one's life among evils and to face the future with confidence in the Lord. The Yahwist text originally did not know about the Exile, which was the focal point of the Pentateuchal text. Originally this programme for trust fitted very well into the special pattern of etiology which was described above as peculiar to the Yahwist: namely, that present suffering is a remedy from the greater evil which results from Israel's sin. When the Pentateuch rereads the Yahwist in the context of the Exile, it fits like a glove. The Exile was a result of human sinfulness, and therefore God sanctioned this evil as a remedy for greater evil. The exiled Jew must accept exile as a providentially provided reality and trust that Yahweh will draw good out of evil. Accepting the Exile, one must proceed to venture into the future trusting God in the midst of foreign nations.

In the context of the Christian Bible, the vocation of Abram remains for all of us. All of our lives lead us to places remote from our origins, places we could not have imagined beforehand, places which God has shown us. If the exiled Jew must accept the Exile, so the Christian must accept the death of Christ, because this too is an evil which God sanctioned because of the sins of humankind. And we must accept our own smaller deaths in union with Christ, since all of this is a remedy for greater evil and willed by God for greater good. Within that context, the Christian reading the Yahwist will feel drawn to endure the pains of present alienation and face future "deaths" and dangers with trust in God who will bless the whole world through our obedience.

The literal meaning of this Yahwist text contains a specific pastoral message of trust for the Christian politician, or business person, or persons about to leave home for the unknown in any way whatever: one must view the future as fraught with ambiguity, peril, and evil; but one must venture into it just the same, because we are called to venture toward a place which God will indicate, and because God will bless us and the world through us.

Note

1. For the controversy, one might begin with Edgar V. McKnight, *The Post-Modern Use of the Bible: The Emergence of Reader-Oriented Criticism* (Nashville: Abingdon Press, 1988) and the literature there cited. For a justification of my position, cf. S. McEvenue, *Interpreting the Pentateuch* (Collegeville: The Liturgical Press, 1990).

2. For the controversy, cf., for example, E. Zenger, "Wo steht die Pentateuch Forschung heute?" *Biblische Zeitschrift*, NF 24 (1980) 101–116, or Hans-Christoph Schmitt, "Die Hintergrunde der 'neuesten Pentateuchkritic' und der literarische Befund der Josefsgeschichte Gen 37-50," *ZAW* 97 (1985) 161–179.

Chapter 6

Truth and Affirmation in Poetry

The questions suggested by the title are very broad indeed. They arise in the general context of defining culture. I would suggest that, whereas every reader of poetry feels that poetry not only delights but also influences (edifies, educates), still it is very difficult to define what kind of influence this might be.[1]

For myself, the question arises specifically in terms of interpretation of Scripture. The Bible is written as literature and yet has been used as a source for doctrines. Is this legitimate? Does any literature, including biblical literature, intend to affirm propositions as true?

To focus the question as sharply as possible, this paper will deal only with poetry and speech which is clearly poetic. Certainly, poetry does not affirm truths in the same sense as do scientific propositions or statements about fact. In what sense, then, is poetry true?[2] What kind of affirmation is made in poetry?

In theoretic language, the answer I shall try to show is that poetic affirmation is not about objectified truths, but rather about subjective states of expectation. It is the affirmation of the, at least ephemeral, value of the author's subjectivity as author, namely, the author's "Foundations" in writing.[3] The paper will not argue on the level of theory, but rather attempt to illustrate in three literary texts (a text from Homer, another from a nineteenth-century North American Indian chief, and a third from T. S. Eliot) that the affirmation of the text is not stated in the text, and yet so powerfully underlies it that the reader either fails to experience the text adequately or else receives this message.

Longinus on Homer

Most of us do not advert to our foundations, although we can do so, and we can study them and define them in part. Foundations are the complex of values and of rules of thought which control how each one goes about thinking and deciding. Some foundations may be learned spontane-

74

ously and subliminally from parents; others may be spontaneous, healthy or neurotic reactions to experience; others may be learned consciously or adopted on the basis of reason and choice. Foundations have been much studied in this century, but the ancients wrote of them, too, in indirect ways.

A first-century Greek rhetorician wrote a very influential treatise on literary theory, which was eventually attributed to Cassius Longinus and given the misleading title *On the Sublime*. In chapters 8 and 9 of his treatise the author enumerates five "principle sources" of greatness in literature and describes the first of these.[4] What he describes we would call foundations.

The first source of greatness in literature, and the most important according to "Longinus," is "strength and greatness of thought." The other four sources are all directly aspects of the text: the subjects treated and the resources of style and language displayed in the text. But the first source is a quality directly of the author. It is not explicit in the text, but a "greatness of soul" which remains implicit, read between the lines of the text as it were.

In trying to define it, he begins, not with an author, but with greatness of soul depicted by an author in one of his characters, namely, Homer's Ajax. He writes: "Hence a thought in its naked simplicity, even though unuttered, is sometimes admirable by the sheer force of its sublimity; for instance, the silence of Ajax in the *Odyssey* (IX, 543) is great and grander than anything he could have said." He adds that "grandeur of conception arises . . . only in those whose spirit is generous and aspiring." Though he was speaking of Ajax, the grandeur of Ajax reveals the grandeur of Homer who had conceived him.

"Longinus" then goes on to give a straight example, namely, the presentation of Poseidon in the *Iliad:*

> Mountain and wood and solitary peak,
> The ships Achaian, and the towers of Troy,
> Trembled beneath the god's immortal feet.
> Over the waves he rode, and round him played,
> Lured from the deeps, the ocean's monstrous brood,
> With uncouth gambols welcoming their lord;
> The charmed billows parted; on they flew.
> (XIII 18–27; XX, 60)

What is great about this text? It does not describe Poseidon at all. It does not even describe the sea, or any of the "ocean's monstrous brood." And yet the reader is filled with admiration for the god. All that is affirmed by the text is affirmed implicitly, by silence, to be read between the lines and in the gaps. What is revealed, but not said, in the text is the approach Homer takes to the god: he does not expect to see the god; rather he invites the reader to leap beyond imagination to a transcendent reality which is only pointed at in nature. What is great in the text is a greatness of Homer, which the reader experiences in the gaps of the text.

It is possible to be more precise about Homer's foundations here. The text tells of tremblings of mountain, ships and tower, and these may be explained by a storm which Poseidon stirs up. But the inhabitants of the sea alone are depicted as knowing and rejoicing in Poseidon. Moreover, these inhabitants are not called "fish," but rather "ocean's monstrous brood." Is not Homer evoking here what Carl Jung would later call "archetypal" images from the unconscious? I suggest that the text invites the reader to release the resources of his deepest psyche in order to understand Poseidon in this text.

If there is any sense to the notion that Homer was writing, not a history, but a story, which nonetheless is true—and I believe there is—then the truth of the story is not expressed in any of the written sentences in the text. The story's truth consists in Homer's affirmation of his foundations, and the demands on the reader to seek for meaning by making the same kind of leap beyond imagination which Homer makes.

If a reader accedes to this demand, and if the reader appropriates Homer's foundations in so doing, then the reader has undergone what, in religious jargon, would be called "conversion."

Speech of Keesh-ke-mun

A second example may be taken from the reported speech of a nineteenth-century Indian chief:

> Englishman! you ask me who I am. If you wish to know, you must seek me in the clouds. I am a bird who rises from the earth, and flies up into the skies, out of human sight; but though not visible to the eye, my voice is heard from afar, and resounds over the earth!
>
> Englishman! you wish to know who I am. You have never sought me or you should have found and known me.[5]

The claim that "you have never sought me" sounds like the youth claim in the '60s that adults did not really listen to them. And the antidote was repeatedly named in the jargon of group-dynamics by the phrase: "I hear you. I really hear you." If it was difficult for a nineteenth-century Englishman to understand what it would be to really hear Keesh-ke-mun, precisely the same difficulty faces us when we attempt to interpret the literature of another culture. Hearing in this sense goes behind the understanding of words and sentences in order to find and know the foundations out of which words and sentences are written.

Keesh-ke-mun said that "you must seek me in the clouds. I am a bird who rises from the earth . . . out of human sight . . . my voice is heard from afar, and resounds over the earth!" Was he crazy? Is this a schizophrenic statement? Keesh-ke-mun was not a bird in the sky. . . .

His mode of speech is, of course, poetic. But in this text he is not merely using a simile, to say that he is like a bird. His affirmation goes deeper than that. What reality is he trying to describe when he says he is a bird? I suggest that he is telling the Englishman about his interior. He is talking about his inner experience in speaking, about his foundations in thinking, about his experience of transcendence. He knows he is not a bird, and not like a bird, but when he thinks and speaks his inner process is out of sight like a bird: it is based on abstract concepts, on logics of universal application, on horizons of meaning which reach toward the limitless. If the Englishman wishes to know Keesh-ke-mun, he must seek his inner self behind his words and sentences, where the inner self is transcendent, "in the clouds," "out of human sight."

This is not an extravagant interpretation of the reported speech. It is a simple attempt to transpose into psychological and epistemological categories what was originally well expressed in poetic form. Either the Chief was psychotic, or he meant something very like the above. A reader, or hearer, who is unaware of inner transcendence, or who is unwilling to recognize it in an Indian, will simply miss the direct meaning of this poetic affirmation. For a racist, an adequate hearing of Keesh-ke-mun will require a conversion of a type similar to the one described in the command to love your enemy. If the Englishman wants to hear his voice which "is heard from afar," he will have to begin by loving him. When Keesh-ke-mun speaks poetically, his affirmation is of himself, his truth is his inner foundation.

The same is true, I submit, of all poetic speech.

The Love Song

T. S. Eliot begins his famous "The Love Song of J. Alfred Prufrock" with a citation from the *Inferno* to the effect that this poem will be self-revealing and terribly unflattering. And, in fact, toward the end of the poem he resumes the "I" depicted throughout in the following terms:

> . . . an easy tool,
> Deferential, glad to be of use,
> Politic, cautious, and meticulous;
> Full of high sentence, but a bit obtuse;
> At times, indeed, almost ridiculous—
> Almost, at times, the Fool.

But it is clear that the poem is more than a witty verse, expressing the self deprecation of a superficial fop, and that the author of the poem has depths far beyond those of the "I" depicted in it. The poem depicts banality in order to invite the reader to accompany its author in desiring to go beyond it.

The central process in the poem is revealed in the title: the first three words. "The love song" invite the reader to expect something passionate, but the following words, "J. Alfred Prufrock," suggest a fussy, self-important fool. This pattern of motion toward a horizon of value, followed by stumbling on immediate banality, describes almost every development in the poem. An "evening stretched out against the sky" becomes a "patient etherized upon the table." A mysterious and suggestive yellow fog which moves through the city like a cat meaninglessly falls asleep. An extended consideration of time and times includes "time to murder and create" but it is dominated by "time to prepare a face to meet the faces that you meet." This is certainly a far cry from Eliot's reflection on time in the *Four Quartets*!

The reduction to banality seems to be blamed on women. He discusses eyes which "fix you in a formulated phrase," and arms which seduce you so that you do not know how to begin, and meaningless voices which "come and go, Talking of Michelangelo," and other voices which emasculate his thought process by interjecting "That is not what I meant at all. That is not it, at all." These are the voices which "wake us" at the end of the poem, "and we drown."

But the poem does not want the reader to drown, or to wake up, or to accept banality as reality. The poem wants the reader to recognize the alternatives. It has formulated banality and left it pinned and sprawling on a wall, in order to demand that the reader join the author in attempting to go beyond it. The author is concerned about "an overwhelming question" at the beginning of the poem. He does not want to formulate it in philosophical language: "Oh, do not ask, 'What is it?' " but prefers to proceed in poetic fashion through consideration of a series of images or cameos: "Let us go and make our visit." The images are, as indicated above, of searching for value and stumbling on the trivial. However, two images go beyond this.

First, in lines 70–73 he asks whether he should begin to search for meaning in Hemingway fashion, through male images; but he rejects this approach, interjecting a totally unexpected alternative:

> I should have been a pair of ragged claws
> Scuttling across the floors of silent seas.

Is one to take this suggestion seriously, or is it satirical, in the sense that he might as well be a crawfish as a Hemingway? As the image is bizarre, and unprepared, one is tempted to read it as satirical. However, that would be a mistake. It is in sea imagery that the poem climaxes, and the wonderful dream which he loses in waking up is a dream of lingering "in the chambers of the sea." It appears that Eliot really longs to be a pair of ragged claws, on the floors of silent seas.

A second image occurs at the climax. It offers the answer to banality. And, as it is women who trivialize him, it will be the feminine which could give him hope and meaning:

> I have heard the mermaids singing, each to each.
> I do not think that they will sing to me.
> I have seen them riding seaward on the waves
> Combing the white hair of the waves blown back
> When the wind blows the water white and black.

In many ways this imagery recalls the text we read from the *Iliad*, and Homer's aspiration for Poseidon. Homer had an image of the god moving toward him, whereas Eliot's mermaids are moving away, out to sea. Poseidon offers strength and decision. The mermaids evoke only a terrible longing. Both speak to the depths of the human unconscious.

"The Love Song" is not at all a love song. Rather, it is a cry for help. It is a protest, which asks where passion has gone . . . is love possible any more? The affirmation of the poem, its simple and elemental meaning, expressed indirectly through complex poetic process, and felt personally by the reader, is a transcendent hunger of the poet. The poem has been universally admired, because this affirmation is a human truth.

Conclusion

The subjective affirmations which are expressed in poetic writing or speech, as we have seen in three examples, can be expressed crudely in propositional form. And they can be accepted as true, or rejected as false. It will be said that this is a question of taste, and the word "taste" may suggest something a bit superficial. However, we accept and reject individual people on the basis of taste, and human relations are not necessarily superficial. When we accept the poems of Homer, or Keesh-ke-mun, or T. S. Eliot as true, we mean that as persons we can resonate to, participate in to some degree, the subjective foundations which they affirm.

Are such affirmations and truths legitimate sources for doctrines? Of course they are. They are not doctrines themselves, as they do not affirm anything about objectified reality. However, questions are inevitably asked and answered about the objective implications of such foundations. That is where doctrines begin.

Notes

1. From Horace to Pope, literary theorists in the Western tradition have taught that the purpose of literature was both to delight and to edify, or educate. Horace's often cited line ran: "Poets desire either to give benefit or pleasure, or else at once to express things both delightful and useful in living—*Aut prodesse volunt, aut delectare poetae; aut simul et jucunda et idonea dicere vitae.*" (Cited from Walter and Vivian Sutton, *Plato to Alexander Pope: Backgrounds of Modern Criticism* [New York: The Odyssey Press, 1966] 3, 80.) In the nineteenth and twentieth centuries this truth has been lost sight of, in favor of either total subjectivity where the poet intends no communication but while writing for her/himself is overheard (John Stuard Mills), or else the poet has no intention whatever and is not a subject (John Keats, Jacques Derrida, Michel Foucault, and others). I do not believe that readers, however sophisticated we might like to be, experience poetry as impersonal or neutral. For contemporary questioning about the educative role of literature, cf., for example, Jonathan Culler, *The Pursuit of Sign Semiotics, Literature, Deconstruction* (Ithaca, N.Y.: Cornell University Press, 1981), chapter 1, "Beyond Interpretation," 3–17.

2. Andrew M. Greeley ends an "Author's Note" at the beginning of his 1981 novel *The Cardinal Sins* with the following intriguing oxymoron: "The book, then, is story, not history or biography or (perhaps sadly) autobiography. It is nonetheless true."

3. The notion of "Foundations" is drawn from Bernard Lonergan, *Method in Theology* (London: Darton, Longman and Todd, 1972) 267–293. For an accurate description of Foundations as they exist as part of the experience of thinking, the reader has to be referred to that book. Within the confines of the present study, an imprecise but still, one hopes, adequate notion will be developed.

4. The texts from Homer and Longinus will be taken from Walter and Vivien Sutton, op. cit., 94–96.

5. Speech of Keesh-ke-mun, Crane Clan Hereditary Chief of the Lac du Flambeau Chippewa, cited by Gail Valaskakis, "The Chippewa and the Other; Living the Heritage of Lac du Flambeau," *Cultural Studies* (October, 1988); the text was taken from William Warren, "History of the Ojibways," *Minnesota Historical Collections*, V, 1885.

Chapter 7

Sense About Endings:
A Reaction to a Detail

Frank Kermode's famous little book about fiction elicited two reactions this year, one in an essay by Ben Meyer and another in an article by Charles Davis.[1] Kermode's focus is on the compelling force of form in story, and he treats form in a Kantian manner as though it were an *a priori* category of the mind which is essentially fictional. The ticking of a clock is a series of identical sounds, and yet we so impose a tick-tock pattern on that data that we actually seem to hear tick-tock; and when we hear a tick we are in suspense until the tock occurs. A story is told always between a tick and tock, both of them fictional. In fact, a story is told in order to get to the tock, and the tock, or ending, determines the shape and meaning of everything which precedes. The space between the tick and the tock is given a specific dimension, whereas the interval between the tock and the ensuing tick has no fixed reality in the psyche of the hearer.

There is a truth to this observation. However, its perfect simplicity and charm is so seductive that its inaccuracy becomes dangerous.

A Critique

First, with the exception of suspense thrillers and detective novels, it is simply, and importantly, not true that the endings of most stories determine the shape and meaning of everything which precedes. Davis points out that John Fowles allows the reader to choose between three diverse endings to *The French Lieutenant's Woman,* and that Charles Dickens changed the unhappy ending he had originally planned for *Great Expectations* in order to please his readers.[2] This observation does not confirm Kermode's thesis. Rather, it tends to suggest that, if the writers could leave endings up to the whims of readers, it is precisely because the endings are not important! Clearly, some overall meaning is changed by such different endings, but when I recall reading those books at a distance of some years I cannot remember the endings at all, though I remember the books quite intensely. That overall meaning which was changed or changeable is relatively unimportant!

Among the novels of George Eliot, *Silas Marner* builds strongly toward an ending, but the endings of most of them are relatively trivial. The novels are about the growth of characters and of relations between them, not about how events turned out. For example, *Romola* ends with the death of Savonarola, and that is an exceptionally dramatic climax for Eliot. But the novel is not about Savonarola. It is about Romola and her husband, Tito. That relationshlp comes to a tragic end too, and its ending had been implicit in the flawed character of Tito which was revealed early in the book. But had Eliot chosen to give Tito a conversion, and to save the day somehow in the last chapters, the novel would have been only superficially changed by that decision. There follows an Epilogue in which all the loose ends are tied up. I doubt if anyone can remember its details! The endings really do not matter.

Other examples can be multiplied indefinitely. Dickens wrote his novels in weekly segments over long periods of time. Each segment had to be a literary success in itself. How much did the end of the novel weigh in the writing and reading, as the episodes filled the columns and the readers' imaginations week by week? Not much surely. If personal reminiscence is more convincing, Muriel Sparks once told me, concerning her own novel-writing experience, that she never had any idea at all about how the story would end, until the moment when it ended under her pencil. Thomas Mallory's *Le Morte d'Arthur* ends sadly, with tragic infidelity rotting and destroying Arthur's kingdom, and that has a powerful message in itself. But does the ending succeed in casting its shadow over the glory of all the preceding stories? Can anyone remember the ending to *Tristam Shandy*? Fellini's *Eight and a Half* has a magnificent ending which recapitulates the whole movie. It is a meaningless dance, in which all the characters join, as in those grand marches which begin or end a circus. That is a strong ending, if ever there was one. Had Fellini simply left that scene out, one would have felt that the movie ended weakly . . . but would the meaning be changed? Similarly, *Pride and Prejudice* is suitably wrapped up with multiple weddings in a perfect ending, the omission of which would be a loss of pleasure, but not a change in meaning. Was the rescue from the cave the closing incident in *Tom Sawyer*? Does it matter? What was the closure in *Huckleberry Finn*? The tick sticks in the memory, as does the interval, but the tock . . .?

Form and Truth

So much as a corrective to Kermode's observation. However, there remains an important truth to it, which needs to be retrieved. Stories move forward on the basis of motivations, desires. Their essence includes an orientation of the characters toward certain perceived goods or goals. Unavoidably, this orientation is toward the future, since the goal is either not yet reached, or, if reached, it needs to be held onto into the future. Therefore, it is in the nature of stories to look forward to some achievement or denouement. That this orientation should finally be cut off by a strong closure or ending is a question of artistic taste—it is a rhetorical flourish rather than the essence of the story. Orientation toward a future goal pertains to human action and therefore to all human storytelling; the actual ending pertains to form.

Literary forms in stories, histories, or biographies, may be visible, or concealed, charming or boring. Some forms, such as a family tree, for example, lend themselves to being factual. Other forms, such as perfect revenge, for example, rarely fit the facts. These forms are not *a priori* categories of the mind as Kermode imagines, nor do they depend upon compelling cultural myths as Davis' discussion might lead one to think. The origin of forms is multiple. Some are learned from others, from language and culture. Some are freshly created. Others may be learned from inner experience, such as the extension of time and the extension of space experienced in an infant's body. Others again may be learned in the womb, as perhaps the tick-tock interval from the sound of a mother's heart. In Lonergan's vocabulary, forms are ideas, not truths. Forms are used to make affirmations; they are not affirmed in themselves.

Forms function as questions which enable the writer to ransack either the resources of imagination, or else the data of history, in order to present a readable whole upon a page. If a form is visible and charming, the text may be read as a fiction, and may even impose itself on the mind as a fiction, whether or not the related events are drawn from the imagination or from historical data.[3] The current fad of "reading the Bible as literature" is very helpful, provided one is aware of the fact that literature is not necessarily fiction, or provided one defines fiction as a genre which can include accounts of reality.

Literary forms should not be thought to be radically diverse from nature. For example, it is gratuitous to assert with Sartre that the reality of living is purely contingent succession, an unordered chaos; and that narratives about living necessarily impose the falsehood of beginnings and endings.[4] Chaos is at least as subjective a category as order. Unless one gratuitously denies the reality of the Creator, there is order in reality: the order of causes and effects and emerging probability. There are also the real beginnings and endings imposed upon real events by human intentions. When Sartre "observes" chaos, he has simply failed to discover the real order. When, on the other hand, an author *imposes* an order (a literary form), he or she has equally failed to note the real order. However, when a writer sets about describing reality, he or she cannot begin in any way other than by trying out the various (literary) forms which lie to hand—does one of them fit the facts? If a pleasing form does fit the facts, it may read like fiction while being history. If it partially fits the facts, the writer may choose to write pure fiction by fudging the facts, or choose to write history by damaging the form.

With regard to the Bible, surely its form is neither so visible nor so pleasing as to impose upon the reader the conviction that we are reading pure fiction!

The Bible does have an ending. And this ending does have the literary impact of closure. However, even if one were determined to read the Bible as pure fiction, this closure would not establish the meaning of the whole text. Such a "sense of an ending" is bad literary theory. It is simply not true that the meaning of Exodus, for example, is shaped and determined by the Apocalypse, any more than that the stories of the Round Table are shaped and determined by the death of King Arthur. Like *Le Morte d'Arthur* the Bible presents an irreducible series of diverse human orientations toward ultimate values.

Theology cannot dispense with the Old Testament, it is true. It is equally true that theology cannot unite the Old Testament and the New in one single perspective of meaning through the sense of an ending. The Bible deals with salvation throughout, and salvation is always in the future for us. However, apocalyptic salvation did not displace the expectancy of Deuteronomic daily bread in the Protestant ethic, or the theology of restoration in Jerusalem in Jewish piety, any more than it determines the shape and meaning of all that precedes in the Bible. This reader of the Bible, for one, is more aware of the many ticks than of the apocalyptic tock.

Notes

1. Cf. Frank Kermode, *The Sense of an Ending: Studies in the Theory of Fiction* (Oxford University Press, 1966, 1967); cf. Ben F. Meyer, "Critical Realism and Biblical Theology," in Ben F. Meyer, *Critical Realism and the New Testament* (Allison Park: Pickwick Publication, 1989) 195–211, esp. 201–204; Charles Davis, "Death and the Sense of Ending," *SR* 18 (1989) 51–60.

2. Davis, op. cit., 54–55.

3. Ibid., 57. Davis draws this understanding of "fiction" from Jonathan Culler as corrected by David Lodge. Kermode's unfortunate understanding of fiction demands that it be restricted to the essentially untrue (39, 42). Cf. Meyer, op. cit., 202.

4. Interpreted by Davis, op. cit., 51–52.

Chapter 8

Northrop Frye, "The Great Code": A Critique

Northrop Frye's historic contribution to literary criticism could not easily be exaggerated, and the extent of his influence should not be underestimated. For that reason, his most recent book, *The Great Code: The Bible and Literature,*[1] which promises to be the first of a two-volume study, demands critical attention.

Frye's personal interest in the Bible is doubtless rooted in his United Church of Canada background, and in his theological training for Church ministry at the University of Toronto. His published view of the Bible displays a consistent approach from *Fearful Symmetry: A Study of William Blake* in 1947,[2] through *Anatomy of Criticism: Four Essays* in 1957,[3] to *The Great Code* in 1982.

In his "Introduction" he makes clear that he views the Bible as more than literature, but as fertilizing English literature from the Anglo-Saxon writers until today.[4] Thus his title is not the Bible *as* literature, but rather *and* literature. Moreover, he has no interest in the original texts of the Bible, but only in publications of biblical texts which have most influenced Western Culture, notably the Authorized Version of 1611.[5] This disclaimer might save him from criticism were it not contradicted by the fact that, first, Part I discusses not the cultural effects, but rather the nature of biblical literature; and second, the fact that the approach established in Part I will be a commanding foundation for all that follows.

It may not be possible to describe a complete philosophy underlying Frye's approach. Certainly he is too subtle and too metaphorical a thinker to be reduced to any straw system. But it will be useful to take two central threads within the cloth he weaves for us: first his rejection of history, and second what I shall call his Platonism. I shall attempt to show that these threads are not only foreign to the Bible but also opposed to it.

Such an attempt presupposes the belief that texts have their own meanings within limits set by their authors. Just as it became intellectually unacceptable to present an interpretation of "linear B" based on Greek roots, grammar and parallels once the Semitic nature of "linear B" had been established, so it will be intellectually unacceptable to present an interpretation of biblical texts based on literary procedures which can be shown to be foreign to biblical authors and to do violence to literary data within the text.

The Rejection of History

First, then, we shall consider that axis of meaning in the Bible which rests upon historical facticity. Frye seems to hate it. His treatment of it is so uncharacteristically crude that one wonders what rhetorical imperative is at work here. He begins quietly by writing, "The general principle involved here is that if anything historically true is in the Bible, it is not there because it is historically true but for different reasons."[6] There is some validity to this observation: the same sort of validity as if I should claim that when I write a letter to my sister I usually relay real events or historical facts, not because they are true but rather because they will interest her, or please her, or amuse her, or somehow express my affection for her, and so on. However, this validity would have been better served had Frye written "not *only* because it is historically true but *also* for different reasons." What leads Frye to believe that historical truth is there without any concern for historical truth?

In the following pages he denies the possibility of retrieving anything of the historical Jesus, though he concedes that "It would be interesting to see, if we could, what the original 'historical' Jesus was like, before his teachings got involved in the mythical and legendary distortions of his followers."[7] One is shocked at the word "distortions" here: surely more gentle words would have been closer to the truth: for example, "interpretations," or "re-interpretations," or "elaborations," or "applications to new contexts," and so forth. What inner rage is Northrop Frye allowing to surface here?

And then he goes on to state: "Nothing said here will be new to Biblical scholars, who are well aware that the Bible will only confuse and exasperate an historian who tries to treat it as history." Well many biblical scholars will have to protest, unless by the word "history" Dr. Frye means some naive ideal of material objectivity which scholars relinquished early in the twentieth century. One of the foremost New Testament scholars in Canada, Ben Meyer, published a masterful presentation of the historical Jesus just three years before Frye published this sweeping claim, with the title, *The Aims of Jesus*.[8] Am I misunderstanding Northrop Frye here? Is his whole argument cast in a different mode than the one I seem to find?

Does he mean only that the Bible may have been written with historical intent, but that now it is difficult to read it for other than its mythical values? He does treat one book in this fashion: Gibbon's *Decline and Fall of the Roman Empire*.[9] He points out that this book, although it was once written with historical intent and read as such, has survived for different reasons: "Gibbon's work survives by its 'style,' which means that it insensibly moves over from the historical category into the poetic, and becomes a classic of English literature, or at any rate of English cultural history." Now, I do not agree that Gibbon's famous *post hoc ergo propter hoc* is adequately analyzed in this way, because I do not agree that it was originally history without poetry, or that it is now poetry without being history. However, I am not surprised at such an affirmation, and I would not be astonished if Frye attempted to treat the Bible in the same way.

However, the fact is that Frye claims the Bible was never written as history in the first place. For example, in Chapter II he discusses the possibility of someone's finding an independent historical record of Jesus' trial, or finding a physical ark on Mount Ararat.[10] Now first of all, by linking these two items as though they were similar he is (intentionally?) obliterating the basis for most judgments of historicity, namely, the diversity of types of text which attest to facts in question. In this case Genesis 6-9 seems to be written in a mythical, or at least legendary, genre; whereas the trial of Jesus is written in a genre which suggests eyewitness accounts. But more than this, Frye goes on to say, "The first thing that occurred to me was that the Bible itself could not care less whether anyone ever finds an ark on Mount Ararat or not: such 'proofs' belong to a mentality quite different from any that could conceivably have produced the Book of Genesis."

That is the whole question. Does Genesis, and by implication the rest of the Bible, have a mentality which is interested in historical proof, or does it not? If not, then Frye's impassioned dehistoricizing is appropriate. But if, on the other hand, historical facticity is part of the biblical focus, then Frye's method systematically misreads the Bible.

Obviously, I think Frye is wrong. But let us begin in the enemy camp, as it were, by taking his own proof text. He refers to the story of doubting Thomas, and to its famous conclusion: "Blessed are they who have not seen and yet believe" (John 20:29).

I shall cite here Frye's statement about this story:

> What it amounts to, I believe, is that credibility, as a factor in the response to the particulars of the Biblical narrative, is very largely a pseudo-issue. When the apostle Thomas demanded visible and tangible evidence for the Resurrection, he was told that he would have understood the Resurrection more clearly if he hadn't bothered with it. I doubt that the implication of this story is that an uncritical attitude is spiritually closer to the truth than a critical

one. I think the implication is rather that the more trustworthy the evidence, the more misleading it is.[11]

I would characterize this argument as clever. First of all, we must note that even if Thomas would have been somehow a better man had he not needed to "bother" with visible or tangible evidence, still the Risen Lord is depicted as providing this evidence when asked, and moreover, the biblical text has bothered to relay this story of visible and tangible evidence to us. Secondly, I can find no basis whatever for saying, as Frye does, that the implication of the story is that "the more trustworthy the evidence, the more misleading it is." Was Thomas the apostle misled by this trustworthy evidence? Who was misled? One is tempted to propose the hypothesis that Dr. Frye holds, on the basis of some *other* argument, that the Risen Lord is one thing and a visible, tangible body is quite another; and that one is liable to be misled by a visible, tangible body: one is liable to be misled into believing that the Risen Lord is a bodily Lord. Now one could conceive that this was Dr. Frye's doctrine about the Resurrection; but one could not conceive that that doctrine was in any sense the meaning of the biblical text. At this point, Frye is not interpreting the text but rather he is fighting it. He is refusing to understand its evident meaning.

It is true that the Bible contains many myths, legends, jokes, parables, and so forth. But it seems to be patently obvious that the Bible also deals in, and focuses on, historical facts even in the most crude sense of the word. By way of proof, allow me to recall some crashingly boring examples.

There are, of course, all the etiologies characterized by the phrase "as to this day" in which the whole point is some historical material object which the hearer can see and touch—a tree, some stones, and in the fantastic Ark Story the golden tumors, the golden mice and the great stone at Bethshemesh (1 Sam 6:17-18). There is a regular museum tag in Deuteronomy 3 where verse 11 reads "For only Og the King of Bashan was left of the Rephaim; behold his bedstead was a bedstead of iron. Is it not in Rabah of the Ammonites? Nine cubits is its length, and four cubits its breadth, according to the common cubit." In these texts the biblical authors lend reality to legends precisely by pointing to arks on Mt. Ararat. And what is Genesis 23 all about, if not about the point made in verses 16-18, namely, a legal, historical claim to part of the land? These authors could not define history with any of the alienated precision of Benedetto Croce, but clearly they are interested in the facts and in meanings rooted in material realities.

The New Testament is equally focused on historical facts. If one thinks of the verses which introduce Luke's Gospel and Acts (which promise research as to the accuracy of the tradition), or of John 20 with its precision about the napkin and the linen clothes rolled up in the tomb, or Matthew's details about rolling back the stone of Jesus' sepulcher and how the guards were bribed to lie about it, and other examples which could be multiplied to the point of boredom, it becomes impossible to agree with Frye that the Bible has a mentality which is not interested in historical proof.

To move now from material details to massive historical claims, it is hard to believe that the biblical text is not concerned with the historic right of the chosen people to the physical Promised Land, or with the historical reality of its kings and prophets. I find it impossible to believe that the prophetic books, for example, are not historical in intent. They seem utterly unintelligible to me unless read as a theological explanation for historically real sufferings in exile, and as validations of the prophets: historical proofs that Isaiah, Jeremiah, and so forth, had accurately interpreted historical reality in the name of Yahweh. To read this material, and systematically to exclude even the possibility of such a meaning, is surely to refuse to understand it.

Frye's Platonism

The second thread to be drawn from Frye's cloth will be merely a broader perspective on the first one. By the word "Platonism" I am trying to designate a somewhat elusive tendency to academic escapism, to a refusal of reality. In Frye, this attitude is trumpeted under the word "centripetal."

What does Frye mean by his distinction between *centripetal meaning* and *centrifugal meaning*? In Chapter III of *The Code*, he offers the following definition:

> All verbal structures have a centripetal and a centrifugal aspect, and we can call the centripetal aspect their literary aspect. In this sense all verbal structures whatever have a literary aspect, even though normally we do not speak of literature unless a pattern of continuous descriptive reference is absent. The primary and literal meaning of the Bible, then, is its centripetal or poetic meaning. It is only when we are reading as we do when we read poetry that we can take the word "literal" seriously, accepting every word given us without question. This primary meaning, which arises simply from the interconnection of the words, is the metaphorical meaning. There are various secondary meanings, derived from the centrifugal perspective, that may take the form of concepts, predications, propositions, or a sequence of historical or biographical events, and that are always subordinate to the metaphorical meaning.[12]

Thus for Frye, the primary meaning of a biblical text will be metaphorical. There will be various secondary meanings, but unless these could be described, to use his own phrase, as "a pattern of descriptive continuous reference," these too will be literary and mythical. Naturally, "various secondary meanings" could be found for any biblical text, none of which would be more true or false than any other, and all true in a purely mythical sense. Since Chapter I has drawn a history of culture in which precisely "a pattern of descriptive continuous reference" is not to be found prior to the Renaissance, one must conclude that the Bible is to be read only for its mythical, centripetal meanings. A poetic reading of the Bible is the only reading, not only for the purpose of lecturing on comparative literature but also because the Bible is a purely poetic book. Despite Frye's disclaimers, this surprising conclusion is inescapably implied by his positions.

It will be helpful and corroborative to see the most general application of this principle expressed in Frye's own words at the beginning of Chapter IV.

> The New Testament insists a great deal on what it calls faith and truth, but its guarantees for such things seem very strange, even when we have understood something of the principle involved. How do we know that the Gospel story is true? Because it confirms the prophecies of the Old Testament. But how do we know that the Old Testament prophecies are true? Because they are confirmed by the Gospel story. Evidence, so called, is bounced back and forth between the testaments like a tennis ball; and no other evidence is given us. The two testaments form a double mirror, each reflecting the other but neither the world outside.[13]

With such a position, it will make sense that Dr. Frye should link law with ritual and make the law collections in the Torah archetypal, mythical, essentially repetitive.[14] One wonders how he could explain that a given law, when actually repeated in the Torah, is not repeated at all, but rather appears in an historically evolved form—a fact which has given a textual base to the immensely rich ethical-legal dialectic within Judaism. Similarly Frye will write about wisdom in the Bible that "wisdom is not identified either with knowledge or with the denial of knowledge. It is an existential wisdom with its centre in human concern, not in the exploration of nature or other worlds," and he cites Job 28:14 "The deep saith, It is not in me."[15] In this, again, Frye's doctrine is a formidable obstacle to understanding the text. Ironically, it would be hard to find a text less helpful to his argument than the one he chose: Job 28. When "the deep" says that wisdom "is not in me," it does not mean Wisdom is not *about* me, that is, not about nature. In the following verse Job tells us that Wisdom is in God. However, these verses prove God's wisdom precisely in terms of "knowledge" and "in the exploration of nature or other worlds."

23 God understands the way of it (Wisdom)
     and he knows its place

24 For he looks to the ends of the earth,
  and sees everything under the heavens.
25 When he gave to the wind its weight,
  and meted out the waters by the measure
26 When he made a decree for the rain
  and a way for the lighting of the thunder;
27 Then he saw it and declared it.

The astonishing fact is that for Job biblical wisdom was very close to what *we* call scientific knowledge, even though it was available only to God. Job has God weighing wind and measuring water like an early Galileo. The Deuteronomistic historian, on the other hand, proves (in 1 Kgs 3-11) that a man, Solomon, was wise. His proof consists of ascribing to him scientific knowledge to the degree that such a thing existed in the Iron Age: namely, cunning in law and politics, virtuosity in engineering and construction, the arts of war and macroeconomics, and simple success in elementary school. One wonders, for example, what sense Frye can make out of 1 Kings 4:29-34. Solomon's wisdom is born of "existential human concern," just as is medical research today, or astronomy, or nuclear physics. Its term is centrifugal knowledge, not just psychic expansion in a centripetal sense. It aims at a mastery over "nature or other worlds," not comfort through altered mental states.

Just what is the doctrine in Frye's mind which forms such an obstacle? One can find no statement of it, but only traces or clues. It has to do with the ancient and recurrent idea that the real world is not the changing and historical universe which we experience through our senses and know through self-transcending activities of understanding, affirming, deciding and acting; but rather the real world is an unchanging and eternal idea which is expressed in our innate archetypes, objectified in cultural expressions, glimpsed through aesthetic sensitivity, and totally unrelated to the phenomenal world and to the human operations usually associated with knowledge and responsibility. This is what I would like to call Platonism. It may explain some respected mystical traditions, but I argue that it is opposed to the text of biblical literature.

Frye seems to indicate a theory such as this when he writes that "Man lives, not directly nor nakedly in nature like the animals, but within a mythological universe, a body of assumptions and beliefs developed from his existential universe. Most of this is held unconsciously. . . ."[16] Later he writes, "But the real interest of myth is to draw a circumference around a human community and look inward toward that community, not to inquire into the operations of nature . . . mythology is not a direct response to the natural environment; it is part of the imaginative insulation which separates us from that environment."[17]

Now I think there is much truth contained in statements like this, and one could live with them, if one were allowed to add a few corrective phrases. However, all of Dr. Frye's own phrases seem to correct in the wrong direction. For example, Chapter I begins with a history of culture in three phases in which cultural change is caused by language change. Knowledge seems to play no role whatever in cultural advance.[18] He then goes on to refute some exaggerations about the role of objectivity and ends up with an opposite exaggeration: "It is not difficult to step from here to the feeling often expressed in contemporary criticism and philosophy, that it is really language that uses man, and not man that uses language."[19]

Some sentences reveal Frye's awareness of the absurdity, and of the peril, of this kind of formulation. But he has no foundation for breaking away from it. His categories distinguish between pure ideas on the one hand and social concern on the other, with no room for truth in between. For example, he sees only conflict between the socially irresponsible integrity of mutually exclusive intellectual disciplines on the one hand and political power with its unifying social concern on the other.[20] It is as though sociology or chemistry were separate thought-bubbles drifting apart. It does not occur to him that the discipline of chemistry, as that of sociology, should exist in order to answer real questions about nature and about human life, about society and its future. Surely they did not emerge or survive as spiritual monads. Except in the sickest preserves of academia, they are not in conflict with, but directly linked to, social responsibility. And with full integrity they cooperate to answer real questions. Truth is in conflict with power only when power ignores reality.

Similarly, in discussing myth in the Bible, Frye comes up with the same two categories, distinguishing two aspects of myth: "one is its story-structure, which attaches it to literature, the other is its social function as concerned knowledge, what it is important for society to know."[21] Once again, no space is allowed between "structure" and "concerned knowledge" for simple truth. Now the term "concerned knowledge" might have been all right had he not gone on to discuss this category by introducing a distinction between *Weltgeschichte*, which he defines as "what I should have seen if I had been there," from *Heilsgeschichte,* which he defines as "the whole point of what was really going on."[22] It all sounds coherent, but these definitions lead one into nonsense. Is *Weltgeschichte* really something seen by a witness? Is secular history coterminus with visibility? Surely secular history is about political passion and about power; and yet both of these are totally invisible. Did anyone actually see the defeat of Napoleon's empire at Waterloo? Even the most limited material aspect of the military defeat on that day is affirmed only as an imaginative construct based on myriad eyewitness reports. The fact is that *Weltgeschichte* is not an account of what was seen, but rather a statement about "the whole point of what was going on." Now Frye defined *Heilsgeschichte* as "the whole point of what was going on." What then is *Heilsgeschichte* as opposed to *Weltgeschichte*? Does he mean the "really real" point, in the sense of the eternal truth? the stable, archetypal myth? Unfortunately, this is just what he means as the next paragraph shows, with its discussion of what he calls the "repeating quality of literature." Frye simply has no category of meaning whereby, for example, the Pentateuch could affirm as true some invisible and yet historical belief such as that the Jewish nation was fused together by the will of God, or that God gave them the land of Canaan. Similarly, the Deuteronomistic History, within Frye's categories, could never mean that the monarchy in Israel was terminated in 587 B.C.E., or that this was due to the crimes of Manasseh, or to the idolatrous practices of many generations. Frye's doctrine and categories exclude meanings which the biblical authors appear to have intended.

Even if we go to places where the Bible seems to affirm truths which are not uniquely historical but rather general and ongoing, Frye's approach excludes what appears on literary evidence to be the simple meaning. For example, Genesis 1:1–2:4a was written as an alternative to the Yahwist's famous story of the fall. The Yahwist's view appears to have been that in the beginning was sin and punishment and these are still with us. The Priestly writer, at the moment of exile and despair in Israel, wrote an alternative: in the beginning the universe was good; man was made to rule; and this is still so. Surely affirmations like these are worth confronting. Surely their juxtaposition, in an order which is not haphazard, expresses a specific spiritual grasp of reality which the reader must either accept, or refuse, or argue with. Now Frye spends eight pages on these chapters, and never once alludes to such simple meanings.[23] Rather, he discusses self-serving motives which could give rise to such narratives, their literary antecedents and echoes, some speculations about the ideas and images he happens upon, and finally the idea that the "essential meaning of the creation story, for us, seems to be as a type of which the antetype is the new heaven on earth promised in Revelation 21:1."[24] Thus, we have a type and an antetype, forming "a double mirror, each reflecting the other but neither the world outside."[25]

Frye's Platonism leads him to find in the Bible a technique for reaching a world "outside" our world, an escape into the spiritual, rather than a discovery of the spiritual. I suggest that this is an abuse of biblical literature.

Notes

1. Northrop Frye, *The Great Code: The Bible and Literature* (Toronto: Academic Press, 1982).

2. Northrop Frye, *Fearful Symmetry: A Study of William Blake* (New Jersey: Princeton University Press, 1947). For example, on 317, he astonishes this reader by presenting the Bible as "the historical product of a visionary tradition . . . a continuous reshaping of earlier and more primitive visions." Others view the Bible as verbal rather than visual, even though the latter is also to be found in some important texts.

3. Northrop Frye, *Anatomy of Criticism: Four Essays* (New Jersey: Princeton University Press, 1957). Cf., for example, 55–56 and 121–122 and 126, where he presents the Bible as a unified mythology, an order of words developing in the creative imagination, totally withdrawn from physics or theology.

4. Cf. *The Great Code,* xvi.

5. Cf. ibid., xiii.

6. Ibid., 40.

7. Ibid., 41–42.

8. Ben Meyer, *The Aims of Jesus* (London: SCM Press, 1979).

9. Cf. *The Great Code,* 32 and 46.

10. Cf. ibid., 44–45.

11. Ibid., 46.

12. Ibid., 61.

13. Ibid., 78.

14. Cf. ibid., 63 and 84.

15. Ibid., 67.

16. Ibid., xviii.

17. Ibid., 37, and longer statement based on Wallace Stevens, 50–51.

18. Cf. ibid., 3–18.

19. Ibid., 22.

20. Cf. ibid., 51–52.

21. Ibid., 47.

22. Ibid., 48.

23. Cf. ibid., 106–114.

24. Ibid., 114.

25. Ibid., 78.

Chapter 9

A Commentary on Manna

Catholic exegesis in this century has tended to learn its trade from our older, more experienced, Protestant colleagues. This strategy has served us well. The Protestant scholar has religiously wanted to return to original meanings, in order to recover an authentic message of a pure revelation, free from any ecclesiastical or traditional corruption. This instinct was open to a radical definition by the Enlightenment, where objectivity became a supreme value. Those of us who were formed in this tradition, have learned to value an interpretation which is based upon precise historical context. The method could be summed up in the question: who said what to whom? And scholarship consisted in bringing ever greater historical precision to the definition of those three entities. The information resulting from this approach, available now in dozens of "Introductions to the Old Testament," must be recognized as a great achievement. Moreover, its discipline remains indispensable, as a decisive step in scholarship as self-transcendence, that is, moving effectively beyond a universe of thought controlled by personal neurosis, or egotism, into a universe of thought clearly understood as controlled by another person, or by a universal viewpoint.

On the other hand, that approach has not been good enough.[1] One often has the impression that exegesis in that style has not delighted or nourished the faithful, or much interested their pastors, or been an outstanding favorite even with theologians. Moreover, the Bible is written in literary genres, and therefore its academic reading must be informed by the best of contemporary literary theory. But, since the 1920s, literary theory, in the English-speaking cultures at least, has rejected historical context outright, and proclaimed a "new criticism" in which the only interpretative context was the internal relationships of the work itself![2] The very methodology which made exegesis academically respectable in the eyes of historians produced a form of interpretation which was academically unacceptable in the eyes of literary scholars.

Over the past decade or more, an ocean of literary theory has washed over the universities. Even to summarize it would require a book. It may suffice to point to the influence of Jacques Derrida, who was so much in demand for several years in the '70s and early '80s that he divided his time between the Sorbonne and Yale. However one evaluates it, this passionate debate about the nature of literary truth has sharply questioned and illuminated the procedures of biblical commentary. We can draw from it important insights to clarify the academic validity of theological disciplines, and in particular of biblical studies.[3]

This essay will attempt to interpret Exodus 16 in a paradigm study, in which are consciously exemplified some principles of interpretation which go beyond the historical-critical method. These principles are academically sound. And they will be seen to yield interpretations which can be directly useful for academic theology, and for the Church.[4]

The Meaning of the Text Within Itself

We shall begin by reading the text according to the "new criticism," observing the internal relations of its elements of meaning. Two methodological principles may be mentioned in connection with this approach. First, historical context, particularly as discussed in terms of the intention of the author, must be excluded as a principle of interpretation. This principle must be understood sensibly. It does not mean that all historical data is taboo when clues about meaning are sought. It does mean that the interpreter must assume that the text in itself expresses all the meaning which is meant, and that commentary or exegesis must argue for its conclusions exclusively on arguments based on the data of the text.[5] This principle is very practical in that it leads the interpreter to go as far as possible in squeezing all the meaning out of the text. It will be seen that other principles of interpretation treated later in this article lead us to go against this one, not because it is false or because its results are misleading, but because once its results are secured they can be richly supplemented by undertaking different kinds of analysis from other perspectives.

A second principle is that one must refuse all paraphrase which attempts to restate "the meaning" of a literary text in abstract summary, using philosophical or psychological or scientific or marxist or feminist terms. Such paraphrase invariably misses the heart of meaning in any literary text.[6] Thus, commentary must radically avoid saying that the text means such and such, or that "the whole point" of the story is thus and so. Especially bad are formulations in past tense: the pericope *meant* this. Such objectifying paraphrases can hardly avoid translating a unique and subjectively rich artistic meaning into an impoverished, pseudo-objective, abstract idea which the author would repudiate as false and absurd. The text means what it means, and means what it meant; and what it means cannot be expressed in any other words. Commentary should define meanings of individual words and phrases, but when dealing with a literary unit commentary should not define meaning but rather point to form and relationship. This does not exclude attempts at translation which recognize the inadequacy of translation. Nor does it exclude creating another literary work, which may employ other literary techniques in an attempt to say roughly the same thing as the text in question. With regard to Exodus 16, for example, one could point to a remarkably faithful restatement of the message of this chapter in the Wisdom of Solomon, where it says that

> "thou didst give thy people the food of angels (i.e., ambrosia, cf. 19:21), and without their toil thou didst supply them from heaven with bread ready to eat, providing every pleasure and suited to every taste. For thy sustenance manifested thy sweetness toward thy children" (16:20-21).

This is not paraphrase, but rather a new literary statement. What is banned is paraphrase; and what is thereby saved is the original, authentic, literary meaning.

The text of the manna story is found in Exodus 16:1-17:1. One can see at a glance that the pericope is framed by two transitional verses (16:1 and 17:1), and ends with an epilogue (16:35-36). The body of the text, as virtually all commentators have complained, is characterized by a confusing discrepancy in detail, apparent doublets and apparent reversals of proper narrative sequence.[7] Undoubtedly, an editor has mixed sources together. However, the body of the pericope can still be seen as a simple ordered whole. It consists of an introduction followed by four unified sections dealing each with different subject matters. I would argue that the difficulty we sometimes experience in reading this chapter comes, not so much from the breaks in narrative logic, but rather from our human reluctance to hear its message.

The sections are as follows. It may be noted that each of the last three sections begins with a speech in which Moses tells of God's instructions.

1) Introduction (vv. 2-8)
2) Fulfillment: Israel sees God's glory in the desert (vv. 9-15)
3) Israel learns trust (vv. 16-21)
4) Israel learns about God's gift of the Sabbath (vv. 22-31)
5) Provision that Israel might always remember these revelations (vv. 32–34)

1) Introduction (vv. 2-8)

The narrative begins when the community of Israel complains, wishing that they had died at the hand of the Lord in Egypt, since Moses and Aaron appear to have instigated the Exodus in order to kill them through hunger. Thus the manna story, here as in Numbers 11, is presented within the context of murmuring in the wilderness.[8] It is helpful to compare these verses to Numbers 14:1-5, where many elements are almost identical, including the explicit murmuring against Moses and Aaron which implies a murmuring against Yahweh.[9] But there is one important difference: whereas the story in Numbers 14 is all about God's angry reaction, in Exodus 16 only Moses will get angry (v. 20b). God adverts to Israel's failure (vv. 4b and 28a), but is presented as expressing only positive reactions throughout the event.[10]

Verses 4 and 5 appear to come from nowhere, and they have generally been presumed to belong to another (earlier) source. They are addressed to Moses alone; they do not advert explicitly to the murmuring which precedes; they contain the notion of "testing" Israel, which does not recur in the pericope or seem relevant; they appear to separate the murmuring of verses 1-2 from a direct answer to it in verses 6-7. On the other hand, they do provide information which helps make sense of verses 6-7, and they contain material which is presupposed by verse 16 and verse 23.[11] One must conclude, therefore, that these verses are inserted here by an editor who fully intended their meaning, and who thereby disturbed what may originally have been a unified story about seeing God's glory (roughly vv. 2-3, 6-15 with alterations), and turned verses 2-8 into an introduction of the whole pericope.

The insertion of verses 4-5 has another dramatic effect. God is presented as intervening precipitately in order to provide food from heaven (v. 4a), without any reaction to Israel's failure in faith. The provision is to be continued on a day-by-day basis, as a test, and it will be doubled on the sixth day. As a result the Introduction interprets the manna incident as a revelation of, and definition of, God as pro-actively caring and intervening. At this point the text makes great demands upon the reader. One is tempted to escape into objectifying reflections about different sources here, rather than to measure oneself against the affirmation of faith one encounters in the text.

Verses 6-7 thematize what is elemental meaning in verses 4-5: something will happen that very day,[12] which will bring the whole community of Israel to faith in Yahweh ("you will know" in the strong sense of that word).[13] If one contrasts this pericope with the parallel story in Numbers 11, one can see that both deal with food and eating. But Exodus 16 sees the food, from the beginning, in terms of revelation. When they see food it will appear as "glory." Moreover, this event will correct their error in complaining against Moses and Aaron, that is, their failure to understand the revelation of Exodus.

Verse 8 adds the notion of flesh, taking advantage of the words "evening" and "morning," which were paired in a kind of hendiadys in verses 6-7. Once again we see a trace of the merging of sources, in which the quail story was added, in a very subordinate role here, to the manna story.[14]

2) Fulfillment: Israel sees God's glory in the desert (vv. 9-15)

If verses 4-5 were omitted, the story begun in verse 2, which is about the murmuring, and the glory of God (in the form of quail and manna), and the faith of Israel, would be completed in this section. The theme of "evening" and "morning" of verses 6-7, 8 recurs in verse 12, and again in verse 13. And the promised "glory" of verse 7a is seen in verse 10b, while the promise that Israel "will know" in the strong sense of verse 6a recurs in verse 12b.

However, the present edited form of our narrative presents this event as the first of three. Hence Israel is not quite presented as "knowing" as yet, since the "knowing" in verse 12b is still promised only (now by Yahweh himself), and since verse 15 has Israel "seeing" without making explicit what they see, and asking theological questions. Verse 15 is really an etymological footnote, rather than a full closure to the original story, and it now functions also as a somewhat awkward transitional verse between the second and the third sections of our narrative. It is noteworthy that the narrative first presents the people as beholding the glory, and subsequently it has the quail and the manna appearing. This was an experience of believing, not primarily of eating.

3) Israel learns that God's gift comes one day at a time (vv. 16-21)

This and the following section, beginning with an instruction of God which Moses communicates to the people, show how the system works if they follow instructions but does not work otherwise, and ends with the people having learned to conform. In this section the instruction is given in two parts: they should collect manna according to their individual need (vv. 16-19), and they should not collect any for the following day (v. 19).[15] Israel disobeys, rot occurs, and Moses is angered (v. 20). But then the people do it properly (v. 21).

What is remarkable here is that there is no punishment. Moses' anger, like the people's murmuring at the beginning, is given no moral significance. It is simply an occurrence which moves the story forward. The story is apparently not about Israel's being tested. Rather, it is about Israel's learning how God operates in taking care of them.

4) Israel learns about God's gift of the Sabbath (vv. 22-31)

The instruction is given very gently, as an explanation of a remarkable experience on the sixth day (vv. 22-26). When some people discover that going out on the Sabbath is fruitless (v. 27), God points out that this is disobedience, but once again he is apparently not angered: instead he explains how he wants them to rest on the Sabbath, and how he has provided manna so that they can do so (vv. 28-29). The unit ends with a reflection on how lovely all this was (vv. 30-31).

5) Provision that Israel might always remember these revelations (vv. 32-34)

This section too begins with a divine instruction, but it does not narrate a learning experience through error. Rather, it is about how the people of all generations should recall and learn the lessons of the manna story. It retrieves the notion of "seeing" (v. 32b and cf. vv. 15a, 10b, 7a), and the definition of Yahweh as the one who brings them out of the land of Egypt (v. 32b and cf. v. 6b), and also the role of Aaron (vv. 33a, 34b and cf. vv. 2a, 6a, 9a, 10a), thus creating a minor effect of inclusion.

The story is about something to be done, something to be maintained (*mishmeret*, vv. 32a, 33b), in a simple way, just as the manna was maintained for the sabbath (v. 23b). It suggests Christ's command about the bread and wine, to "Do this in memory of me."[16] Its purpose is that all generations might see the food as God's glory.

Conclusion

The introduction and second section told a story about how the people experienced God's glory in the manna. The third and fourth sections told of a further experience in which the people learned to trust in a way which made it unnecessary to be concerned for the future.[17] The fourth section comments on a memorial of this experience which was maintained in the Temple and which had enabled all the generations of the Jews to relive this birth of faith.

The reader of this story may never have seen Jerusalem, the Temple, or the jar of manna. But the story invites the reader to share the experience of those who have. It is an intolerably sweet story. I suspect that many readers are instinctively drawn toward reactions of anger at Israel's paranoid murmuring and repeated disobedience, so that the narrative seems hard to follow, though we have seen it is perfectly in order. It rubs the wrong way. It demands that the reader change expectations about the role of God in this world. Such a reader is like the prophet Jonah whose attitude was so unhealthy that he could not understand that God really cared for the people and animals of Nineveh (Jonah 4:11).

The story is based on zoological and biological phenomena which occur even today in the Sinai Peninsula and upon tribal memories. However, the story, while it uses these realities, is concerned with a different sort of affirmation. It is about defining the care God has for Israel. And it affirms (in a way which makes the reader uncomfortable perhaps), a positive attitude of expectancy about this care. The text demands hope. It does not offer a historical truth (i.e., constructed on the basis of precise time, sequence, and causality), or a theological truth (i.e., constructed on the basis of precise systematic conceptualization and philosophically grounded principles), but rather what the Second Vatican Council termed a "salvific truth."[18] This is the sort of truth which is characteristic of literary genres. Readers who accept the authority of such texts allow them to form their own subjectivity. If a reader, because of the manna story, goes through the internal sea change of replacing habitual negative with habitual positive attitudes, perceiving God's loving care in every moment and event, this will be a coming to faith. It will be psychologically true insofar as the inner shift has really occurred, and is not just a facade.[19] It will be "realistic" insofar as it is a subjective expectancy (as was the previous negativity), which is used to interpret real data, and not to support illusion. It will be spiritually true insofar as one's deepest being is attained, and raised to awareness as being-in-relation to the Infinite Love which causes us, calls us, and awaits us. The reader will have experienced the "performative meaning" of the text.

The Meaning of the Text in its Historical Context

Having got this far with the "new criticism," we shall now change methods, and admit the historical context as a factor in interpretation. There is the historical reality of tamarisk sap and migratory African quail in the Sinai Peninsula, and also the trace of historical memories of a migration of Jewish families from Egypt through the desert. But more important for meaning is the history of the relevant literary objects, namely, the discernible written sources of this pericope.

Sources

Source critics agree in assigning the major portions of this pericope to the Priestly Writer, thus placing the historical context of the final form of the story most probably in the late exilic or early post-exilic experience of Israel. It is disputed whether the non-Priestly verses should be dated earlier,[20] or later,[21] but this dispute is too wide-reaching to be addressed here. It will be sufficient to consider the historical context of the Priestly writer. A following section will touch upon evidence from earlier tradition history.

The Priestly Writer was concerned to rewrite the history of Israel, leaving aside elements of conditional covenant, sin and punishment, and establishing the prescribed practices of the cult in Jerusalem as the key to assuring God's blessing for Israel. It is a document of Zionist hope.[22] He appears to have written before the Temple was restored, and based his work on memories of former times. He may have had present some of the Temple furnishings, such as some of the gold and silver vessels and possibly the menorah.[23] In this context, the memory of a jar, containing food God had given Israel to eat while freeing them from Egypt, forms a very striking climax to the story. It invites belief that God will enable Israel to fully repossess Jerusalem, and to build the Temple there according to the plan laid out in Exodus 24ff, restore the sacrifices legislated in Leviticus 1-9, and once again behold God's glory in their midst.

Here, as in Genesis 2:2-3, the Priestly Writer presents the sabbath, not as a requirement of law, but rather as a divine gift, as a time provided for rest.

Tradition history

Whatever position is taken regarding the dating of Pentateuchal sources, it is clear that, prior to Exodus 16, the manna story had more than one form. One must deduce this on the evidence of the differences in detail in its description, in the vocabulary used, and in its manner of being eaten, which may be seen especially in Exodus 16:13-14, 23, 31; Numbers 11:7-9; Psalm 78:24-25. Moreover, the mention of anger or disapproval, which appear in Exodus 16:20b and 28b, remain undeveloped and irrelevant to the story, and thus appear to be traces of fidelity to earlier versions of the present story.

There is no hope of recovering an original form of this story. One suspects that there was once a form of the story which was a simple miracle story. However, in Numbers 11 and Psalm 78 the manna tradition has been associated with a quail tradition. And both have been appropriated by "Pattern II" of the murmuring tradition, and associated with sin and divine wrath, punishment, death.[24] Numbers 11 presents the people as sick and tired of manna!

Exodus 16 is a complex of sources. It retains the murmuring tradition, and also a mention of the quail tradition, and slight traces of anger and disapproval in verses 20b and 28b; but all the connections to sin, divine wrath, punishment and death are eliminated. This is in keeping with the Priestly Writer's agenda. The editor of Exodus 16 has embroidered and sharpened the elements of hope and trust in God, a message of particular religious value either to exiled Jews, or to Jews under oppression in Seleucid or Roman oppressed Judea.

Conclusion

The consideration of historical contexts, in this case, serves only to confirm and sharpen the perception gained through "new criticism."

The Subject Matter of the Manna Story

It must be pointed out in passing that advances in biological science have enabled us to understand manna itself better than did the Jews. However, it cannot be said that this advance yielded new meanings of the text, because the subject matter (or object) of the text is not manna itself, but rather it is the pro-active gift of God as received through the manna.

The gift of God was symbolized as glory in this account of the manna experience. It was a learning of trust. This reality was once based on a physical fact, but at the time of writing it has become an object of contemplation through memory (much like the song of "The Solitary Reaper" or "The Daffodils" of William Wordsworth),[25] supported possibly by the jar of manna. Texts deal with objects, and the better one understands a text, the better one understands the object it deals with; conversely, the better one understands the object, the better one can understand the text.[26] Often a reader's knowledge of the object discussed by a text surpasses that of the writer. For example, "The Star Spangled Banner," the American national anthem, speaks of American national courage and pride as symbolized in a specific flag. Since Francis Scott Key wrote that song, both the flag itself and the pride of the American nation have changed and developed through growth and defeat and triumph. When one hears that song, possibly at the Olympic games, or at the inauguration of a new president, one understands in it something far beyond anything its author, Francis Scott Key in prison, could have conceived. One understands far more than the author understood.

The manna recurs in Numbers 11, but there the subject matter of the text is not the pro-active gift of God leading to trust, but rather the sinfulness of Israel regarding manna and God's reaction to that. Israel remembered the meat, the cucumbers, the melons, the leeks, the onions, and the garlic in Egypt, and that memory made their throats feel dry because now they could look forward only to manna! (11:6). This is a story about the recurrent human strategy of finding grounds for resentment in order to escape the radical discipline of love. This is not a development in the subject matter of Exodus 16.

Joshua 5 and Deuteronomy 8

But a development in the subject matter of Exodus 16 did occur on the day when the desert period came to an end and Israel entered the promised land. At that point, as we read in Joshua 5:12:

> And the manna ceased from the following day, upon their eating the produce of the land. And no more was there manna for the sons of Israel. This year they fed from the crops of the land of Canaan.

Now the pro-active gift of God leading to trust was revealed in the experience of the land of Canaan. Of course, the production of grain in Canaan, however less startling, was no less an act of creation than the production of manna in the desert. God's gift in this case was clothed in the miraculous conquest of land by the chosen people under Joshua, just as in the former case it was clothed in astonishing zoological and biological phenomena of manna and quail in the desert. Moreover, this pro-active care was clothed in the revelation of the wisdom of the Torah, whereby Israel was able to prosper and eat well in the land (Deut 4:5-8, 32-40).

The divine gift of the land of Canaan is a theme which invites almost limitless comment. For present purposes, it must suffice to point out that it differed from manna in that Israel was called upon to administer the land—not just in terms of trusting a day-by-day schedule, but in terms of establishing and managing a whole just economy. The rules for this were provided by God, and recorded in the rest of the Pentateuch. Respect for God's directives regarding the land, as regarding the manna, would result in prosperity, and the disappearance of poverty and suffering, for all the people and for all time.[27] Deuteronomy 8 explains this very carefully, and verse 3 ("one does not live by bread alone but by every word that comes from the mouth of the Lord"), which is specifically an interpretation of Exodus 16:4,[28] makes the key point: the experience of eating manna in the desert, just like the experience of living from the land of Canaan, is not only about eating, but also about knowing God's gift and recognizing it as glory.

Thus, the jar of manna in the Temple, as long as it was there, served both as a memorial of the desert experience of manna, and as a revelation about the meaning of their current prosperity in the land of Canaan. After the exile the jar of manna seems to have disappeared, as we do not hear of it again.

What is notable here is that the object of Exodus 16 is a grace of trust based on a historical reality which existed no longer when the story was told, but which once was real and was now remembered as a revelation of glory. Similarly, the object of Joshua 5 and of Deuteronomy 8, at the time when these texts became Scripture, was the same trust. It has, however, now become more complex because it is based on a complex historical reality (i.e., the possession and administration of the land according to Torah) experienced over centuries. This complex reality is no longer in existence, but it was once real, and is now remembered as a revelation of glory. The object we are dealing with includes both a historical reality and its human appropriation as revelation, both of which change through time.[29]

Wisdom of Solomon

The whole burden of this book is, once again, an intolerably sweet message about God's pro-active goodness, which may meet resistance in the reader. It teaches, in categories familiar to its first century Greek readers, how God intervenes through the elements of nature to preserve the Israelites and to give them eternal life. Its method is to review the historical events of the Exodus as presented in the Book of Exodus, evoking trust by recalling a past experience of trust (19:10). The introduction expresses it this way:

> Because God did not make death,
> And he is not happy when the living are cut down.
> For he created all things that they might be;
> And the basic elements of the world are wholesome.
> In them there is no lethal chemistry.
> Nor does Hell have any power upon the earth.
> For goodness is immortal (1:13-15).

John 6

With the fall of the Northern Kingdom in 722 B.C.E., the subsequent incessant state of siege of Israel over the next century, and finally with the subjugation of Judah, the fall of Jerusalem, and the beginning of diaspora Judaism, the land/Torah ceased to nourish Israel in the manner of manna. It became an object of longing, rather than a paradigm of care. Even after the return under Ezra and Nehemiah, or in modern Israel, where the land was and is seen as a gift of God. Still, its torn history makes it a poor candidate as replacement for manna. Is there, then, any object to give continuity to the message of Exodus 16? Where can one find its subject matter today?

In John 6, Jesus explicitly makes himself the "bread of life," replacing the manna. Jesus' discourse begins in verses 25-34 explicitly as a meditation on the texts we have been discussing. Jesus makes a contrast between eating bread for the sake of eating (v. 26) with seeing bread as a sign, namely, doing the work of God which is believing (v. 29). The people make the same error here as in Exodus 16:2-3, in that they thought it was Moses and Aaron who were acting. Like Moses in Exodus 16, Jesus in John 6 tells them it is not Moses, but the Father who gives them the bread of life.

St. Augustine's reading of John 6 illuminates the text in a manner which is helpful precisely in reference to the gift of God we are discussing.[30] The following comments on John 6:25-59 will be drawn from Augustine. In verses 26-27 the contrast between perishing food and the food of life is not a contrast between manna and the Eucharist; rather, it is a contrast between eating with faith and eating without faith. For one who eats of the real bread of heaven without faith "eats and drinks judgment to himself" (1 Cor 11:29), and he or she will die. Conversely, Moses, Aaron, and Phinees ate manna and they lived. In verses 30-31, the crowd claim that Jesus gave only barley loaves, and thus Jesus is not as great as Moses, but Jesus refutes this in 32-33. In verses 47-49 again the real contrast is not between manna and the Eucharist, but between the faithless murmurers then and now and those who believe. And finally in verses 57-58 the same correction must be made. Thus God sends manna, and his Son. Both are the bread of life. Those who receive it with the gift of faith enter eternal life.

It is true to say, then, that the same reality discussed in terms of manna in Exodus 16, was again revealed as gift of the land in Deuteronomy, and finally recurred in the form of Jesus Christ as bread of life. We must note right away that, here again, we have a historical reality (the historical Jesus), given to us as a revelation (glory) of God's active care for us, which is no longer present since his ascension into Heaven. "It is to your advantage that I go away, for if I do not go away the Advocate will not come to you; but if I go I will send Him to you."[31] In place of Jesus we have the Spirit, who enables us to remember and recall Jesus in the daily Eucharist.

This final development of the object of Exodus 16 evokes a future enhancement: the same historical Jesus who has left us will return on the last day, and hence his memorial in the Eucharist invites us to know God's glory in the past, and also his glory in the future. This bread of life is really the body and blood of Christ for us when we really "know," namely, really believe, that is, when we live as Paul put it: "now not I, but Christ lives in me."

The gift of God in Jesus Christ is often seen in terms of suffering and martyrdom and penance and poverty. The gift of his body and blood is directly linked to his death. But there is another perspective which is equally revealed. The body and blood of Christ is also presented in the Bible, and can also be seen and known and believed, as a fulfillment of the Exodus 16 tradition, in terms of delight and life, nourishment and prosperity. When we recall Jesus, it is to feel safe and well, because in him we know that God wants us to be healthy and prosperous. When we ask for bread, will the Father reach us a stone? The lilies neither sow nor reap, and yet not even Solomon was so gorgeously attired. Jesus came that we might have life, and have it ever more abundantly. Not that we should take health and wealth, and let the faith go. But that faith should not be reduced to a mental trick for explaining and enduring suffering!

Meaning of the text for its ideal reader

Every literary text implies something about its reader, and by this implication affects its own meaning.[32] The implied something may be only the knowledge of a specific language. But some texts imply that the reader know mathematics, or history, or that the reader wants to travel. The Bible, because it is composed of many layers of sources which constantly comment on each other, and which carry perspectives from very different centuries and ages, implies a reader capable of sophisticated analogical thinking. And because it expresses often the same faith experience in diverse symbols, it demands a spiritually sensitive reader. In fact, because it is so complex, and was written in three different languages, it supposes a whole Church community for its interpretation.

The Bible was in fact made into a unified book by two communities: the Jewish community for the Old Testament, and the Christian community for the whole Bible including the Old Testament. These complex and historical communities form the implied, ideal readers of the Bible. It will be helpful, for present purposes, to consider the hermeneutical implications of recognizing the Christian community as the implied reader of Exodus 16. Insofar as this reader, at successive points in its history up to the present and not excluding the future, is the implied reader of the text, the meaning of that text is progressively deepened and broadened through the centuries.

The Liturgy

We see the community directly interpreting Exodus 16 in the liturgy. The most pervasive example is the "Our Father," a prayer learned and recited by all Christians. In it the phrase "Give us this day our daily bread" literally recalls the gift of God as sustaining bread, and qualifies it as "daily," a word which evokes the daily distribution of manna, but equally well suggests the regular support of nourishment from the land. The Greek word translated by "daily" is ambiguous: it could also be translated as "tomorrow" (i.e., the bread of the last day) or as "supersubstantial" (i.e., supernal). This one phrase in the Our Father says the whole content of this essay. The other obvious example is found in the readings in the Roman Lectionary for the Feast of the Body and Blood of Christ (Corpus Christi). The Gospel Acclamation and the Gospel are drawn from John 6:51-59. The first reading, preparing for the Gospel, is about manna. It is drawn from Deuteronomy 8:2-3, 14-16. These texts were discussed above, but it must be added that the Deuteronomy text selected here begins "Remember," and ends "Do not forget." If we were told to celebrate the Eucharist "in memory of me" as Christ said, and were to recall the manna when seeing the jar preserving it in the Temple, we must also remember and not forget the trust in God's word which accompanied the whole desert experience and which made the land fruitful. The third reading is from 1 Corinthians 10:16-17, a text which tells of our community through sharing in the one bread. Associated with the Feast of Corpus Christi is Thomas Aquinas' hymn *Pange Lingua* which celebrates the gift of God (*nobis datus*) in the food which Jesus gave with his own hands, replacing the old rite with a new one (*Et antiquum documentum novo cedat ritui*), and also the very beautiful hymn *Panis Angelicus* celebrating the bread of angels.

Many Christian readers will approach Exodus 16 with this kind of liturgical tradition already in their minds and hearts. However, the ideal reader of Exodus 16 will not exist until the Last Day, when we will know the gift of God in the beatific vision. It may be helpful to point out other major attempts to express the subject matter of the manna, the land, and the bread of life in other powerful systems of thought or symbols.

The Holy Grail

The medieval legends connected with the Holy Grail originated in Celtic tribes in Brittany, Ireland, Wales, and Cornwall, and eventually were connected with the stories about King Arthur whose popularity in the twelfth century was extraordinary. The best source we have is the early thirteenth century *Queste del Saint Graal*, written in Middle French, and readily available in English.[33] According to this account, Percival's saintly aunt explains the whole thing as follows. Jesus Christ presided at the last Supper, and gave his followers the bread of heaven. This power was carried in the Holy Grail, namely, the vessel in which the bread was broken and the blood drunk. Joseph of Arimathea came to England with four thousand followers, carrying with him the dish in which Jesus had eaten the Paschal lamb, and he established a Table of the Holy Grail where many miracles occurred. Later Merlin established a magical Round Table, whose knights under Arthur would set out to find the Holy Grail. The point of finding it was to receive its revelation. Eventually, a chosen knight, a virgin, Galahad would succeed in finding the Holy Grail. He would be dressed in red armor like the flames of the Spirit at Pentecost through which Jesus visited his disciples "comforting them and banishing their misgivings."[34]

This story deals with a historical object, now lost to us, namely, the Grail, and three special tables (banquets) associated with it, and its subject matter is a gift of God in continuity with the bread of heaven. It demands hope in eventual reception of revelation, which seems to be similar to beatific vision. Connected with this hope is a demand for sexual purity. It is a tale powerfully told and its influence in Holland, France and England throughout the medieval period and up to the sixteenth century, and its further flourishing in English readers through Mallory's adaptation, and eventually Tennyson's, are hard to overestimate.[35]

The Holy Spirit

Thomas Aquinas showed that the gift of God, like all other free gifts, consists in the first instance of a gift of love. The gift of love is in some degree a gift of self, and it is expressed secondarily in various objects called gift. And he asked whether "gift" should be considered a personal name of God, and, if so, to which Person did it belong. He argues that the Holy Spirit is the Love which is given by the Father and the Son. It is, in our vocabulary, a self. It can give itself to us to be enjoyed by us insofar as we participate in the Word to know God, and in Love to love God. He concludes that "gift of God" is a personal name of the Holy Spirit.[36]

In this analysis, the Holy Spirit is the uncreated reality which is given in the first instance, and which may then be expressed in gifts: the created bread of heaven, the promised land, the Eucharist. In all of these is found a revelation leading to hope. If we see God's glory as did the Jews in Exodus 16, or if we receive the bread of heaven worthily, we will possess the Holy Spirit, and joyfully cry "Abba, Father." In this understanding, the subject matter of Exodus 16, of Joshua 5 and Deuteronomy 8, and of John 6, was what we now know as the Holy Spirit.

Transubstantiation

The Council of Trent, in its preparatory documents if not in the actual conciliar texts, dealt with type and antetype, and was very concerned to express the notion that what was said about God in Christ was not said by way of metaphor, or image for comparison, but rather as a fullness of reality. Thus whatever types, or images, were used to affirm the mystery of Christ, these were to be understood as designating, not a pious idea, but a substantial reality.[37]

In this sense the bread and wine at Mass, which could be discussed in a series of typological comparisons with the sacrifice of Melchisedek, or the manna, or the multiplied loaves, and so forth, should not be left in that endless unreality of speculation. The conciliar text itself refers to the bread of Angels (Ps 77:25), explicitly linking the manna tradition with the Eucharist.[38] But the focus of the Council was upon affirming that Jesus did something which was substantial (i.e., not metaphorical). He gave bread and wine at the Last Supper and it was real. The bread and wine became his real body and blood even before the Apostles had received it to eat and drink.[39] He gave his body and blood on Calvary and that was real. His resurrected body is in heaven and that is real. We had moved from figure or type to substance. The Eucharist remains for us, then, as a present object in which we remember the historical Christ, and are taught to trust in an eternal life given to us day by day as a gift of God.

Conclusion

It is, at times, troubling to read Exodus 16, just as we are at times doubtful about the goodness of life, or of the created universe. We doubt the gift of God in many other ways. To read Exodus 16, with all the resources of academic interpretation theory, and to accept it, is only possible insofar as one has already begun to share in the Last Day.

This essay proposes that biblical exegesis should embrace the "new criticism" and use all its resources to recover the timeless meaning of the text within itself. A second phase should turn to "historical criticism," not in order to limit meaning to a hypothetically constructed original context as we were taught, but rather in order to enrich our understanding by adding dimensions of time and existential involvement. In a third and fourth phase, by recognizing the historical character of the "subject matter" and of the "implied reader," the meaning of the text is shown to be modified by its *Wirkungsgeschichte* in subsequent tradition. It is hoped that such a complex approach will be seen using the resources of contemporary philosophy and hermeneutic theory to restore some of the lost power of patristic interpretation.

Notes

1. This point is fully discussed in the first two chapters of S. McEvenue, *Interpreting the Pentateuch* (Collegeville: The Liturgical Press, 1990).

2. This is true of the English-speaking world at least. It was brought about principally through the influence of the great Cambridge scholar F. R. Leavis, who lectured extensively, not only in the British Isles, but also in North America and Australia. In the U.S. it was supported by German philosophical thought through the work of Rene Wellek: Wellek and Warren, *Theory of Literature* (first published in 1949 and still available in Penguin books), became a standard university textbook, and is still widely consulted. In Canada, N. Frye, with his "centripetal meaning" follows this view to extreme lengths. (Cf. *The Great Code, The Bible and Literature*, [Toronto: Academic Press, 1982].) One merit of the Pontifical Biblical Institute in Rome was its introduction of one aspect of the "new criticism" into the methods taught its students, namely, the painstaking identification of objective literary structuring in biblical texts.

3. Cf. T. R. Wright, *Theology and Literature* (Oxford: Basil Blackwell, 1988).

4. An attempt to provide a framework to systematize these may be read in chapter 3 in this volume, "A Mandala for Biblical Commentary," pp. 40–46.

5. This principle became institutionalized in the prestigious "Oxford editions" of literary texts, which followed the doctrines of F. R. Leavis in omitting historical introductions

to the literary works, and all footnotes beyond textual criticism. The principle was then extended by the often cited article of W. K. Wimsatt and M. C. Beardsley, "The Intentional Fallacy," in W. K. Wimsatt, *The Verbal Icon: Studies in the Meaning of Poetry* (Lexington: University of Kentucky Press, 1954) 2–18. It is a useful self-control in interpretation, but it becomes absurd when critics give the text complete authority over meaning, without any reference to the original author. For a discussion with Gadamer and Derrida on this point, cf. S. McEvenue, *Interpreting the Pentateuch*, 17–28.

6. The case for this is most persuasively made in Cleanth Brooks, *The Well Wrought Urn: Studies in the Structure of Poetry* (New York: Harcourt Brace Jovanovich, 1947).

7. An excellent brief account of these can be found in Brevard Childs, *The Book of Exodus: A Critical, Theological Commentary* (Philadelphia: Westminster Press, 1974) 276–280.

8. Cf. George W. Coats, *The Murmuring Motif in the Wilderness: Traditions of the Old Testament Rebellion in the Wilderness* (Nashville: Abingdon Press, 1968). Brevard Childs distinguishes a "Pattern I" story, in which the murmuring is about something real and results in God's solving the problem (which is the case here), and a "Pattern II" story in which the murmuring is not justified, and punishment ensues. Cf. *The Book of Exodus*, 258–263.

9. In Numbers 14, the murmuring against Moses and Aaron is thought to belong to the JE tradition (vv. 1b, 3-4), whereas the blasphemy directed at Yahweh belongs to the Pg tradition (vv. 1a, 2, 5). Both traditions have it result in dire punishment. In Exodus 16, the Pg source has itself appropriated this confusion, making the people misunderstand the object of their murmuring, and having Moses and Aaron correct them, i.e., vv. 2-3, 6-7.

10. In the Pg tradition in Numbers 14 and 20 Moses and Aaron fall on their faces when they hear the murmuring, because they recognize it as blasphemy. In Exodus 16, it is quite different.

11. It must be pointed out that v. 32, parallel to vv. 16 and 23, presupposes a communication which is simply not found in the text.

12. Something like that is the sense of "evening" and "morning" in v. 6b, which must be understood as parallel rather than contrasting or sequential.

13. Cf. Walther Zimmerli, "Das Wort des göttlichen Selbsterweises (Erweiswort), eine prophetische Gattung," *Mélanges bibliques rédigés en l'honneur de André Robert* (Paris: Bloud & Gay, 1957) 154–164.

14. In Numbers 11 it is the quail which dominate the narrative.

15. This instruction was given to Moses in v. 4, using a different vocabulary. In neither place does it sound like a law, or like something to be nervous about!

16. Cf. 1 Cor 11:24-25.

17. This kind of teaching recurs in wisdom form in the familiar New Testament text in Luke 12:22-32.

18. Cf. chapter III of "Dogmatic Constitution on Divine Revelation," promulgated on November 18, 1965, by the Second Vatican Council.

19. Many techniques have been developed as therapy techniques, to bring about such inner changes. The religious approach has identified two components: the component of "grace" on the side of God (i.e., divine love has to be present in created reality), and the component of repentance, prayer, and sacrament on the side of the person and the person's community.

20. This is the traditional view. Cf. Childs, *op. cit.*, 276–280.

21. Cf. Eberhard Ruprecht, "Stellung und Bedeutung der Erzälung vom Mannawunder (Exod 16) im Aufbau der Priesterschrift," *ZAW* 86 (1974) 269–307, cited as irrefutable by Erhard Blum, *Studien zur Komposition des Pentateuch* (BZAW 189) (New York: Walter de Gruyter, 1990) 146–148.

22. Cf. Karl Elliger, "Sinn und Ursprung der priesterlichen Geschichtserzählung," *ZKT* 49 (1952) 121–143. For a complete summary of recent research on the Priestly Writer, cf. Norbert Lohfink, "Die Priesterschrift und die Geschichte," *SVT* 29 (1978) 189–225.

23. Cf. Ezra 1:7–11. For the menorah, cf. S. McEvenue, "The Style of a Building Instruction," *Semitics* 4 (1974) 1–9.

24. Cf. note 8 above.

25. For William Wordsworth, each of us had a glimpse of God before birth, a forgotten revelation: "Our birth is but a sleep and a forgetting." However, quiet revery could occasionally not only evoke memories of lovely experiences of nature, but could also recover traces of the divine ('intimations of immortality") emerging in the memory: "For oft when on my couch I lie, They (the daffodils) flash upon that inward eye, Which is the bliss of solitude."

26. Cf. Bernard Lonergan, *Method in Theology* (London: Darton, Longman & Todd, 1972) 156–158, 165–166.

27. Cf. Norbert Lohfink, "Poverty in the Laws of the Ancient Near East and the Bible," *Theological Studies* 52 (1991) 39–49.

28. Exodus 16:4 begins by telling of raining "bread," but goes on to say that they will collect this *"dabar"* (= stuff, word) day by day. The "word" of Exodus 16:4 has become the whole teaching of Deuteronomy.

29. This kind of truth used to be designated as "typology." But it is best to simply drop that designation, as it evokes a theory of knowledge and a method of theology which made sense in a neo-Platonistic thought world, where the "really real" are eternal ideas, not historical and contingent beings. That approach makes no sense in our current intellectual culture.

30. Cf. *St. Augustine: Tractates on the Gospel of John,* trans. J. W. Rettig (Washington: The Catholic University Press, 1988) 251–271.

31. Cf. John 16:7.

32. Cf. Jane P. Tomkins (ed.), *Reader-Response Criticism: From Formalism to Post-Structuralism* (Baltimore: John Hopkins University Press, 1980).

33. P. M. Matarasso, *The Quest of the Holy Grail* (London: Penguin Books, 1969).

34. Cf. ibid., especially 97–101.

35. Cf. ibid., 28.

36. Cf. *Summa Theologica,* pars prima, quaestio 38, art. 1 & 2.

37. For the Council of Trent, cf. Josef Wohlmuth, *Realpräsenz und Transsubstantation im Konzil von Trient,* 2 vols. (Bern/Frankfurt: Herbert & Peter Lang, 1975). For a post-Tridentine discussion cf., H. J. Klauck, *Presence in the Lord's Supper,* trans. B. Meyer (Macon, Ga.: Mercer University Press, 1992).

38. Cf. Denzinger/Rahner, *Enchiridion Symbolorum Definitionum et Declarationum de Rebus Fide et Morum* (Freiburg and Rome: Herder, 1960) #882.

39. Cf. *Idem.* #876.

Chapter 10

The Rise of David Story and the Search for a Story to Live By

If Lonergan is right in claiming that scholarship has sealed off all the familiar avenues between theology and Scripture,[1] then it seems misleading to speak of biblical theology and it appears a deception to teach the Old and New Testaments, as presently understood, in departments of theological studies. However, Lonergan himself has made notable use of Romans 5:5. Moreover, many otherwise sensible scholars cannot make head or tail of Lonergan's approach, and in reading the Lonerganians they find little which they can understand, reason about, or deliberate upon! A seventy-fifth anniversary, twenty-two years after the publication of *Insight*, is a fitting occasion for at least one student of the Bible both to acknowledge gratefully that Lonergan's thought has been perking through the grains in his cranium and to rise to the colossal challenge of "migrating from a basis in theory to a basis in interiority."[2]

The *Rise of David Story* is a redactional unity stretching roughly from 1 Samuel 16 to 2 Samuel 8.[3] The story ends with a triumphant summary, rounding off David's accession to power over an empire. Its opening chapter contains an editorial creation which clearly makes a point: the outcome was determined by Yahweh from the very beginning, when Samuel, after finding the boy Cinderella-fashion and noting that he "was ruddy, and had beautiful eyes, and was handsome," anointed him at the Lord's command. The organizing theme is that David blamelessly replaced Saul as the dynastic head of Israel. The full theme appears most clearly, perhaps, in the twice recounted confrontation between David and Saul, in which Saul is the persecutor and David asks only to be spared.[4] The confrontation ends with Saul asking David's forgiveness, and recognizing David as his son (i.e., legitimate successor), and as destined to be king over Israel.[5]

Now if one allows oneself to interpret this story in a cynical frame of mind, a frame of mind all too easily adopted by critical-historical methodists, one can see here a purely political intention: to support David's kingship first by stilling whisperers who must have argued that David had come to power through bloody assassinations, and second by claiming divine authority for the outcome. But this is a massive anachronism: no author in the ancient world had purely political intentions. We must read for compact mentalities in which religion and politics and history are not adequately differentiated.

Similarly, if one indulges in facile forms of biblical theology, one might point out a purely theological intent, an intent made visible by the last editor who, in writing 1 Samuel 16:1-13, has drawn materials from the heroic legend of David and Goliath (cf. 1 Sam 17:12-15 and 42) in order to spin a yarn about an anointing of David at the hands of Samuel.[6] This approach relieves any anxiety we may have about the unhistorical tone of this tale. Moreover, by making its author a "late" interpreter of this material, we can easily imagine such a process of theological abstraction and fabulation. This is the line taken, for example, by Gerhard von Rad.[7] It has two drawbacks: first, it is once again untrue to the compact mentality of ancient authors, who express religious experiences not theological doctrines; and second, it gets us into a theological trap. If this were a theological doctrine, namely, that God acted with prevenient grace in the case of David's kingship in a manner paralleling the vocation narratives (e.g., Jer 1: 5), then we are committed to a certain form of divine causality. It could seem true, indeed, *de fide divina*, that God foreordains the salvific acts of at least certain of his saints, and maybe *proxima fidei* that he foreordains all gracious acts. However, we need not fall into this trap, if we insist that the author was not writing doctrine, but rather compactly expressing the meaning of experience. Interpretation, then, would need to reach into the historical, socio-cultural context to imagine creatively and feelingly the experience which was conveyed to the first readers of this story.[8]

What general historical context should be indicated? Scholarship leads to a dating in a period after David and prior to the end of the monarchy. The story was composed after David because some time must be allowed during which the David stories could grow variants (e.g., 1 Sam 16:14-23 and 17:55-58; 1 Sam 24 and 26; 1 Sam 21:10-15 and 27:1-7), and one could forget just who had killed Goliath (cf., 2 Sam 21:19). And it was composed before the end of the monarchy because the core text of the Deuteronomistic history is generally viewed as having been completed under the monarchy.

A socio-cultural context involves a specification of the role of the king of Israel, and most particularly the centralizing role of the monarchy of Jerusalem. First of all, kings in the ancient world, and right up to the turn of this century, were very powerful symbols. That Psalm 2 could be written, and retained in the canon, shows that Israel appropriated the near idolatry surrounding kings in the ancient world. We North Americans tend to think of kings in comical terms, and we do not easily go beyond words like "super-stition" in trying to recapture feelings about the monarchy which we come across in history. The overwhelming feelings and passions which link us with parents, as analyzed by Freud, and which are ruled by archetypes, as described by Jung, were once quite unanalyzed and overpoweringly pres-ent in relation to kings. Like all powerful symbols, the kings of Israel were ambiguous figures.

What then would a Judean feel about the king at any point during the monarchy?[9] One could easily imagine a subject tortured with doubts: "If I obey the king's orders, will I be doing the will of God or cooperating with the devil?" Our own religious experience extends very easily to im-portant uncertainty in religious matters. We can sympathize with an an-cient Judeans' anxiety when Hezekiah stopped all sacrifice in the homes and villages, centralizing religious practice in Jerusalem (2 Kings 18:22). "We can no longer expiate our sins, and commune with God, in the coun-try. . . . Has Hezekiah, like Saul before him, come under an evil spirit, receiving instructions from the witches at Endor? Is God on the side of this king in Jerusalem? Didn't David usurp power from the Benjaminite Saul? Was it not the Benjaminite Joshua who conquered this country for Yah-weh? Are there not many Benjaminite families living here now who have never trusted the Ephrathites? Oh for the days when kings went to war, and we could soon know whose side Yahweh had chosen. . . ."

This situation is significantly mirrored in the Deuteronomistic historian (Dtr) for whom the monarchy remained theologically ambiguous. He has absorbed the *Rise of David Story* into his work, a story in which David ap-pears as beautiful to look at, a military darling and super-hero, successful in everything, enhanced by the contrast with Saul, chosen and anointed by Yahweh and by all Israel to be king. But Deuteronomy has then placed beside it the *Succession Narrative* (2 Sam 9-20; 1 Kings 1-2). In this, David is presented as weak in dealing with Bathsheba (2 Sam 11; 1 Kings 1), with Absalom (2 Sam 13:39; 19:1-8), with Adonijah (1 Kings 1:6); David is presented as politically devious in dealing with Ziba and Mephibosheth (2 Sam 9:9-13; 16:1-4;19:24-29); David is presented as hypocritically vicious in dealing with his enemies (1 Kings 2:5-9); and finally, he is presented as criminal in dealing with Uriah the Hittite (2 Sam 11). Even more impor-tant in the *Succession Narrative* is the fact that the choice of Solomon to re-place David is not seen as blameless or directly influenced by God, but rather as the result of a corrupt court life in which rivals have been murdered; and the weak, doddering, impotent, old king David has been manipulated by Bathsheba and a secularized Nathan (1 Kings 1). Moreover, Dtr has re-tained the admiring tradition regarding Solomon (1 Kings 3-11), but he himself has evaluated Solomon negatively: into the law for kings in Deuteronomy 17:14ff. he has introduced warnings which clearly aim at Solomon (Deut 17:16-17); and he has written a programmatic speech for Samuel in the same terms (1 Sam 8:4-22). Again, Deuteronomy presented Hezekiah and Josiah in a favorable light precisely because of their centralizing reform, but condemned virtually all the other kings of Israel and Judah for sins to the contrary. Other texts in his work and in the book of Jeremiah (despite Deuteronomy editing), retain clear evidence that not every contemporary Judean agreed with such views (2 Kings 18:22; Jer 44:15-19). Finally, Dtr clearly felt that the kingship was over (2 Kings 25:27-30) and yet he retained the prophecy of Nathan that there would always be a son of David on the throne (2 Sam 7:11b-16).[10]

All of this is a schematic indication of what was surely a far more complex chaos at times in the minds and hearts of villagers under the king; political uncertainty, religious confusion, personal anxiety, social chaos, all contributing to one another. At some stage there emerged a creative unifying vision: "The power of the king in Jerusalem comes from Yahweh, and has been so willed since he chose David. Our present confusion is due to our failure to believe that Yahweh alone has brought about the present political-religious structure." The vision is expressed and written, not in analytic terms, but through the accumulation of stories about the origin of the Jerusalem monarchy, and their selective integration in a manner which supports this vision. The *Rise of David Story* catches on, unifying the country, comforting souls, releasing creative energies, renewing faith throughout Judah. Even a modern theologian could not quarrel with this: whatever the nitty-gritty human facts, and whatever the theory of divine causality, it remains true that insofar as the kings' power was real it came from God. One could only praise God in it, and proceed to deal with it.

It must be pointed out that the author did not write a parable. He has not created a timeless paradigm in order to teach a lesson. Rather, he has creatively gathered carriers of "incarnate meaning,"[11] to form a new meaning relevant to issues which tortured his community. The writer discovered and portrayed a personal vision of contemporary reality within community memories. This is not timeless: it is his world as he felt and meant it. It is not a lesson, but a transformed and transforming interpretation of reality. It was not a doctrine, but primarily a faith-perspective for himself and communicated to others. He has not made a judgment, but retold a story. He has not just had an insight, but rather has undergone an incarnate conversion. He is not thinking about prevenient grace, but feeling toward order in the world he inhabits.

At this point, let us see where we stand with regard to functional specialties. We have made use of the functional specialty of *research* in establishing a text for interpretation. Research has progressed beyond the work of

Wellhausen and Eissfeldt who exhausted the possibilities of identifying continuous strands in the sources of the books of Samuel and Kings. It has established redactional unities which existed prior to the final Deuteronomistic redaction. A unity, which could be described as the *Rise of David Story*, with the theme we have indicated, certainly can be discerned. Research is still active in determining the exact boundaries and text of this unity, but the further determinations which are possible will probably not change much in the discussion.

We have further initiated work on the functional speciality of *interpretation*, focusing on 1 Samuel 16:1-13, and drawing out its meaning on the understanding that it is itself a summary of the meaning of the whole unit.

In interpreting we appealed to *history*, but not as something "going forward"—rather as cross-sectionally delimiting a social context. We also entered into some *dialectic* insofar as we pointed out the cynical bias implicit in any "purely political," and so forth, interpretation of this story, and we adduced the notion of "compact consciousness"[12] to establish a perspective on interpretation alternative to both the purely political and the purely theological perspectives from which interpretations have been attempted. However, all of this has been done in order to point towards interpretation. Within that pointing there has been no attempt at theology, and one might conclude that the product of this considerable effort is merely interesting or curious, valuable for a scholarly article to be published in a review to be deposed in the many tombs of university libraries.

My training as a "scholar," and my bias as an "academic," would indeed lead me to stop there. And I would note that all further inquiry on my part will be incompetent to begin with and unprofessional as well. However, as a human being I am dissatisfied, and if I dare call myself "theologian" instead of "scholar" then it will not be unprofessional to go further with due caution about competence. I am dissatisfied on two minor points and one major.

My first dissatisfaction is around the psychological, social, religious role of the king of Israel. Current social science has a great deal to say about this, and it has not been said. Because my foundations include a hermeneutic which requires a scientific perspective on reality, I have to be dissatisfied with the very vague description I gave about the role of the kings in a Judean's consciousness. The social history of Israel has yet to be written. Roland de Vaux began the task with his study of the institutions of Israel, and the first volume of his *Histoire Ancienne d'Israël*.[13] His death has been a monumental loss to this enterprise. The sporadic attempts of psychologists to enter the field have not dealt with the psycho-dynamics of a divinely appointed king, and in biblical areas have been singularly lacking in critical sense for history.[14] Norman Gottwald has applied sociology to the

Old Testament,[15] and in conjunction with Frank Frick has formed a study group within the "Society of Biblical Literature" with the title "Social World of Ancient Israel Group."[16] So far their attention has been directed to premonarchial Israel. Still, a social study of the tribes, and particularly of their relations to each other, will eventually be essential to an understanding of the role David played between Judah and Benjamin, and the other Northern tribes, as he established regal power in Jerusalem. My dissatisfaction will have to wait.

A second dissatisfaction lies in the functional specialty of *history:* what was going forward at the time of David? First of all, did David kill off the Saulides, or was he really as open to God's will as portrayed in some texts? In any event, what can be said of the religious meaning of the execution of political enemies in fundamentalist theocracies today or in Israel during David's lifetime? Secondly, what institutions and social phenomena created a national consciousness of which we have evidence in the biblical document written by "the Yahwist"? These questions arise because my foundations include a heuristics of revelation and tradition: my knowledge of God is dependent on those who knew him before me, and specifically on the affirmations about God made by David and David's era. Were those people credible only because later ages lived through the culture they created, or were they worthy of belief in themselves?

However, my main dissatisfaction with stopping at interpretation arises in the area of politics and religion. My foundations include heuristically an imperious demand for knowing God now. I do not believe that God appoints political leaders now, and establishes civilizations for me to enjoy spiritually. Did he ever do this, and if so what can I conclude about political theology for the present? This question invites the theologian to participate in a *dialectic* which is visible in our tradition.

Immediately following the *Rise of David Story,* we had a very different religious experience in the area of Israel's king, namely the *Succession Story* which (as indicated above) presents the kingship of David without any trace of direct, divine interference and little trace of human virtue,[17] and in particular presents the selection of Solomon (1 Kings 1) as the result of manipulation of David once he is impotent in every sense. This presentation would tend to deny rather directly any idea that God's will for David as expressed in 1 Samuel 16:1-3 was repeated in the anointing of subsequent kings of Israel. The Deuteronomistic editor ends up by relegating the whole experience of the Jerusalem monarchy to an irreversible past,[18] even though he leaves uncommented, and as yet unfulfilled, the Nathan prophecy in 2 Samuel 7 that there will always be a son of David protested by God upon the throne. The Deuteronomist's vision includes a succession of eras with clear transitions: a golden age of Joshua, a charismatic era of judges terminating in 1 Samuel 8, and a decisive era of the monarchy. His vision for the despairing Jews in exile embodies both a disastrous past in which God is shown as nevertheless fully in command, and a few glimmers of hope for the future. For purposes of the present dialectic, his experience supports the view that Yahweh's involvement in politics, as known in the past, is now over.

The Bible presents other experiences subsequent to this. In Chronicles, salvation centers around the Temple and its cult, and this salvation has been placed on earth by God working through the political power of David. Another, and probably parallel vision, makes the High Priest take over the robes and role of the king, and, in that sense, fulfill Nathan's prophecy.[19] In the New Testament, of course, Jesus is the Messiah, and the multiplicity of meaning around this word as used in the New Testament has been the subject of an infinity of recent scholarly literature. For our purpose it will be sufficient to say that Jesus was indeed king, and his kingdom was not of this world.[20] St. Augustine believed that there was an earthly kingdom, and a *civitas Dei* beside it. In all of this tradition, God sent the priest, the crucified Messiah, the Pope, the Church, and so forth, and had a direct will in their work, but really he left the rest of life to the Seleucides, or the Romans, or the kings.

There followed another tradition drawn from both biblical and pagan sources, in which the Emperor at Constantinople was divinely appointed, as were Charlemagne and the leaders of the Holy Roman Empire. This tradition survived in the Russian empire right up until the abdication of the last Romanov, Tsar Nicholas II, March 16, 1917. In the West, Boniface VIII believed that he held the ''two swords'' in his own hand insofar as spiritual power was more excellent than temporal (DB 469). As the medieval papacy lost ground, a new basis for divinely directed temporal power was built upon the doctrine of ''the divine right of kings,'' as set forth most cogently in *Basilikon doron* by James VI of Scotland (James I of England), and contested by Suarez and Bellarmine.[21]

All of this dialectic would require more reading than a biblical scholar could easily undertake before publishing the present article. And yet even this leaves completely untouched such areas as theories of divine kingship in Egypt and the ancient Near East, Plato's *Republic* and the continuous outpouring of commentary on it, Machiavelli and his very real influence on irresponsible forms of bureaucratic governments in the West, all controversy about individual rights versus state rights, not to mention forms of government sacral and otherwise in the Orient. Yet all of this clearly lies within the horizon of inquiry which is relevant to determining a doctrine about God and political authority. It bases solidly the case for functional specialization.

One could conclude from this discussion that it is absurd to devote time to studying the Bible. The Bible is so demanding, and yet so remote that no *doctrine* about God and politics could arise from it. No biblical argument could in any case have more than a straw's weight in such a massive study. However, this is refuted at the personal level. This Bible set in motion a personal *dialectic* which must be pursued with a hermeneutics of suspicion: why do I absolutely not believe that God appoints civil governments, and why have I, over several decades of reading theology, read so little in the area of political theology? And why am I so upset at the biblical writer's insistence that David was beautiful to look at? And why did I use the words "biblical argument" above? There is a lot to examine here: being brought up as a defensive Roman Catholic in Toronto with its Protestant establishment; a Manichean-Jansenist tradition of rejecting the body; a tradition heavy with deductivist rationalism; a scholarly tradition detached from modernity; and so on. These are important biases, which disable my reading of the *Rise of David Story*, and which have closed my mind to a huge area of intellectual and religious concern. My foundations[22] are in need of significant correction. The Bible text, and the questions which it elicited in this case, demand conversion of me. And the acknowledging of that demand itself is a conversion which has made me a member of a modern theological community ready to support the advance into modernity in the areas I now perceive to be neglected. And while such an initial conversion and its follow-up may not enable me to make up for wasted years, it will alter important areas of my present experience, understanding, reasoning, and deliberation, in living, in scholarship, and in teaching.

The question why one should start with the Bible, however, returns in a new form: granted, on the one hand, that the Bible is both demanding and remote and, on the other, that one can draw some profit of conversion from reading it, why should one choose to begin one's questioning with the Bible rather than with a more immediately promising source such as Rahner or Weber? Here are some tentative sketches of an answer. First, the Bible is the collection which the Jewish and Christian communities recognized as authentically expressing their beginnings. It is a collection of those texts which contained the collective memory and self-appreciation of the "factions" within Judaism and Christianity which emerged as dominant and normative. These texts have influenced, in more or less valid ways, all significant phases in the development of our communities. We would lose our roots, and suffer collective amnesia, if at least some part of our scholarship were not dedicated to biblical studies. Secondly, the Bible is the only text common to Jews and Christians, and the only text common to all Christians. It is the place where divisions of Western civilization can discuss most radically what they hold in common and what irreducibly separates them.

It is also the text for worship in all these communities. Thirdly, the Bible objectifies compact consciousness's experience of God which our differentiations of consciousness have caused us to fracture in some degree, and which we aspire to repossess when consciousness is finally reintegrated after some centuries of this migration through interiority.

Notes

1. Cf. B. Lonergan, *Method in Theology* (London: Darton, Longman and Todd, 1972) 276, "Scholarship builds an impenetrable wall between systematic theology and its historical sources, but this development invites philosophy and theology to migrate from a basis in theory to a basis in interiority."

2. I did not, and could not have, risen to the challenge without the continuous encouragement and guidance of Philip McShane, Visiting Fellow at Lonergan College during 1979–80.

3. The literary criticism of the book of Samuel has a complex and inconclusive history. For a summary cf. Brevard Childs, *Introduction to the Old Testament as Scripture* (Philadelphia: Fortress Press, 1979) 266–271. That a *Rise of David Story* is a unity which can be recognized is not universally adverted to, but it is generally agreed upon by those who look for redactional units beyond original sources: e.g., M. Noth, *Überlieferungsgeschichtliche Studien*, 1943, 3rd ed. (Tübingen: J. C. B. Mohr 1967) 62; G. Fohrer, *Introduction to the Old Testament* (Nashville: Abingdon Press, 1968) 220–221. The exact limits of this unit are debated. 2 Samuel 6–7 are often thought to introduce the Succession Narrative (2 Sam 9–20; 1 Kings 1–2), and not to be a part of the *Rise of David Story:* cf. e.g., David Gunn, *The Story of King David: Genre and Interpretation* (Sheffield, Eng.: University of Sheffield, 1978), who gives a thorough review of opinions and reasons. I would contend that 1 Samuel 15 became part of the *Rise of David Story* at some redactional point, since the links with ch. 16 are marked, and since there is a very similar framing of a Saul story and of a David story by the concluding summaries of 1 Samuel 14:47-52 and 2 Samuel 8:15-18. None of these points bear on the discussion we will pursue in this paper.

4. Cf. 1 Samuel 24 and 26. The accounts are introduced by divergent "travelling legends" (24:1-7 and 26:1-12), which serve to base dramatic confrontations of very similar content.

5. There can be no doubt that the author strives to establish these postures throughout the narrative. Cf. David's relationship with Jonathan (1 Sam 18:1-4; 20:13-17 and 30-31). Cf. also the author's constant concern to point out that David could not have killed Jonathan or Saul, or Abner or Ishbosheth (1 Sam 29; 31; 2 Sam 1; 2:31-39; 4).

6. In the rest of the *Rise of David Story* there is no sign that David was aware of such an anointing. In fact, in 2 Samuel 2:4, David is king of Judah, and in 2 Samuel 5:3, he is anointed king over all Israel.

7. Cf. Gerhard von Rad, *Old Testament Theology*, Vol. 1 (Edinburgh and New York: Oliver and Boyd, 1962) 309. The same line of thought is implicit in recent commentaries, v.g. Peter Ackroyd, *The First Book of Samuel,* Cambridge Bible Commentary on the New English Bible (Cambridge: Cambridge University Press, 1971) 131–132.

8. Cf. B. Lonergan, op. cit., 172–173.

9. Clearly we are raising questions here which, as indicated below, demand extensive new research.

10. For further discussion cf. Georg Fohrer, *History of Israelite Religion* (New York: Abingdon Press, 1972) 149–150; M. Noth, op. cit., 56–58.

11. B. Lonergan, op. cit., 73.

12. Cf. Eric Voegelin, *The Ecumenic Age* (Baton Rouge: Louisiana State University Press, 1974) 2.

13. Roland de Vaux, *Ancient Israel: Its Life and Institutions* (New York: McGraw-Hill Book Company, 1961); *Histoire ancienne d'Israël: des origines à l'installation en Canaan* (Paris: Lecoffre, 1971).

14. Notably Sigmund Freud's *Moses and Monotheism* (New York: A. A. Knopf, 1939), and C. J. Jung's *Answer to Job* in the *Collected Works*, vol. 11 (Princeton, N.J.: Princeton University Press, 1969) 355–470.

15. Cf. Norman K. Gottwald, *The Tribes of Israel: A Sociology of the Religion of Liberated Israel, 1250–1051, B.C.E.* (Maryknoll, N.Y.: Orbis Books, 1979).

16. This group proposes to prepare a complete bibliography in this area for the AAR-SBL meeting next year.

17. For this reason this story has often been called "The Court Narrative," emphasizing the tone rather than the point of the story. David Gunn (op. cit.) characterizes this story as "serious entertainment," and, although I cannot accept his conclusion, the term itself suggests the point I am trying to make.

18. Discussion of Deuteronomy's intentions has its own history. Cf. M. Noth, op. cit. (Tübingen, 1943), and G. von Rad, "Die deuteronomistische Geschichtstheologie in den Königsbüchern," *Deuteronomium Studien; Teil B* (Göttingen: Vandenhoeck Ruprecht, 1947) 189–204, and reprinted in *Gesammelte Studien zum Alten Testament* (Munich: C. Kaiser Verlag, 1965); H. W. Wolffe, "Das Kerygma des deuteronomistichen Geschichtswerkes," *ZAW* 73 (1961) 171–186; N. Lohfink, "Bilanz nach der Katastrophe: Das deuteronomistische Geschichtswerk," in *Wort und Botschaft* (Würzburg: Echter-Verlag, 1967) 196–208; P. R. Ackroyd, "The Deuteronomic History," in *Exile and Restoration* (Philadelphia: Westminster Press, 1968) 62–83; F. M. Cross, "The Themes of the Book of Kings and the Structure of the Deuteronomistic History," in *Canaanite Myth and Hebrew Epic* (Cambridge, Mass.: Harvard University Press, 1973) 274–289.

19. Cf. the supplements to the Priestly document in Leviticus 8 where the priest wears a crown and is anointed, and the extended praise of Simon son of Onias in Sirach 50.

20. Cf John 18:33–38.

21. For the medieval period, cf. discussion and bibliographical information in J. J. Ryan, *The Nature, Structure, and Function of the Church in William of Occam* (Missoula, Mont.: Scholars Press, 1978) 26 and 49. For the divine right of kings, cf., for example, *New Catholic Encyclopedia*, vol. IV (New York: McGraw-Hill Book Company, 1967), under the entry "Divine Right of Kings"; *Catholicisme* (Paris: Letouzey et Ané, 1952) entry "Droit divin des rois"; or James Broderick, *Robert Bellarmine: Saint and Scholar* (London: Burns & Oates, Ltd., 1961) chapter 10. For a moving portrait of the religious self-awareness of a Tsar, cf. R. K. Massie, *Nicholas and Alexandra* (New York: Atheneum, 1971).

More recently Christian political thought has moved from divinely appointed authority to divinely motivated insurrection: Marxist insight has enriched the debate, spearheaded by the political theology of J. B. Metz and worked out in Europe through the Christian-Marxist dialectic of the "Paulus Gesellschaft." In South America liberation theologies have been developed by G. Gutiérrez and others. For recent discussion and publication cf., for example, J. M. Bonino, *Christians and Marxists: The Mutual Challenge to Revolution* (Grand Rapids, Mich.: Eerdmans Publishing Company, 1976); J. G. Davies, *Christians, Politics and Violent Revolution* (Maryknoll, N.Y.: Orbis Books, 1976).

22. I have not here explicitly gone beyond indications regarding the first five functional specialties. Clearly, however, the discomforts expressed reach into doctrines, systematics, communications and life.

Chapter 11

The Elohist at Work

Source criticism is not a popular sport among most Pentateuchal critics these days. Research concerning an author is frequently disdained in favor of inquiry about the meaning of the text.[1] As a result, studies which depend explicitly on the "documentary hypothesis" may seem out of date. Two major books might be referred to here. Rolf Rendtorff's *Das Über-lieferungsgeschichtliche Problem des Pentateuch* (BZAW, 1977) rejects traditional source criticism as methodologically incompatible with form criticism. Brevard Childs, in several publications over the past ten years, and massively in his *Introduction to the Old Testament as Scripture* (1979) has effectively stressed the importance of the final biblical edition/tradition in establishing the scriptural meaning of the total text including its sources.[2]

These theses have to be popular with all who have grown weary with uncertainty about the details of source criticism. As Chesterton's *Lepanto* had it: "The North is full of tangled texts and tired eyes." Popular also with those who feel that Julius Wellhausen is a too heavy authority over the Bible. Popular, finally with those who have discovered the futility of identifying historical sources using a methodology which does not go beyond a history of ideas (ill-named "biblical theology"), that is, a succession of interesting but now irrelevant religious concerns.

At the other extreme of the pendulum are those who, equally disdainful of classical source criticism, have in fact returned to source criticism in an iconoclastic mood. One might cite John Van Seters, *Abraham in History and Tradition* (1975) and Peter Weimar, *Untersuchungen zur Redaktionsgeschichte des Pentateuch* (1977).[3]

However, as contemporary scholarship develops fertile new approaches to the Bible, it would be a tragedy if we failed to systematize the results of several centuries of traditional source criticism, collecting those data which have proven to be dependable, and picking from the welter of uncertainties those data which can be substantiated. Clearly, the Elohist is the area most in need of research at this point. And among texts generally ascribed to the Elohist, the first major block, Genesis 20-22, climaxing in the sacrifice of Isaac, is an obvious place to start. This segment of the Pentateuch contains three major stories. "The Patriarch's Wife," a "Hagar Story," and "The Testing of Abraham," which will be seen to form a sort of trilogy.

We shall begin with what has traditionally been designated as the Elohist text here, without argument. If stylistic study reveals no contradictions or counter-indications, but rather supports the hypothesis of continuous authorship, we shall conclude that this much of the final Pentateuchal text was in fact the product of one author, traditionally called the Elohist. For the three stories, the text will be: Genesis 20:1-18; 21:8-21; 22:1-13, 19. Genesis 21:1-7 is generally thought to be Yahwist and Elohist materials. For discussion of source critical questions, the reader is referred to the classical commentaries,[4] and to a study by J. Grindel which reviews this material and concludes to some clear probabilities.[5]

First then, we shall read chapters 20-22 rapidly, pointing out a remarkable identity in narrative procedure within the three central stories, apart from the continuities of vocabulary and formulae which have led classical source critics to see here a single author. In a second step, proceeding more slowly, we shall read each of the stories separately to point out the demands they make on the reader. In this process we shall understand what may prove to be the chief narrative technique of the Elohist.

I. Identities in narrative procedures

Even though the atmosphere and focus in these three chapters seems to vary a great deal, it is relatively easy to point out four characteristic aspects of narrative style which are identical in each: sequence of events, role of God in the story, focus on inter-personal feelings, a religious horizon which explicitly touches both its internal and external expression.

a) Sequence of Events

One way of discerning the concern of a story-teller, or the *Tendenz*[6] of a story, is to distinguish between the "real" sequence of events and the narrative sequence. This is particularly helpful in understanding Genesis 20, as we shall see in the second part of this paper. The identity to be shown here is in the "real" sequence of events: namely, the order in which the writer and reader finally understand they must have occurred.

In each of the three central stories the following four-phased development is evident: 1) God intervenes with an instruction which sets up a horrific human situation; 2) Abraham obeys; 3) Dangerous consequences ensue; 4) God intervenes to bring good out of evil. The four phases can be seen in the following schema:

Patriarch's Wife	*Hagar Story*	*Testing of Abraham*
1) God tells Abraham to wander—Sarah accompanies him as his sister (v. 13)	God tells Abraham to obey Sarah and send Hagar and child away (v. 12)	God tells Abraham to sacrifice his beloved son (v. 2)
2) Abraham obeys (vv. 1-2a)	Abraham obeys (v. 14)	Abraham obeys (v. 3)
3) Abimelech "takes" Sarah; a disease in Abimelech's court (vv. 2b, 18)	Hagar's (i.e., Abraham's) child is dying of thirst (v. 16)	Abraham prepares to slaughter his son (vv. 9-10)
4) God prevents the adultery; tells Abimelech to return Sarah; restores health to the court (vv. 6, 7, 17)	God's angel shows Hagar a well; takes care of growing child (vv. 19-20)	God's angel saves Isaac and provides an alternative form of sacrifice (vv. 11-13)

b) Role of God in the story

It strikes one immediately that in each case it is God who causes the problem, setting up the tensions which are the essential motor of the story. God is also the source of the solution to each story. In saying this, we are not pointing so much to narrative technique as to the author's instinctive cosmology, since the above data is from the story as the author supposed it "really" occurred, not as he actually undertook to tell it. (We shall see later that it is equally true of the actual telling of the stories.)

In Genesis 22, to begin with the clearest case, God starts the story by commanding Abraham to sacrifice his son.

In Genesis 21:9-10 the scene opens with Sarah being troubled about Hagar's child. She instructs Abraham to send the two of them away. However, Abraham does not agree (v. 11), until God decisively intervenes to tell him to do so (v. 12). This may be contrasted with the Yahwist parallel. In Genesis 16, the action is not only initiated by Sarah, but it is also entirely carried out by her with Abraham's acquiescence (vv. 2-6). God does not intervene at all.

In Genesis 20, God intervenes to tell Abimelech about the true relationship between Sarah and Abraham (v. 3), thus initiating the action. This too should be contrasted with the Yahwist parallels: in Genesis 12 we are simply not told how Pharaoh found out, and in Genesis 26:8 Abimelech discovers it by catching a glimpse of them through the window. Clearly,

God is given powers of a transcendent order, but in Genesis 20, 21 and even 22, at the level of dramatic action, the Elohist presents God's initiating intervention at the same level of action as anyone else in the drama. He is one of the players on stage.

Similarly, in the conclusions God intervenes with striking directness. In the Yahwist parallels this is not the case, God does nothing to help Hagar in Genesis 16, beyond integrating the Ishmaelites in his general view of human history; in Genesis 12 God sends a plague to help Sarah, but that is not made explicitly contributory to the development of either the action or the resolution; in Genesis 26 God simply does not interfere in the events.

This view of an all-encompassing God who directly intervenes in these human events is surely not unique in the Bible. Still an intervention, at the dramatic level of human actors on stage, upon household or family (i.e., not national) affairs is foreign to the Yahwist, as we have seen. Moreover, it is importantly different from the view of the Priestly Writer. In the Priestly Writer, God is primarily the Creator, and therefore certainly all-encompassing. Moreover, his narrative proceeds precisely in terms of a divine Word, followed by its inevitable fulfillment.[7] However, in the Priestly Writer, God is not one of the actors upon the stage; his transcendence is absolute. Where the Elohist has God reacting to events, and to human decisions (as, for example, reacting to the dispute between Sarah and Abraham about what to do with Hagar and her child, or reacting to the sound of the infant crying in the desert, or reacting to the tragedy of Abimelech's error with Sarah) the Priestly Writer presents God as initiating, never reacting. Moreover, whereas the Elohist is writing a dynamic story with real interaction, the Priestly Writer has characters without personal interiorities[8] and a history without dynamism. It is rather a set of paradigms than an unfolding drama, a static image rather than moving story.[9]

It is clear that the role of God in each of these three stories is identical, and is sharply distinguished from that of the Yahwist on the one hand, but unlike that of Pg on the other.

c) Focus on inter-personal feelings

In each story the initiating event involves a situation of extreme emotional tension. Abraham is to undertake the life of an unprotected wanderer in foreign lands in chapter 20. As we shall discuss more at length later, he has no choice but to expose Sarah to the whims of men in authority wherever he goes. This is put most poignantly in verse 13, where we learn that he did not tell her simply to call herself sister, but he asked her to change the nature of her commitment (*ḥesed*) to him. His relationship with God demands an excruciating change in his marital relationship. In chapter 21

Abraham is to send off his lover Hagar, and his son to an unprotected exile in the desert. Death is the most probable prospect for them, either through starvation or through violence. That he suffers in the face of this is explicit in verses 11 and 12. But he must do it in obedience to God, because God wants his name to be carried by Isaac rather than his son by an Egyptian woman. Finally, in chapter 22 Abraham is told to sacrifice his beloved Isaac. Each of these stories begins in a situation of extreme human anguish.

Moreover, the author has spared no pains in making the reader feel the anguish. In fact, at times a scene is exploited for its emotional content in a way which is unprecedented in the rest of the Bible. For example, in chapter 22, verses 6-8 can be simply eliminated without harming anything in the action of the story. These verses are there purely to evoke the reader's emotion. They portray, with soul wrenching dramatic irony, how Issac sees all this without understanding it. Twice the reader is made to contemplate the two of them, father and son, walking along together. They portray the unsuspecting trust of Isaac, and invite the reader to imagine the storm in Abraham's heart as he answers Isaac that God will provide the victim. Similarly, in Genesis 21 the reader is asked to contemplate the anguish of Abraham as he sees Hagar and the child off in the morning (v. 14a), and then the sorrow of Hagar as she waits for her infant to die of thirst. Again, the whole of verse 16 could be left out without disturbing the action of the story. Here we see Hagar unable to bear the sight of the dying child. And then we hear the child's voice crying, and realize that Hagar cannot escape hearing what she cannot bear watching.[10] Finally, in verse 17a, God too hears the baby crying!

It is clear that this narrative style not only tells a story but also makes special demands on the reader. This aspect will be the central theme of the second part of this paper. At that point further examples of focusing on feelings, including examples in Genesis 20, will be given.

d) A religious horizon including internal and external expressions

With regard to the internal expression of religion, it is quite clear that Genesis 22 deals explicitly with a divine trial of Abraham (v. 1), which is later explained as a trial of Abraham's "fear of God" (v. 12). Without attempting an exact indication as to what this term denotes, it is certainly some internal, or psychological, state of commitment to God. It appears to be a theological focus throughout the Elohist document.[11]

The other two stories may be less explicitly focused on internal expressions of religion, but they do touch on them. In Genesis 20 the fear of God among the Philistines is a very important element in the story (v. 8). Abraham was forced to expose Sarah to dishonor because originally there was no fear of God in Gerar (v. 11).[12] Moreover, the structuring of the story in two parallel panels gives emphasis to this:

A. Transition and Setting   (v. 1)
B. The Complication   (v. 2)
C. The Action   (vv. 3-17)

I God and Abimelech	II Abimelech and Abraham
1) The Protest (v. 3)	1) The Protest (vv. 9-10)
2) The Exculpation (vv. 4-5)	2) The Exculpation (vv. 11-13)
3) God's actions (vv. 6-7)	3) Abimelech's actions (vv. 14-16)
4) THE RESULTS (v. 8)	4) THE RESULTS (v. 17)

D. The Closure (v. 18)

The structure proposed above lays out the dramatic flow of the narrative. It seems to correspond to the way the story is told, although the structure is not emphasized by the writer. He has not used techniques of inclusion or echo to underscore beginning and endings of units or their parallel nature. What we have called THE RESULTS in verse 17 are the main resolution of the story, namely, the curing of Abimelech's court. The parallel RESULTS in verse 8 are given significant emphasis by this structure, and they terminate in the clause "and the men feared greatly." Moreover, that verse begins with the observation that "Abimelech rose early in the morning." Now this clause designates significant actions, and usually godly actions. It might be noted that Abraham gets up early in the morning in Genesis 22 as well. It is the first proof of his obedience (v. 3). Right at that point the reader knows how Abraham will respond to the horrific divine command in the preceding verse. And Abraham does the same, to the same effect, in Genesis 21:14. I conclude that Genesis 20:8 refers to some religious interiority among the Philistines.

Finally, in Genesis 21, internal expression of religion is not as prominent, but is still touched on. This whole story is cast in the area of feelings: the feelings of Sarah and of Abraham about Hagar and her child, and the feelings of Hagar. Abraham's obedience in verse 14 is depicted externally, but is understood internally. Abraham's obedience is displayed here in passing, although it will not be thematized until the next chapter.

With regard to the external expression of religion, each story receives its dynamism precisely through a conflict between personal emotions on the one hand and external religious constraints on the other. Genesis 22 deals with doing away with human sacrifice in the religious practice of Israel.[13] Genesis 21:8-21 deals with mixed marriage. It begins introducing Hagar explicitly as "the Egyptian" (v. 9a), and ends by having her find a bride for her son "from the land of Egypt." These words receive emphasis by their position, and by their forming an inclusion. This chapter, as a distant forerunner of Ezra 9 and 10, restricts family relations in ancient Israel. This is an external religious constraint. It is far removed from the Yahwist parallel in Genesis 16, which is concerned with integrating within the Yahwistic politico-theological synthesis the political animosity of Ishmaelites for Israel.[14] Genesis 20 and 21:22ff. deal with the appropriate relations between Israel and the Philistines, recognizing the fear of God among non-Hebrews. Whatever the exact historical detail, these chapters sensitively define how Israel should deal religiously with non-Jews. They are in sharp contrast with other (Southern?) undifferentiated condemnations found throughout the Pentateuch concerning "Canaanites." Moreover, the complication which needs to be resolved in Genesis 20 is explicitly the most external taboo imaginable: a guilt acquired because the Patriarch's wife has (innocently) dwelt in the court of Abimelech. Thus, all three stories are written with a religious horizon which includes both internal and external expressions of religion.

In connection with Genesis 20, and the relation between Jews and non-Jews, it may now be pointed out that Genesis 21:22-34 appears to belong immediately after Genesis 20 since it deals with Abimelech and Abraham, mentions the kindness Abimelech showed to Abraham in chapter 20 (cf. 21:23), and establishes a covenant between them at Beer-sheba in a rite which Abraham initiates (v. 27) just as Abraham prays for Abimelech in 20:17a. The question arises: how did it get misplaced here, after the whole incident with an Egyptian concubine? For an answer one does not need to wait for a harmonizing R, who ravelled J and E together. If the Elohist was focusing on relations, not specifically with Egyptian or Ishmaelite, or Philistine, but rather with non-Hebrews, this resolution through ritual covenant at Beer-sheba may well have seemed an appropriate conclusion to the stories about Abimelech and Hagar.

e) Conclusion

This initial study of Genesis 20-22 provides us with a fairly strong confirmation on stylistic grounds of what classical source criticism established on other grounds, namely, that the three central stories here were written by a single author. Several consistent characteristics of this author's style have been pointed out. Some reason has been given for accepting the Beer-sheba story in 21:22ff. as part of the Elohist text, in its present position.

II. A dominant narrative technique

In reading these stories, we are well aware that they are very different stories, with differing atmospheres and focuses. In a second study of the chapters we shall first show a stylistic peculiarity in Genesis 22, and then look for it in the other chapters. It will be shown to be operative in chapter 21, and seen as decisive in solving the problems, and in identifying the *Tendenz*, of chapter 20.

In Genesis 22 the story begins with a transition and announcement of theme in verse 1a, and continues in 1b-2 with a placing of the complication in God's speech. This speech is constructed in a way calculated to force the reader to participate actively in the scene. It begins, "And he said to him 'Abraham.' And he said: 'I am here.'" In this half verse there is no content to what is said. There is an establishing of mutual presence, God-Abraham, while readers learn nothing new—they merely contemplate. They feel their own presence to this meeting. And the text continues, "Take that son of yours, your only son whom you love, I mean Isaac."[15] Three designations for the son are given, climaxing in his name. The narrative style here again elicits the participation of readers. The otherwise meaningless repetition gives time to feel what Abraham must have felt about taking this person. And finally the horrific command is given to go and slaughter him as a sacrifice, on a hill to be designated by God later.

Readers know from verse 1 that Abraham is only being tested. Still by this manner of telling the story in the ensuing verses readers are led to contemplate the scene as a participant, and to feel what Abraham must have felt, and to undergo the same test which Abraham underwent. Readers have seen Abraham placed carefully in the presence of God in verse 1b. They now await Abraham's answer. But Abraham does not answer! That scene does not even end. Instead the scene shifts unexpectedly to the next morning (v. 3). Readers are left all alone in the presence of God to formulate their own answer.

Verses 3 to 6 present Abraham going through nine or ten actions which express his obedience without naming it. When he speaks (v. 5) it is with dramatic irony, and to those who know nothing of his problem. Again, this very silence makes readers participants. They must formulate Abraham's unspoken answer on the data placed before them. This is a distinctive literary technique. It is at the polar opposite of Job, for example, who, when he is tested with God's permission, shouts his answer through many chapters. It cannot be said to be unique in the Elohist. For example, the silence of the Levite in Judges 19:20b-28 is used to exactly the same effect. However, used so massively as here, and with such subtle emphasis, it is a literary technique with a distinctive signature to it.

In the ensuing scene (vv. 7-8) once again the presence in dialogue of Abraham and Isaac is established, and readers feel themselves participants in the scene. No "aesthetic distance" is possible. Readers themselves share in the terrible emotional storm in Abraham's heart as he says what he can say in answer to Isaac's ironic question. Again readers are tested: what answer can he give?

In verses 9-10 the meticulous details are heart-rending. This is not suspense. Readers already know that nothing terrible will happen. It is participatory suffering-testing: who am I when God's voice tears through my most basic human instincts?

In verse 11 the same technique of establishing presence is used: "And he said, 'Abraham . . . Abraham.' And he said 'I am here.' " There is no rush to break the tension. Tension is the whole point here. And when the solution comes in the following verses it is presented in so neutral a fashion that readers are left with the tension, and with the test. By the solution God is off the hook, just as Abraham is off the hook by his explanation in 20:11-13. But readers are left on the hook. This precisely is the effect intended by the author.

This narrative technique entails several narrative devices which aim directly at making readers participants in the story. All narrative does this indirectly insofar as readers are led to identify with plausible characters and to "believe" plausible plots. But the Elohist has gone far beyond this. He directly involves the reader by pausing to focus on the personal presence to each other of the actors in the drama, by drawing out the emotional values, by allowing Abraham to speak to those only who do not know what he is thinking while having him remain silent about the central issue, and in particular by the rapid shift of scene in verse 3 when the test of obedience is proposed, a test which is universal in its challenges. If readers do not allow themselves to be drawn into this challenge, if they do not participate, if they maintain aesthetic distance, then they must reject the story out of hand as presenting God in an intolerable light. This narrative technique is essentially performative in that it effects a shift in the reader's consciousness. It is written precisely for this purpose, and must achieve this if it is to succeed as a story. We shall call the literary technique described here "participant focus."

Turning then to Genesis 21:8-21, a similar "participant focus" is evident. The story begins on a pun (in the Hebrew text) on the word "playing" and the name Isaac (v. 9). This is not a pun which Sarah makes for herself, nor a pun she makes for another actor in the drama. Nor is it a pun directly between the writer and the reader. It is a pun between Sarah's mind and the reader's. The reader has to "get" it.[16] Verse 8 places us in a great banquet, and verse 9 has the child playing. Suddenly in verse 10 we find Sarah speaking in tones of contempt and anger. No attempt is made directly to explain the shift.[17] Participation by readers is demanded by these three verses: they must move from the pun into Sarah's mind, and create there the reasons for anger in the following verse. By this device for "participant focus" the reader becomes author.

In verses 12-13 we have God intervening and instructing Abraham. Again Abraham is not allowed to answer God, but rather verse 14 presents actions objectively, silently, in five verbs. The actions are expressive: he gets up early in the morning; he takes bread and water; he gives them to Hagar; he settles the child on her back; he sends her away. These silent details evoke in the reader who contemplates them a realization of the tenderness and sorrow in Abraham's mind. Similarly, in verses 15-16 the reader is led to share the fear, despair, and grief of Hagar.[18] In verses 17-18 no solution is given and no action taken. Rather, the emotion is dragged out as Hagar (and the participant reader) is placed in the presence of God who hears the child, as we are told twice in verse 17, and as Hagar is told to rise and take her child back into her arms. Finally, verse 20 tells us nothing beyond the presence of God to the growing child.

This story deals with the personal feelings of Sarah, Abraham and Hagar. These feelings rise to great storms of anger and grief because of the effects of racial-religious taboos. The reader is led to focus upon all of this, but never is it directly mentioned. The essence of the story is never articulated by the author; it depends entirely, for its articulation, upon the participant reader.

We turn finally to Genesis 20, which is the difficult unit in this trilogy. A contemporary reader, no matter how sophisticated, has to overcome two obstacles to feeling this story in the way it is intended. And since "participant focus" evokes feelings, the importance of these obstacles is greatly increased. The first obstacle is the primitive concept of guilt which is taken for granted in this story. It is guilt contracted and eventually healed, in a manner which seems to us superstitious or magical. Even though God knows that Abimelech had been completely misled about Sarah and was unaware of any adultery in taking her, and even though God himself has prevented Abimelech from actually approaching Sarah sexually (v. 6), still God begins his conversation with Abimelech by telling him that he is condemned to death for adultery (v. 3), and ends with a savage statement in verse 7 that if he Abimelech does not send the woman back, then Abimelech and his whole household is condemned to death. In this view, a guilt which is merely imputed is still treated as meriting divine wrath and radical punishment. Moreover, sending the woman back will not of itself heal the guilt. God further requires that Abimelech ask Abraham, whom he calls "a prophet," to pray for him (v. 7). Eventually, after Abraham has prayed, and after Abimelech has made extremely generous gifts of land and money to Abraham and Sarah (vv. 15-16), only then is the curse removed.

The second obstacle which a contemporary reader must overcome is the social role this story presupposes for women in that society. It is not harder for us to accept that Abraham exposes Sarah to dishonor her than to accept that he sends off Hagar and Ishmael to a slow death, or that he slaughters his beloved son Isaac. But the case of Isaac was labelled a test; and the obedience regarding Hagar was based on God's promise that he would protect Ishmael because he was Abraham's son (21:13). Here, in the case of Sarah, no assurance is given, and the aspect of doing this in obedience to a divine command is also not explicit. We learn, in verse 13, only that God ordered Abraham to wander. It is Abraham who solves the resulting problem by telling Sarah that her wifely *ḥesed* during this exile would no longer be fidelity in the ordinary sense. How are we to react to this? It is clear that for the author it is fine. He presents God as being offended at Abimelech, but not offended in any degree by Abraham. Moreover, he has Abimelech make amends to Abraham directly, and only indirectly to Sarah (v. 16).

It may be easier to grasp the mental process of the writer here by looking at a similar case in Judges 19. Here once again the writer has written a story with maximum emotional effect by inviting contemplation of scenes without writing explicitly about the underlying emotions, where once again the story is in motion precisely because of the love between a man and a woman, although the narrative barely alludes to it.

In Judges 19 it is the woman's feelings that begin the story in that she runs home, away from her husband. The husband follows her to win her back. He does win her back, but this is not directly mentioned. Rather, it is expressed through the very extensive talk of hospitality and mutual affection between the husband and the father-in-law (Judg 19:3-l0).[19] Some social or narrative convention seems to dictate that approach. The woman's presence is felt, but yet invisible, mirroring in literary form the veiled and invisible presence of women in some parts of the oriental cultures.

The crime is narrated in verses 22-26. The men of Gibeah want the guest returned to the street so that they can kill him and seize his wife.[20] Desire for this woman, and the woman's outrage, in this story as in Genesis 20, is hardly alluded to in any explicit way, and yet it is the subject of the story. That she is finally dismembered (v. 29) is a ''fitting'' climax. Finally she will speak: when she is dead.

The author is telling a horror story. He portrays the horrors, not by describing the violence in detail, but by revealing the mind of the woman involved; revealing not through speeches, but rather by describing the external actions of the husband.[21]

Only when we have come to terms with the notion of imputed guilt on the one hand, and with literary conventions in narratives about women on the other, can we attempt a fair reading of Genesis 20, looking for the technique we have called ''participant focus.''

The story begins in verse 1 with a pun on *gûr/grr* (''sojourn''), a pun between writer and reader which is otherwise meaningless. It invites reader participation, or attention, without saying anything important. Then in verse 2a, without any explanation, Abraham says about Sarah his wife that she is his sister. Again a reader-directed device.[22] As in Genesis 22, the reader is almost certainly supposed to know that there is an explanation, and that the story will turn out well. Still, in reading this story, one's mind always goes on the alert at this point. Then in verse 2b the reader's inquiry about reasons turn to concern for Sarah's welfare when the king "takes" her.

In verse 3, still without explanation, we have God intervening to warn Abimelech of danger to himself because of this disorder. The participant reader feels that God is in control, and everything is going to be all right. With aesthetic distance, the reader would go astray here, thinking that God should not be threatening death. The Elohist is writing for another reaction. He expects the reader to be delighted to discover God interfering directly in the mind of a Philistine king. God in control everywhere!

In verses 4-5 we have Abimelech's exculpatory protest, and in verses 6-7 the reader is again delighted to discover that God was there before him: God knew all this, and God even prevented the actual act of adultery, and God can solve the problem: He instructs Abimelech to restore the prophet's wife so that the prophet might pray for him and save his life. We have learned by now not to read this as narrative nonsense. The Elohist has had us contemplate the indignation, anger and fear of Abimelech for two verses. We participate in those feelings and are delighted to find the solution with him.

In verse 8, the Elohist makes his point about the fear which results. Then in verses 9-10 we listen to high rhetoric from Abimelech. This is drawn out for our benefit. The second introductory clause, which begins verse 10, seems so redundant that one is tempted to wonder if we have the trace of a second source here. The whole unit invites the reader to contemplate and participate in Abimelech's indignation.

There follows in verses 11-13 Abraham's explanation. At an aesthetic distance Abraham looks weak and whiney here. The participatory reader has a different reaction. Verse 9 had begun by having Abimelech address Abraham. Their presence to each other is not developed here as in 22:1 and 7. However, the second introductory clause in verse 10a has a similar effect. The reader hears this indignation in full awareness of the humiliation involved for poor Abraham. Abraham's patient and humble exposition of his case, which the reader may feel finally explains the ancient problem of Abraham's lie in the Yahwist parallels, certainly has the delightful effect of making the reader feel that God was in control of the whole thing before the story began.

Verses 14-16 may then be seen as a confirmation, a sort of expressive ritual, of the fact that Abraham and Sarah are blessed. In this case the blessing comes through the hands of a non-Hebrew. And finally, in verses 17-

18, the radical control of God over the whole situation is again brought home to the reader. Commentators have always been struck with the apparently lame manner in which verse 18 is somehow information given too late here.[23] A good storyteller would have talked about this infertility in connection with the prevention of adultery in verse 6. Commentators are drawn to consider the verse as a gloss, or an editorial addition of some sort. However, for a writer whose focus is on the participant reader, this evidence of God's omnipresent control provides a very fitting closure to a story whose essence has been to make the reader progressively discover the radical nature of divine providence.

The three central stories in Genesis 20-22 may, therefore, be read as a trilogy which begins with the purpose of having the reader discover God's power radically present in historical events, and present both inside and outside Israel. It ends with the opposite pole to such a discovery: it challenges the reader to radical trust in God, to the point of absolute conformity to God's will.[24] It invites the reader to discover God's trustworthiness on the one hand, and God's radical demands for commitment on the other. This is not a "theological narrative," in the sense of "roman à thèse," in which the story is only a vehicle for a basically abstract idea. The participant reader is invited to understand feelingfully rather than to articulate a universal doctrine. This is performative writing, like a parable, which tells a story, not so much to teach something but rather to invite conversion.

Thus "participant focus" is a narrative technique found in all three stories. It is, in fact, the essential key to understanding the *Tendenz* of Genesis 20.

One further point must be made. The Elohist has written his trilogy as a complement to the Yahwist's Abraham saga. Genesis 20:2 makes sense only for a reader who has just read Genesis 12:10ff. In its own way, that verse refers just as clearly to Genesis 12 as does Genesis 26:1. It must be supposed, therefore, that it was the Elohist (and not some later R) who inserted verses 9 and 10 into Genesis 16, in order to make room for his additional Hagar story in chapter 21. In this case, chapters 20 and 21 must be understood as partially corrective treatments of stories which are already sufficiently important in Israel's religious self-understanding as to merit both preservation and reformation. And Genesis 22 must be understood as an addition to the tradition, supporting corrective aspects, and adding something new. What apparently needed correction in the Yahwist was his chauvinistic tendency to overlook the action of God upon other nations, and his exclusively God-and-country perspective which overlooked the presence of God in our daily lives. The new idea which the Elohist added in Genesis 22 was the radical demand for faith on the part of readers.

What the Elohist meant

It is clear, then, that the Elohist meant to produce something in the reader: an attitude of looking expectantly for the loving hand of God in one's daily life, one's family life, one's love life. Moreover, by writing a text which in some respects is unintelligible except when explained by the Yahwist text, he meant that his story must be read in the context of the Yahwist. Thus, the Elohist's meaning cannot be stated without reference to this context. This context may be roughly stated as follows: The world is cursed because of sin (Gen 2-11); the family of Abraham has been placed as aliens in the cursed world in order to interact with other nations and be a blessing to them (Gen 12:1-3); God promises extensive progeny to Abraham, and secure possession of the land of Canaan (Gen 15); threats to the fulfillment of this promise arise but are all overcome (*passim*). The Elohist presumably buys all of this, but is not satisfied with a political-theology perspective. He presents God's interventions as occurring frequently, directly and intimately. There is implied here a doctrine about Providence which I, for one, would not venture to formulate in analytic terms. Still a distinct attitude, a spirituality demanding some practices, is inculcated. This spirituality demands, among other things, that theologians mediate their own cultures in such a way that God's providential activity in our daily lives be discoverable!

What happened to the Elohist's teaching within his tradition? After the Elohist himself had written his text into the Yahwist book a Pentateuchal editor added 22:15-18. This editing took place, of course, at a point in history where Israel feels totally united by defeat and radical exile, and when the time of Abraham is as distant and fabulous to them as is the period of King John, the Magna Charta and Robin Hood to us. The editor retained the Yahwist-Elohist Abraham complex with some few additions. The point of the editorial addition in chapter 22 is that Abraham's merit in being ready to sacrifice Isaac assures Israel that God's promise is maintained and God's providence is immediate: "because you have done this, and have not withheld your son, your only son, I will indeed bless you, and I will multiply your descendents . . . And your descendents shall possess the gate of their enemies, . . . because you have obeyed my voice." The editor has retained the Elohist's teaching, but has made it seem more probable to the readers, more trustworthy (i.e., still believable, despite the intervening teachings of prophets and deuteronomists about Israel's sins wiping out the covenant), by inventing a doctrine of merit. Christianity has, of course, picked up this view in the doctrine of redemption through the merits of Christ, or else transposed it to the intercession and motherhood of Mary. A contemporary theologian will have a similar challenge to make this doctrine believable because of the intervening doctrines about doing one's own thing.

If one turns to the Targumim, one finds that the story of the testing of Abraham (Gen 22) is retained in its edited form, but with a remarkable addition: Isaac has been moved center stage, and his merits become the source of blessing for Israel. I shall cite the Neophyti text from Bovon and Rouiller.[25]

> 10 Then Abraham raised the hand and took the knife to sacrifice his son Isaac. Isaac began to speak and said to Abraham, his father: "My father, bind me well so that I do not make any kicks of a sort that your offering be rendered invalid and that I be precipitated into the pit of perdition in the world to come." The eyes of Abraham were (fixed) on the eyes of Isaac and the eyes of Isaac were turned toward the angels on high. Abraham did not see them. At that moment a voice descended from the heavens which said: "Come, see two unique (persons) in my universe. The one sacrifices and the other is sacrificed: he who sacrifices does not hesitate and he who is sacrificed bends the neck."
> 11 But the angel of Yahweh called him (from above) from the heavens and said: "Abraham! Abraham!" He said: "Here am I!"
> 12 He said: "Do not extend your hand against the boy and not do anything to him, for now I know that you fear Yahweh and that you have not refused me your only son."
> 13 Abraham raised his eyes and saw that there was a ram among the trees, (held) by his horns. Abraham went and took the ram and offered it as a sacrifice in the place of his son.
> 14 Then Abraham worshipped and invoked the name of the Word of Yahweh, and said: "I pray you, by your mercy (literally: by the mercy before you), Yahweh! All things are manifest and known before you. There has not been any division in my heart from the first moment when you told me to sacrifice my son Isaac, to reduce him to dust and ashes before you. But immediately I arose early in the morning and quickly carried out your words, with joy, and performed your commandment. And now, when your sons find themselves in a time of distress, remember the *aqëdah* of their father Isaac and hear the voice of their supplication. Hear them and deliver them from all tribulation. For the generations to come will say: On the mountain of the sanctuary of Yahweh where Abraham offered his son Isaac, on this mountain the Glory of the Shekinah of Yahweh appeared to him.
> 15 The angel of Yahweh called Abraham (from above) from the heavens, a second time, . . .

This transposition is also featured in the New Testament, where obviously the merits of Isaac are more easily seen as parallel to those of the crucified Jesus.[26]

In all of these transpositions and additions the original intent is retained. All that changes is its applicability, or rather its availability to the reader.

We have, then, a clear example of a normative tradition. It has been normative in the sense that we see both Judaism and Christianity retaining it, and reactivating it. It has been actively normative, or normative in a positive sense. It would doubtless continue to be normative in a positive sense if individuals could manage to do both the exegetical work and the philosophical work required to formulate this truth in current language, which takes for granted that God is not outside time, and as a result does not make promises, foresee results, provide for the future.

But the point which needs clarification can be touched by the following question: what precisely is normative? the meaningful story? the spiritual attitude which it inculcates? a doctrine about God which it states without philosophical precision? In other words, is "the tradition," insofar as it is normative, a set of texts and practices, or is it a spiritual attitude, or is it a set of doctrines? All would agree that the texts and practices are objectively the tradition. This paper, by stressing the performative (as opposed to significative) aspects of these texts, and by pointing to the focus on reader participation in the Elohist, leans toward making the normative tradition consist of a spiritual attitude.

I believe that the argument could easily be made that within Scripture doctrines have not been considered normative. Contradictory doctrines are retained in the canon without discussion. Moreover, scriptural scholarship, which may not have been entirely without intelligence or value, has developed various methods of discovering the meaning of texts, all of which are aimed at establishing appropriate contexts for the interpretation. The point of establishing the right context is that one is looking for the intention of the text: How has the author taken a stance within the given context? Why is authorial intention so paramount? Do not the words mean what they mean? The answer is that Scripture has seemed to scholars to be preaching rather than explaining, and inculcating attitude rather than truth.

Notes

1. Such a distinction contributes inevitably to the uprooting of meaning from historical context, and eventually from historical reality. It was implicit in the "New Criticism" so influentially taught by the Cambridge literary critic F. R. Leavis, and philosophically systematized by R. Welleck and others. At the same time Hans-Georg Gadamer (in his *Truth and Method,* 2d ed. [New York: The Crossroad Publishing Company, 1989—original German 1960]) has taught us that a text once written has its life and meaning independently of its origin. In 1957, Northrop Frye introduced literary circles to "archetypal" criticism, which he has

presented in modified, but unimproved, form in *The Great Code: The Bible and Literature* (Toronto: Academic Press, 1982) in which the source of meaning transcends the author on the one hand, and in which the text is to be read "centripetally," namely, without historical reference on the other. Since Frye, literary critics, apart from the "consciousness critics" (George Poulet, the early Hillis Miller, etc.), have embraced theories of reading which move farther and farther away from the author: "structuralist" theories and "semiological" methods often applied in a manner so abstract as to be absurd, or "deconstructionist" techniques of showing that a text does not mean one thing more than another. The power of these influences is not to be overlooked. For a good account of contemporary literary criticism, explained along with its philosophical roots, cf. Frank Lentricchia, *After the New Criticism* (Chicago: University of Chicago Press, 1980). Uncertainty in the area of cognitional theory has occasioned this hectic search for meaning in new modes. Academia is not sure it knows "the real world," and so it has a pleasure dome decreed. Bernard Lonergan's *Method in Theology* (London, Darton, Longman and Todd, 1972) and other publications, provide the philosophical underpinnings for the approach taken in this paper.

2. For a discussion of the positions developed by Brevard Childs, cf., for example, the whole issue of *JSOT* 16 (1980) articles by Barr, Blenkinsopp, Cazelles, Kittel, Landes, Murphy, Smend, and Childs himself.

3. Ideally, a refutation of all these positions and others should precede the writings of the present paper. Still, the argument of the paper is both intelligible and defensible, whatever the final decision on sources and dates, and it is in itself a small contribution toward refutation.

4. Consulted for this paper were H. Gunkel, *Genesis,* 7th ed. (Göttingen: Vandenhoeck & Ruprecht, 1966); G. von Rad, *Genesis: A Commentary,* trans. J. H. Marks (Philadelphia: The Westminster Press, 1961); B. Vawter, *On Genesis: A New Reading,* (Garden City, N.Y.: Doubleday & Company, Inc., 1977); C. Westermann, *Genesis: A Commentary,* trans. J. J. Scullion (London: SPCK, 1984ff.). For a most useful summary of research concerning Genesis 22 cf. Jean Duhaime, "Le Sacrifice d'Isaac (Genesis 22, 1-19); l'heritage de Gunkel," *Science et Esprit* (1981) 139-156. Westermann's commentary expresses great reservation about the Elohist, and specifically he finds that when Genesis 20 is compared to Genesis 21:8-21, one is forced to conclude that the two must have been written by different authors at different times. This paper points to evidence to the contrary.

5. The results of this study have been presented progressively at recent annual meetings of the Catholic Biblical Association and are soon to appear in print. Uncertainties which remain about some details of the Elohist text seem to change nothing in the argument of this paper. The only significant textual note concerns the Septuagint's additions in 20:2a and 21:9b. In both cases we remain with MT, as do the commentaries cited.

6. This German word is clear, and preferable to the overly suggestive English word "meaning." Whereas one may be tempted to paraphrase the "meaning" of a story without realizing that the substance has been left behind, one does realize that to define the *Tendenz* of a story is more like indicating the angle at which a tower leans, than like describing the tower.

7. Cf. S. McEvenue, "Word and Fulfillment: A Stylistic Feature of the Priestly Writer," *Semitics* 1 (1970) 104–110.

8. Cf. S. McEvenue, *The Narrative Style of the Priestly Writer* (Rome: Biblical Institute Press, 1971) 32–33, 78, 83, 125–127, 182.

9. Cf. Norbert Lohfink, "Die Priesterschrift und die Geschichte," *SVT* 29 (1978) 189–225.

10. Cf. Gunkel's commentary for textual discussion, and for the aspect of feeling in this scene.

11. Cf. H. W. Wolff, "The Elohistic Fragments in the Pentateuch," *Interpretation* 26 (1972) 158–173. In later Wisdom literature, "fear" denotes the most central and profound internal religious experience. Cf., for example, J. Haspecker, *Gottesfurcht bei Jesus Sirach, ihre religiöse Struktur und ihre literarische und doktrinäre Bedeutung* (Rome: Biblical Institute Press, 1967).

12. I would disagree with Wolff's contention that "Abraham is acquitted but at the same time condemned because he did not take into account the fear of God in that place." Cf. H. W. Wolff, op. cit., 162. As we shall see below, modern sensibilities mislead us here. Nowhere is Abraham "acquitted." The story does not find him guilty. Nowhere does the story claim that the fear of God was in that place before God intervened. On the contrary, Abimelech will be "acquitted" only if Abraham, who is a "prophet" (!), prays for him (v. 7). Effectively, when Abraham does pray, then God cures Abimelech, his wife and his servant girls (v. 17). Clearly the writer and first readers of this text understood from the beginning that Abraham would be shown to have done no wrong at all, and needed no acquittal.

13. Cf. the commentaries and R. Kilian, *Isaaks Opferung: Uberlieferungsgeschichte von Gen 22* (Stuttgart: Verlag Katholisches Bibelwerk, 1970).

14. Cf. S. McEvenue, "A Comparison of Narrative Styles in the Hagar Stories," *Semeia* 3 (1975) 64–80.

15. The translation attempts to take into account, in some manner, the thrice repeated *'et,* which slows the reading and gives solemnity. If one is prepared to accept Kilian's division of the text (see note 13 above) into an early source and Elohist additions, it will be seen that all the materials focused upon in the present analysis belong to the specifically Elohist additions.

16. Naturally, the pun could not be carried by translations: hence the addition in translations since the Septuagint of "with her son Isaac."

17. Gunkel's commentary points out that later tradition felt a lack here and invented explanations such as the idea that Ishmael persecuted Isaac (Gal 4:29), or that he practiced idolatry. (Cf. 228.)

18. This observation is confirmed by Westermann in his commentary who hit upon the same word to describe the narrative technique, namely, *"Teilnehmender"* "participant" (cf. 418). In his summing up of Genesis 22, he points out once again that the story addresses itself not to "spectators" ("Zuschauer"), but rather to "participants," and this observation (which he does not recognize as one of stylistic technique) provides him with the clue to understanding the "Ziel" of Genesis 22.

19. For this analysis of Judg 19, cf. Hans-Winfried Jüngling, *Richter 19—Ein Plädoyer für das Königtum: Stilistische Analyse der Tendenzerzählung Ri 19, 1–30a; 21, 25* (Rome: Biblical Institute Press, 1981).

20. Cf. ibid., 149–152 and 193–195.

21. This same convention seems to shape Matthew 1:18-25. Luke 1–2 followed another convention. The Yahwist also followed another convention. He tells his stories through the eyes of the women. (Cf. McEvenue, "A Comparison of Narrative Styles in the Hagar Stories," 68–73.).

22. The Septuagint translators felt this so strongly that they simply added the required explanation: "for he feared to say 'She is my wife' lest the men of the town kill him on account of her."

23. Westermann feels that the whole pericope can hardly be considered a narrative at all, but rather it is a meditation or an interpretation of Genesis 12:10ff. Cf. further the analysis of Klaus Koch, *Was ist formgeschichte? Neue Wege der Bibelexegese,* 2d ed. (Neukirchen-Vluyn: Neukirchener Verlag des Erziehungsvereins, 1967).

24. This understanding of the trilogy can be further founded if one follows Westermann's contention that the meaning of Genesis 22 is given in verse 14. He translates (431):

And Abraham gave this place the name "God sees"
Even today we say of it
Upon the mountain: God reveals himself.

He comments that the story aims, not at praising the faith of Abraham, but at praising God who reveals himself, as promised in verse 8 (cf. 446–447). In this reading, the trilogy begins and ends with the discovery of God's intervention in human affairs. Despite the compelling logic of Westermann's position, it may not be entirely convincing. The text is so powerful in presenting Abraham's suffering that the reader may not feel the impact of verse 14 as Westermann argues he should.

25. F. Bovon and G. Rouiller, *Exegesis: Problems of Method and Exercises in Reading (Genesis 22 and Luke 15),* trans. D. G. Miller (Pennsylvania: The Pickwick Press, 1978).

26. All of this is studied at length in a monograph of James Swetman, *Jesus and Isaac: A Study of The Epistle to the Hebrews in the Light of the Aqedah* (Rome: Biblical Institute Press, 1981).

Chapter 12

The Basis of Empire:
A Study of the Succession Narrative

The Succession Narrative may be read in 2 Samuel 9-20; 1 Kings 1-2.[1] Our study will attempt to discover the meaning of text by searching out the focus of creative effort manifest in the telling.[2]

Historical Interest

The literary quality of this story is so striking that it may be wise to begin our study in a counter direction, by stressing its bias toward what we might call hard historical facts. First of all, in a general way the author, without quite achieving the anti-hero cynicism with which we are familiar from the dominant literary modes of the sixties, still wrote a story quite without heroes. There is a refusal of myth at the heart of this writing, as we shall see in detail below, which would tend to present king, soldier, wise man, prophet, and priest as weak human beings, or worse. This refusal leaves the author little to work with except historical facts.

Secondly, one must admire the skill with which the author provides each personage in the story with a distinctive and consistent character, and the narrative art with which these personages are introduced and interwoven in a complex plot development. However, we must also note that some personages are introduced, and given no character, and not interwoven with any narrative skill whatever. For example, we are told that Mephibosheth, before David brought him to Jerusalem, was living with Machir, the son of Ammiel, in Lo-debar (9:4, 5). Much later in the story, when David had fled to Mahanaim, we are told that Machir, the son of Ammiel, from Lo-debar came there to help him out (17:27). This personage appears nowhere else, and seems to generate no narrative meaning in the text. He appears to be mentioned in the text only because he participated in the events. The same is true of an otherwise unknown Shobi, the son of Nahash, who appears in the same verse apparently just because he too turned up in

Mahanaim. More striking is the mention of Mica, the son of Mephibosheth (9:12). In a succession story, a great grandson of Saul either should not be mentioned, or else, if mentioned, his role as threat to the throne or as successfully neutralized should be narrated. But our author is so distracted by facts, away from story forms, that he names Mica in chapter 9, and then never mentions him again. One can only conclude that he mentions Mica simply because he was there, and that he narrates nothing further simply because he knows nothing further about him. Similarly, the mentions of Ittai the Gittite (15:19-22; 18:2, 5, 12), and of Barzillai the Gileadite (17:27-29; 19:31-40), appear to carry no narrative value beyond the value of facticity. Again, the details of Shimei's error in 1 Kings 2:39-40 are otherwise irrelevant, and therefore must be understood as historical facts. Finally, even the artful presentation of David's uncertainty in the disposition of Saul's wealth between Mephibosheth and Ziba (16:4; 19:29) must be historical, if only because such wealth was too visible to be lied about, at least for many generations afterwards.

This paper is concerned with the historicity of the text only to the point of establishing what kind of narrative this is. These few observations should be sufficient to show that this writing is historical, in the sense that it is truly rooted in historical facts and realities.

Narrative Structures

The narrative proceeds by a series of vignettes, each of which is skillfully turned. Moreover, the clever interweaving of separable stories about Mephibosheth, Ziba, Joab, Shimei, Nathan and Bathsheba, through the larger story of David and his sons, serves to knit the incidents into a continuous development. But beyond this there is a further continuous story line, which the reader feels obscurely as a deeper unity, even if one cannot easily identify it. What is the underlying narrative about?

Leonhard Rost recognized a narrative line from Yahweh's election of Solomon in 12:24-25, through the elimination of competitors (Absalom and Adonijah) to the establishment of Solomon on the throne in 1 Kings 2:46. There is no reason to doubt that that narrative line exists in the text. However, it is difficult to agree that it is the point of the text, or that it does justice to the concerns of the author. For example, if the story is about Solomon, how does one explain that Solomon himself plays a very brief role in the story line? And if it is about succession, how does one explain that the idea of succession is adverted to only at the very end? And how does one explain the wealth of material in the text which is very remotely, or not at all, connected with this story line? The story line itself is so obscurely present in the text that one major study denies its very existence.[3]

Moreover, one can point to a second underlying story line which is equally present in the text: namely, a story of sin and punishment, in four phases. This story begins with David the king attempting to do good things, (to take care of the descendants of Saul in 9:1, and to be loyal to the Ammonites in 10:1-2), and with Yahweh very firmly on David's side in 10:12-14, 18. In a second phase, the focus is on sin. First, David sins: adultery leading to an odious murder. God promises punishment (chaps. 11–12). Then David's son Amnon also perpetrates a sexual crime, and another son, Absalom, also becomes guilty of an odious murder, while assuming the role of punisher of sexual folly. Absalom then proceeds to punish David, but finally ends up murdered himself (13-18). In a third phase of the story, David has done penance (12), has accepted the curses heaped upon his exile by Shimei (16:11-12), and has accepted as from God's hands all that he suffered from Absalom (18:5, 33). In a final phase of the story, David is restored to his kingdom (19-20); and his son by Bathsheba is established on the throne (1 Kings 1-2). That is a plausible reading of the text. It is a story line which is undeniably present in the text, even if its presence is just about as obscure as that of the succession story.

A third underlying story line can be pointed out. It might suggest further source analysis, and it may be closer to propaganda than story, but it is a unifying theme within the text. And it is clearly tributary to the main succession narrative. It is the story of David's vindication: how he is proven not guilty of the blood of Saul. David is a devious and sinful man, but he is not guilty of regicide. The political value of such a story to Solomon, or any later successor of David, is obvious.[4] This story line is carried with particular clarity in the vignettes about Shimei. Shimei curses David, precisely because he believes that David's defeat is a proof that Saul's blood is on his head (16:8). It is important to note that David himself is presented as not being sure but that Shimei may be right (16:12). When the rebellion has been defeated, Shimei realizes he was wrong and begs forgiveness (19:18-20). David states that he too has recognized a proof of his innocence in this victory, and he is so overjoyed that he will not allow Abishai to kill Shimei (19:22). Finally, the death of Shimei forms a kind of climax in a series which reaches beyond Shimei: all those who endangered the consolidation of Solomon's succession to the throne are killed or exiled: Absalom, Adonijah, Abiathar, Joab and, finally, Shimei. The first three are punished because they contested Yahweh's choice of David and then Solomon for the throne. Joab is punished because he had brought blood on the head of David and his family. Shimei is punished for imputing blood guilt to David and his house.

The reader must ask why these plots are so interwoven as to be almost hidden in the text. One could imagine three possible answers to this question. It could be because the author is struggling with too many historical details, and unable to bring out clearly the points he wants to make? Or it could be because the author is a wisdom writer, who chooses to write in an indirect riddling style, inviting the reader to figure out what lies beneath the surface? Or, finally, it could be because the author uses the story lines as an underlying framework, but does not focus on them because his or her main interest does not lie in story at all, but elsewhere?

It can hardly be the first, because there is not a single sentence in the text in which one can see the author struggling to establish any clear points. There are no generalizations. There are no summaries. There is no introduction, and the conclusion is only one half verse in length.

The second is more plausible, but it too has to be rejected, when one thinks concretely about the points actually in question. This brilliant writer simply cannot be imagined to have written so complex a document in order to invite readers to riddle out these three lessons. There is no riddle about the fact that Solomon was chosen by God. This must have seemed all too obvious to those Jews who lived during the splendor of his empire or within memory of it. Or again, that David had sinned, been punished, and then restored to power, is a truth which is not so much subtly concealed in this story, but rather one which is weakened and almost denied by the graceless ending to David's life which is portrayed in the final two chapters. Finally, that David is vindicated of blood guilt by his victory over Absalom, and by the crowning of Solomon, might justify a riddling treatment. However, this theme can explain only the last part of the narrative, leaving the whole of chapters 9 to 15 unmotivated.

Now it is true that wisdom is much discussed in the text, and that, as we shall see below in some detail, much of the author's genius is involved in portraying communication by indirection. However, it is also true that the author does not really admire indirection, as he or she consistently associates indirection with unsavory accomplishments. For example, Jonadab is described as "wise" (13:3) when he shows Amnon how to go about raping his sister, an act which is later characterized as folly (13:12-13). Joab sends a "wise" woman of Tekoa in order to wheedle David's consent to the idea of restoring Absalom, an idea which proves to be a disastrous mistake. When David figures out the manipulation, the author compares his "wisdom" to that of the angel of God who knows all things. In this context, even angelic wisdom turns out to be a dupe! Another "wise" woman (20:16) intervenes as a negotiator, and succeeds by betraying Sheba the son of Bichri. David calls Solomon "wise" (1 Kings 2:9) because he will be able to kill Shimei, circumventing David's oath. Similarly, Solomon's "wisdom" will enable him to bring Joab to an evil end (1 Kings 2:6). Even the more elegant word "counsel," reserved for the great courtiers Hushai, Ahithophel, and Nathan, signifies nothing more elevated than astuteness, craft, or wiliness on the pen of this author (cf. 16:23; 17:7, 11, 14, 15, 21, 23; 1 Kings 1:12). The author has the wise woman of Tekoa flatter David by comparing his "wisdom" to that of the angel of God (14:17), but when the author himself, or herself, seriously praises the "counsel" of Ahithophel, she compares it, not to God's "counsel," but to God's "word" (16:23). In this case Ahithophel's "counsel" was correct, but Yahweh intervened to defeat this good counsel (17:14). This author describes astuteness and manipulative communication within history, but places God, and the story's unidentified narrator, outside it. Such an author can hardly be expected to relate to his or her own readers in this mode.

As a final argument, I would ask whether the reader's pleasure in reading this story is enhanced when these hidden story lines are pointed out. When we read the text, with the hypothesis that these plots govern the basic meaning, that they are the "whole point" as it were, do we not feel rather disappointed and bored? Do we not feel that we are missing something, or else that this clever author could easily have made these "points" more effectively?

We must conclude, therefore, that the third explanation is correct, namely, that the author is interested in something other than these hidden story lines. The central meaning of the text is to be found elsewhere.

The Central Focus

If the author of The Succession Narrative draws upon history, and uses interwoven story lines, where does he or she apply and display creative interest, original thought, passionate talent? What are these stories really about?

A first answer, and an important one, is that at their best they are about communication, deception, manipulation. This can be seen in a rapid survey of the major stories. Chapter 9 is, in fact, a good example, but we will reserve it for later consideration. Chapter 10 deals with war, and climaxes in definitive victory over Syria. However, that part of the story is told as a colorless chronicle. All the authorial creativity has been concentrated in relating the misinterpretation of David's intentions in sending mourners to the Ammonites, and in their humorous response. Chapter 11 is a story of adultery and murder, and yet almost no time or effort is spent depicting those events. Even the emotional and moral aspects are reduced to a single verse (11:26). All the energy in the story is derived from contrasts in communication. On the one hand, the directness of David's communication to Bathsheba (11:4, 27; 12:24), and to Joab (11:6), and of the servants' communication to David (11:10), and of Uriah's to David (11:11) provide a uniform background. On the other hand, another series of communications form a very striking contrast against it: namely, the manipulative deception of David's communication to Uriah (11:8,12), and the detailed portrayal of circumspection and indirection in Joab's communication to David (11:18-24; 12:27-28). This element absorbs the whole interest and creative energy of the story. Similarly, the sequel in chapter 12 is not at all a straightforward story of prophecy and repentance. First, we see Nathan employing an indirect approach (12:1-4), remote from prophetic forms but similar to that of the wise woman of Tekoa in chapter 14. Second, David's grief turns out to be not just grief, but rather a posture in prayer. Third, the author focuses the readers' attention on a communication problem experienced by David's servants (12:18-23). Finally, the end of the chapter wraps up the war with the Ammonites begun in chapter 10, but the focus of interest is not on the victory, but rather on Joab's astuteness in having David secure the image of victor for himself.

Chapter 13 presents the rape of Tamar, and it focuses on the technique of tricking her. Tamar's reaction centers only on appearances and reputation (13:12-13), and then on a technique of communicating her state to the family (13:19). The rest of the chapter deals with the concealment (13:20), the delayed deception by which Absalom takes revenge, and the way in which David finds out about it (13:20-36). Chapter 14 deals with Absalom's return to Jerusalem, but the author has conceived it as a story about communication and persuasion in the royal court. Chapter 15 presents David's defeat in Jerusalem, and chapter 16 deals with his flight. The interest in the story is maintained by reflections on how Absalom created a good opinion of himself (15:1-6); how he deceived David (15:7-12); how David set up a communication system for himself (15:24-28) and a perverse wisdom for Absalom (15:32-37; 16:15-19); and finally how Absalom communicated his victory to the common people (16:20-23). Chapter 17 deals with the contest in persuasion between "counsellors," and the messenger system set up by David. Chapter 18 relates the death of Absalom, but even here the whole of verses 19-33 are dedicated to the story of how the news of it was brought to David. Chapters 19–20 present David's complete return to power in a manner consistent with the foregoing, though not remarkably focused on communication.

Finally, 1 Kings 1-2 relate Solomon's accession to the throne, and David's final advice and death. Chapter 1 is exclusively about communication: it is a kaleidoscopic study of creating appearances and manipulating information in order to create power. The point is not that Solomon became king, but precisely the manipulative process by which Solomon became king. Chapter 2 then deals with craft in government.

It must be concluded that, to an astonishing degree, the central and almost exclusive interest of this author consists in his or her ability to depict the role of communication, deception, and manipulation in history.

A second answer to our question about the focus of our author's creative interest is intimately related to the first. The Succession Narrative is a clever study of David, provided by a narrator who has no access to David's inner thoughts, but who appears to be a member of the court (9:11: "Mephibosheth ate at *my* table, like one of the king's sons."), who witnesses David's actions and gestures and decisions from close-up. The author has no privileged information about David's motives. He or she does know what individuals said to David in relative privacy, as in chapter 19 where Joab urges David to cease grieving for Absalom; and also what such individuals might have reported of their private conversations, as in chapter 14, for example, the conversation with the wise woman of Tekoa. But there is never a glimpse of David's own thinking. The genius of the presentation is that David is consistently shown as acting or speaking, on the basis of motives which are unknown or ambiguous. There results a figure who sits very convincingly at the center of a story of communication, deception and manipulation.

Ambiguity arises at the very start, in chapter 9. The reader's doubts will be slight at first, but they will grow even larger as David's duplicity is revealed, and as the author allows ambiguities to accumulate without ever giving counter-indications about David's motives. The story opens with David proffering a generous gesture toward a grandson of Saul. David says he intends to "show him the kindness of God" (9:1, 3). However, the reader is left unsure about David's motives. Mephibosheth is to live in Jerusalem and eat at the royal table. Is this an honor, or a form of imprisonment? The reader must note that Mephibosheth's helplessness is mentioned in 9:3, and then placed as a final comment on the story in 9:13. Moreover, David now places Ziba in control of all the land of Saul, and tells him to bring in all the produce for Mephibosheth. What will Mephibosheth do with it, now that he is to eat at the king's table? David considers Ziba himself to be a servant only of Saul, not of Mephibosheth (9:9-10). Later in the story, Ziba will lie about Mephibosheth, and as a result David will give him all that had belonged to Mephibosheth (16:4). Later again, when Mephibosheth clears his name, and David does not know whom to believe, David will show no trace of "the wisdom of Solomon," but rather will hastily divide the land between Mephibosheth and Ziba as though it were a matter of small consequence (19:29). In this sequence we see David's initial magnanimity take on an ambiguous note, and then gradually be revealed as a political manipulation. And David's inability to decide which was the liar, Mephibosheth or Ziba, somehow leaves David in complicity with deception.

In chapter 10 the author gives us only David's word for it that his purposes in regard to the Ammonites is only condolence. We see David letting Joab lead the battle until the king of Syria appears on the scene. Then David takes to the field (10:17). This is uncommented in the text. Later, in 12:27-30, David will again take to the field, this time for the moment of glory. In chapter 18:2-4 there is a great discussion about whether David should risk his neck in battle, and the decision is that he should not. Again the author gives no clue as to the real motives, and the reader is left just slightly unsure about David's military honors.

Of course, the Uriah story presents David at his deceptive worst. Moreover, in chapter 12, David's impressive grief over the loss of Bathsheba's first child, and his immediate recovery upon the child's death, leaves the reader wondering. Is this strong religion, or weak theater? Here again the author chooses to leave the ambiguity intact.

David's relationship with Joab is ambiguous. Clearly they begin as allies in war and in crime in chapters 10-12. Clearly they end up as enemies, and David explains that it is because of Joab's murder of Abner and Amasa (1 Kings 2:5). However, the reader knows something of Joab's contempt for David from his manner of instructing the messenger in 11:18-21, and the wise woman in 14:1-3 about how to manipulate David. And we know that Joab directly disobeyed David in murdering Absalom, and then hypocritically assumed the honest-statesman role, convincing David that he must resume his leadership and cease his indulgence in grief (19:1-8). Just five verses later we see David appointing Amasa to head the army! The author makes no comment about this implicit demotion of Joab. The reader is puzzled. Did David learn who had murdered Absalom? Or was this simply astute politics, promoting a former enemy? Later, in chapter 20, Joab manages to kill Amasa, and simply reassumes his position at the head of the army. What did David think of this? Again the author leaves the reader without any clues, until the end, when David tells Solomon to kill Joab.

David's concern that Absalom not be killed, and subsequent grief, in chapters 18-19, seem authentic. But then we immediately see David securing his power in Judah and in Israel by manipulation and violence (19:11-15; 20:6). One cannot doubt, after reading the Shimei encounter in 16:5-14, that David firmly believed that his kingship was given him by Yahweh. However, it is equally clear that David felt called upon to use every means, fair or foul, to protect Yahweh's choices! In this context, the grief over Absalom appears to be both genuine and also a political gesture.

In the final scenes, we see David blatantly manipulated by Nathan and Bathsheba to give the nod to Solomon. In his own words, his decision is based on his oath to Yahweh (1 Kings 1:11-31). And his dying advice to Solomon begins with an admirable exhortation to virtue (1 Kings 2:1-4),[5] but this is followed by a return to the scheming and vindictive politician, assuring rewards for his friends and revenge on his enemies (1 Kings 2:5-9).

The ambiguity about David is accompanied by other more minor ambiguities in the narrative. Some characters are relatively colorless: for example, Absalom, Amnon, Zadok, and Abiathar. Others are stereotypes, such as Bathsheba, "the dumb blond," or Joab, a prototype of contemporary images of the Pentagon. However, Mephibosheth and Ziba remain enigmatical to the end of the story. And Nathan is remarkably ambiguous: he is given prophetic responsibility for Solomon in 12:25; and in 1 Kings 1 he is again called a prophet in verses 22-23, and he plays a decisive role in securing the throne for Solomon. Moreover, he is allowed to use the formula "Thus says the Lord" in 12:11. However, his style is that of a wise man in chapter 12, and of an unscrupulous courtier in 1 Kings 1. The reader does not know what to make of him as a person, even if Yahweh has used him to his own purpose.

Such then is the genius, the charm, and creative contribution of this writer in narrating David's end and Solomon's accession to the throne. The author writes of deception and ambiguity. Presented this way, it sounds like a situation comedy. But it is clearly far more serious than that. We see here a literary technique by which the author, and hence the reader, does not finally know the human reality which underlies this history. Or rather we know that the human reality was always ambiguous, and never decisive. However, there was a decisive reality underlying the events, namely, a series of divine decisions. And this reality is largely taken for granted, though quietly mentioned, by the author. It demands faith on the part of the reader. It is the tension between these two elements of ambiguity and certainty which makes this not only a clever but also a powerful text. It is to the divine reality that we must now turn.

The Interventions of Yahweh

The belief system which forms a background to this story understands that God is very much in charge of outcomes. "Man proposes but God disposes" is very much the view of history represented here. For example, when Joab is set to go to battle against the Ammonite-Syrian coalition, he understands that his battle is in defense of the "cities of our God; and may Yahweh do what is good in his eyes" (10:12). A New Testament translation of this wish is "Thy will be done." And this must not be taken for a meaningless phrase, for we see this to be a serious principle in a later story, which determines David's actions. In 15:25-26, David expresses readiness to be restored or to come to an end as God sees fit, and this pious affirmation is shown to be operative in chapter 16. There, David fleeing the city, is cursed by Shimei for the murder of Saul's family. Abishai wants to kill Shimei, but David is very much afraid that Shimei is right and that his present suffering is due to Yahweh's intervention. Killing Shimei would not, therefore, stop Yahweh. Rather, it would remove all chances of satisfying God's wrath with some punishment short of death. David hopes for a reprieve in return for suffering this insult: "Possibly Yahweh will witness my guilt-suffering, and Yahweh may restore blessing after his (Shimei's) cursing today" (16:12). Thus, for David, all manipulation of persons and events by himself is powerless against divine decisions, and indeed might prove counter-productive.

In this line of thought, one might further reason that all manipulation of persons and events toward furthering divine decisions will be appropriate. Our author offers no such generalizations, but this one would explain and justify David's remarkable shift from passivity, in chapters 14–18, to decisive and energetic activity towards restoring his position in Jerusalem, once he is sure that Yahweh wants him to continue as king, in chapters 19–20. It would also explain the shift from David's hands-off policy regarding his sons throughout the story (particularly Amnon and Absalom), to his decisive action in securing the throne for Solomon, once Adonijah has threatened that divine decision. Moreover, it is clear that the wise woman of Tekoa held this doctrine (14:11, 17).

In this story, Yahweh is not at all involved, and is almost never mentioned, in the world of intrigue, of communication, of manipulation. However, the author presents very specific moments of divine intervention, which it will be well to enumerate. First, if we are to trust Joab's and David's piety in leaving the outcome in Yahweh's hands, as we saw above, then we must conclude that Yahweh gave the victory over the Syrians and Ammonites in chapters 10 and 12. Moreover, we shall see below that Yahweh is said to have given David the victory over his foes, though this is a slightly different category.

Second, we are laconically told that Yahweh was displeased with David's adultery-murder (11:27), and then that Yahweh will punish the crime by causing armed strife in David's family, by humiliating David sexually, and by taking the life of the illegitimate child (12:10-14). These three threats are carried out in the ensuing story. In regard to the second and third of these, the text itself explicitly points out the divine intervention (12:15, 22; 16:21-23). Similarly, the punishments which Solomon gives to Abiathar, Joab, and Shimei, are attributed to Yahweh (1 Kings 2:27, 32-33, 42-46).

Third, it becomes evident that Yahweh has decided, in fact, that David should be returned to the throne in Jerusalem. We are told that David prayed Yahweh to confuse the counsel of Ahithophel (15:31); and later that Yahweh had decided "to defeat the good counsel of Ahithophel, so that Yahweh might bring evil upon Absalom" (17:14). Three times it is said that Yahweh has given David victory over his enemies (18:19, 28, 31). In 19:22 David says that "this day I know I am king over Israel." However, the author does not choose to indicate how David knows, or to confirm this with another specific statement.

Fourth, we are told that Yahweh loved Solomon at his birth (12:24-25), and that the throne was given to Solomon by Yahweh (1 Kings 2:15). Moreover, we are assured that Yahweh will grant eternal peace to this dynasty (1 Kings 2:33).

In summary, Yahweh intervenes to give victory in war, to punish evil, and to choose the monarch.

The Subliminal Teaching of this Narrative

The theological teaching of this text is not at all obvious. It contains a teaching about divine intervention, outlined in the previous section, but this is more a background than a positive affirmation of the text. If any biblical text can be said to be secular, this witty piece surely is it.

Within the context of the Deuteronomic history, one could align it with those texts which are opposed to the monarchy. An exilic Deuteronomist, who wrote Deuteronomy 17:14-20, and who edited 1 Samuel 7-12 by the insertions of 7:3-4; 8:6-20a; 10:18-19; and especially 12:6-25, and who viewed the monarchy as a corrupt institution from the start, and destined to bring about the end of Israel, would certainly have enjoyed this story as exemplifying royal corruption.[6] Such a reading would rightly argue that the conclusion of a text usually indicates "the point" which is intended. In this case, 1 Kings 2 consists mainly of David's malicious advice, and Solomon's craftiness in following it. And the closing incident shows how Shimei is killed on the pretext of a trivial offense. The final closure consists of a single sentence, which reads: "And the kingdom was established in the hand of Solomon." The closure seems to signify that Solomon's imperial power is to be explained by the foregoing narrative, namely, its origin lies in the political manipulation which brought Solomon to the throne and in the devious violence which secured him there.

However, this paper would like to seize the original meaning of The Succession Story prior to specific subsequent moments of interpretation through larger contexts of the canon.[7] It would like to do so, partially because that meaning is still there, however much subsequent biblical and post-biblical tradition may have overlooked it; and partially because the canon, or the Deuteronomistic history, have seldom, if ever, been read as continuous units by the faithful in the churches or synagogues. Our faith has been formed on the basis of small segments of texts, and the voice of this faith must not be lost.

The fact is that, even if it is not articulated textually, there is a distinctive message in The Succession Story which leaves its mark on the reader. There is a Voice in the text, which is the creative aspiration of the original writer, and which is obscurely heard in every pericope. This writer remains ambiguous about David and Solomon as human persons. However, he or she did not use any words such as "malicious," or "devious," or "violent." The author does not condemn these kings as we have done in the last paragraph. We feel the author's pleasure in revealing ambiguity, but we do not detect any trace of indignation or anger. If the author lived during the time of Solomon, or shortly after, then he or she lived in a period of Israel's history where the kings provided political stability, personal security, financial wealth. The author's voice invites the reader to recognize the deception of appearances, and of political postures, and to embrace these human beings for what they were. At the same time, it invites the reader to identify and rely on the divine decisions which form reality and give shape to history.

In formulating this message, one is tempted to take modern proverbs such as "The Lord writes straight with crooked lines," or else to return to ancient authors such as Plato who taught his disciples to seek "truth" (*aletheia*), in preference to "opinion" (*doxa*). But the voice of this text, while counting on the straightness and truth of God, does not spend much time on it. Its focus is not there, but rather in the complexity of deception. There is an iconoclastic message in the text, which demands that we abandon awe before royalty, since it presents David and Solomon as ambiguous at best; abandon admiration for the army, since Joab is presented as a ruthless schemer; abandon the cult of prophets, since it presents Nathan as a court politician; abandon respect for wisdom, since the wise are presented as manipulative and deceptive. It is so certain about well-being at the hand of God, that it takes pleasure in laying bare the uncertainty of human institutions through which God operates. It lays them bare, without hating them. It embraces life, reality, without myth, because that is where God does operate.

This is a unique literary genre. Where the edifying literature of the Deuteronomist explains prosperity (blessing) by civic virtues, or prophetic literature explains doom by human sins, or much of wisdom writing invites us to seek the causes of events in the hidden patterns of human nature, the sparks of divinity within creation, this writing delights in showing that human virtue and vice and the patterns of nature are only shifting appearances, froth on an ocean of reality. This is an approach which loves discussing ambiguous human process, precisely because it relies on divinely determined outcomes. This genre could be called adult, realistic, history. It is truly adult, because it is not cynical, or satirical. Rather, it understands and embraces human ambiguity, instead of withdrawing in distaste. And it is truly realistic, in the sense that it finds God's work within human lives, rather than by covering these with myths or aesthetics.

There are biblical proverbs, which are close to the thought of this text, and which will help to clarify its meaning. We may begin by first citing two helpful texts from the Succession Narrative itself: first, Joab's code that we should do our best, leaving the outcome in the hands of God:

> Be of good courage and let us play the man for our people, and for the cities of our God; and may Yahweh do what seems good to him (10:12).

Second, David makes several rapid decisions, and expresses the same code, as he flees Jerusalem:

> Carry the ark of God back into the city. If I find favor in the eyes of Yahweh, he will bring me back and let me see both it and his habitation; but, if he says "I have no pleasure in you," behold here I am, let him do to me what seems good to him (15:25-26).

Some proverbs make humans responsible for the antecedents of events, but God alone is responsible for the public event which occurs, even distinguishing preparatory thoughts from publicly uttered words. This view is close to that of our author, for whom the public acts are real, but the motives are shadowy, and ambiguous, hidden under devious words which fascinate but are finally irrelevant. We might consider the following three Proverbs:

> Commit your work to the Lord,
> And your plans will be established (16:3).
>
> A man's mind plans his way,
> But Yahweh directs his steps (16:9).
>
> The plans of the mind belong to man,
> But the answer of the tongue is from Yahweh (16:1).

In particular, it is the decisions of the king, and his actions, which are real, and created by God. David flees from Absalom precisely because he is not sure, as we saw above, about his own blood guilt, and whether Yahweh wanted him or Absalom as king. Only when this question is answered by the death of Absalom does David take charge again. This belief in the divine right of the king has been supplanted in our time by rights based on majority vote, or the divine rights of the people. In our society, a leader must wait for a new mandate by the electorate before enunciating new policy. For us the divine will is expressed by democratic process; for David, as we saw, the divine will is expressed in success in war, in life and death, and in the ceremonies of enthronement. Consider the following Proverbs:

> It is the glory of God to conceal things,
> But the glory of kings is to search things out (25:1).

> My son, fear Yahweh and the king,
> And do not associate with those who change;
> For disaster from them will rise suddenly,
> And who knows the ruin that will come from both (24:21-22)?

> Inspired decisions are on the lips of a king;
> His mouth does not sin in judgement (16:10).

Even though what matters is what the king does or proclaims, still it remains true that it does not finally matter what the king thinks:

> Many seek the favour of a ruler,
> But from Yahweh a man gets justice (29:26).

> As the heavens for height, and the earth for depth,
> So the mind of kings is unsearchable (25:3).

With such a view of reality, it is little wonder that our author studied the words and deeds of David so attentively, presenting them as they were with subtle innuendo and implied questions, but ultimately little concern about the motives which lay behind them. It was not in creation, or in nature, but rather in politics that this author could experience the reality and love of God. The realm of his or her search was the ambiguity of human communication, but divine action was found in the stable realities of political power. The voice of this author, subliminal and therefore all-powerful in the mind of the reader, demands a similarly adult and realistic way of living religiously.

For many readers, this text may seem to teach nothing at all regarding the topic of this symposium, namely, the implication of biblical texts for Church and state relationships. The easiest way to show implications, if it is an allowable one, may be to indicate the challenge this text directs to myself, with my own peculiar history. I was brought up as a member of a despised religious minority in the city of Toronto, during the 30s and 40s. During those years I learned to feel that government was simply corrupt and corrupting, foreign to true religion, and totally within the purview of what I believed to be a heretical religious establishment. In other words, my attitude to political authority was analogous to the position of the exilic Deuteronomist toward the king, as I mentioned earlier. Personally, I was unaware of the exilic Deuteronomist until recent years. Rather, my attitude seemed to be sufficiently justified by glib interpretations of Jesus' words: "Render to Caesar the things that are Caesar's, and to God the things that are God's." However, later in life, when I no longer felt powerless, or marginalized in society, or free from social responsibility, well then that angry escapist attitude was not enough! It did not constitute an adequate political theology, to say the least. And yet the subliminal message of this text is so inimical to all those early feelings that it has taken me fifty years of living with it, and of growing in other ways, before I could understand and accept its challenge.

Conclusion

The author of this narrative chose to write about the succession because these were the major events he or she had lived through as an involved spectator, and mostly because he or she had searched for and discovered a traditional faith, not in the past, not in traditional myths or language codes, but in the experience of ambiguous human interaction. The reader who seeks "objective" historical data, or who admires literary skill, will find much to praise in this text. But the reading will be somewhat sour, unless one habitually lives as a radically responsible citizen.

Notes

1. Cf. Leonhard Rost, *Die Überlieferung von der Thronnachfolge Davids* (BWANT III 6), (Kohlhammer, Stuttgart: W. Kohlhammer, 1926) translated into English as *The Succession to the Throne of David* (Sheffield: Almond Press, 1982). A most accessible and complete literary study of this narrative, with a useful survey of prior scholarship, may be found in R. N. Whybray, *The Succession Narrative: A Study of II Sam 9-20 and 1 Kings 2 and 3* (London: SCM Press, Ltd.; Illinois: Alec R. Allenson, Inc., 1968). He characterizes the work as a "propagandist narrative" (54), intent at the same time on illustrating specific proverbial teaching (95), written by a wisdom teacher who was influenced by Egyptian models of "political novels" (115–116). The present paper might be considered an attempt to fill a lacuna to which Whybray makes allusion: "The question why the author chose to recount the events which led to Solomon's accession to the throne rather than some other story still remains unanswered" (50). What were the aims of the author? For further bibliography cf. James W. Flanagan, "Court History or Succession Document? A Study of 2 Samuel 9-20 and 1 Kings 1-2," *JBL* 91 (1972) 172–181; and also Anthony Campbell, *Of Prophets and Kings: A Late Ninth-Century Document (1 Samuel 1-2 Kings 10),* (CBQ Monography Series 17) (Washington: The Catholic Biblical Association of America, 1986) especially 82–84. Campbell's claim that 1 Kings 1 is part of a different prophetic document is hard to accept, as the image of Nathan in that chapter is radically diverse from the image of prophets elsewhere in his proposed "Prophetic Record."

2. The objectives and the justification of the method employed in this study are presented in chapters 1–2 of Sean McEvenue, *Interpreting the Pentateuch* (Collegeville: The Liturgical Press, 1990).

3. Cf. James W. Flanagan, op. cit., who argues that the material concerning succession (i.e., the Bathsheba incident and 1 Kings 1-2) are a separate story, from a different source. For the purposes of this paper, it is not necessary to refute the source-critical arguments of Flanagan and others. Whatever the history of the weaving of this text, this paper addresses continuities in narrative, attitude, and style in this slice of the present biblical text, which produce a specific effect in readers of the Bible.

4. The vindication of David seems also to have been one of the main concerns of the "Rise of David Story," which may be read roughly in 1 Samuel 15–2 Sam 8. For a history of research cf. the classical introductions to the Old Testament, and especially Brevard Childs, *Introduction to the Old Testament as Scripture* (Philadelphia: Fortress Press, 1979) 266–271. Cf. further, David Gunn, *The Story of King David: Genre and Interpretation* (Sheffield, Eng.: University of Sheffield, 1979) and chapter 10 in this volume, "The Rise of David Story and the Search for a Story to Live By," pp. 113–121.

5. These verses are sometimes ascribed to a Deuteronomistic editor.

6. For the source analysis and themes of the exilic Deuteronomist in Samuel and Kings, cf. Norbert Lohfink, *Rückeblick im Zorn auf den Staat, Vorlesungen zu ausgewählten Schlüsseltexten der Bücher Samuel und Könige* (Frankfurt, 1984) 44–110, especially 61.

7. For critical discussions of the powerful hermeneutical principles proposed by Brevard Childs, written within the same basic philosophical presuppositions, cf. *JSOT* 16 (1980) the whole issue, and also *Horizons in Biblical Theology: An International Dialogue* (1980, vol. 2, section 2) 113–211. My own critique is published in an article, "The Old Testament, Scripture or Theology," *Interpretation* 35 (1981) 229–42, and further in a book review in *CBQ* (1980) 535–537.

Chapter 13

The Authority of Text and the Liturgy

It would be hard to say what motivated Vatican II to introduce such a concentration of biblical texts into the liturgy. But that concentration has happened, and I would say that the results are uncertain at best. In the liturgy in which I most frequently participate, the biblical texts are read without solemnity from the little liturgical leaflet. Moreover, the reading is uniformly either inaudible, or unintelligible. I take this, not as evidence of a lack of ability on the part of readers, but rather as evidence of an all too generally held conviction that these texts will mean nothing to the faithful.

In this paper I shall concentrate on Old Testament texts, because, even though the problem is identical with texts from the New or Old Testaments or any ancient source, still it is most acutely felt in Old Testament texts, and therefore most easily identified and faced.

In general, ancient texts are a little boring! For example, if you consider the Old Testament reading for the second Sunday in February this year, Isaiah 58:7-10, you discover an exhortation to share your bread with the poor.

> Is it not to share your bread with the hungry, and bring the homeless poor into your house; when you see the naked, to cover him, and not to hide yourself from your own flesh?

This is fine, but in comparison with the various plays we saw on T.V. around Christmas time, carrying this same exhortation, like the musical "Annie," or a familiar Mickey Rooney rerun, or Dickens' "Christmas Carol," poor Isaiah does not have the same impact, to say the very least! And study of the ancient texts does not help. In fact, the more one penetrates to the precise meaning of any ancient text, the sharper and deeper does the problem become. These texts are almost invariably context-specific when read accurately, and only indirectly applicable to diverse contexts of the modern world. For example, the text assigned for the last Sunday in February this year, Leviticus 19:1-2,17-18, urges us to not bear grudges but to love our neighbor as ourselves. That sounds wonderful. However, a closer reading reveals that the neighbor there is specifically defined as a fellow Jew, and the reason for loving that neighbor as oneself is that both of you are different from other people, because Jews are "holy" as others are not. Suddenly the text is a hot potato: we must explain the text away, almost excuse it, rather than be inspired by it!

The problem arises because we tend to look for useful lessons for today in the text. And most homilists feel they have two options: either to simply bypass the readings or to urge their lessons. Moreover, the authorities who chose and assigned these texts appear to have grouped them in ways which favor this approach. This is a crucial error in dealing with ancient texts, and it has led to disaster in our liturgies.

That this is an error is most clearly demonstrated in Bernard Lonergan's wonderful analysis of truth and meaning in *Method in Theology*.[1] He distinguishes a sequence of eight distinct operations which are required to move from ancient text to sermon: first, there is *research* which establishes the actual text accurately in its original form; second, there is *interpretation* which recovers the precise original meaning; third, there is *history* which recovers the significance for life of that meaning in its original context; fourth, there is *dialectic* in which the reader encounters the writer in order to decide whether or not to follow him/her; fifth, there are *foundations* in which readers articulate the criteria for truth which will rule their thinking and choosing; sixth, there are *doctrines* in which readers affirm certain truths on the basis of the foregoing five steps; seventh, there is *systematics* in which a coherent theoretical pattern of explanation is worked out to link doctrines in intelligible systems; and eighth, there is *communication* in which such systematic truth is applied to concrete circumstances of daily living and expressed in appropriate terms. This analysis is extremely precise, and very helpful for anyone working in theology. It is also quite easy to grasp in broad outline, and compelling: all of us do in fact presuppose that all those steps have been taken care of, whether or not we take time to notice it. The point to be made, in the context of this paper, is that when one has arrived at the original meaning of an Old Testament text through *interpretation*, one has not arrived at a lesson for today. There are five further distinct theological operations to work through (history, dialectic, foundations, doctrines, systematics) before one can move from the original meaning of a text to formulating a lesson for today! Between the authority of a text and the urgency of a sermon there must be interposed the complex apparatus of truth. It is the failure to realize this which has been a fundamental error on the part of liturgists and preachers, and which has contributed in some measure to the abandoning of our Churches by all but the most patient of the faithful.

If, therefore, one should not look for lessons in these texts, what should one look for? What is the use of the Old Testament in the liturgy? Clearly preachers could not hope to bring the audience through all of Lonergan's operations in less than three or four hours, even if they were such towering intellectuals as to get through them themselves! This paper will try to answer this question, using for illustration the text assigned for the first Sunday in February this year, namely, Zephaniah 2:3; 3:12-13.

> Seek the Lord, all you humble of the land,
>   who do his commands;
> seek righteousness, seek humility;
>   perhaps you may be hidden
>   on the day of the wrath of the Lord.
>
> For I will leave in the midst of you
>   a people humble and lowly.
>
> They shall seek refuge in the name of the Lord,
>   those who are left in Israel;
>
> they shall do no wrong
>   and utter no lies,
> nor shall there be found in their mouth
>   a deceitful tongue.
> For they shall pasture and lie down
>   and none shall make them afraid.

First, it is essential that readers take notice of their reaction to this text? Did you skip it for the moment, with a view to getting on with the argument? Did you skim it swiftly? Do you feel confused and slightly depressed, or elated by it? At precisely what point in the text did the confusion, depression, or elation occur?

Second, readers should take note now of how they would set about preparing a sermon on the text. Do you think the text is a good basis for a sermon on humility? Or what basis for anything do you find here? Reader reaction is not interesting to the reader alone, and not just anecdotal. Liturgical texts are artistic creations, whose purpose is to express and provoke a reaction. The reaction of the reader tells us a lot about the "meaning" of the text. If you originally didn't really read the text, then perhaps you have joined the majority who expect to learn nothing from Old Testament texts. If you read it, but were merely depressed by it, then possibly the text is bad art. In either case, the sermon will have to begin precisely here.

In this case, as often, the text is not an authentic Old Testament text. Rather, it is a composite of two texts from separate chapters, joined because of commonality of theme. The liturgical authority invokes our respect for the Bible in order to read us a non-biblical text! In doing this, the liturgical authority is carrying on a very ancient tradition: the Bible itself is a composite of texts, and the individual books of the Bible were edited as composites, as anthologies which sometimes have a narrative or logical coherence, and sometimes have a purely extrinsic principle of order. Zephaniah itself, for example, was edited to follow a pattern set for most prophetic books: oracles of doom are heaped together at the beginning, and oracles of salvation are heaped together at the end, with little or no concern for the historical order of their utterance, or even for thematic coherence. In this case, the liturgical authority has linked an oracle from the doom collection with one from the hope collection, thus duplicating in the liturgy the overriding pattern of the Biblical book.

Moreover, Zephaniah, like other prophetic books, was carefully characterized as ancient by an editorial introduction (Zeph 1:1), indicating the precise historical era when the prophet preached. Similarly, the liturgical authority has characterized its text as ancient by ascribing it to Zephaniah, a name from a fabulous past. This technique is designed to produce an effect in the reader. Whether or not we reflect on it, we do not hear these words as addressed to ourselves; rather, we overhear them, as officially recalled for us, being addressed to others in a remote past.

It follows from these two editorial interventions that this text in the liturgy is essentially a dramatic presentation, an artistic event, a performance of literature. If the performance does not succeed, because the audience is ill-disposed to the Old Testament, or because the literary text is artistically deficient, then the homilist must begin by solving these artistic problems. Before we get to lessons, or even to truths, we must deal with literature as art.

What do we overhear in Zephaniah? First there is, in fact, a confusion, because the first verse is spoken by the Zephaniah who threatens doom, whereas the second and third verses, without transition, are spoken by God who promises salvation. The first verse exhorts to humility, but it is a humility born of terror: "perhaps you may be hidden on the day of the wrath of the Lord." This clause bears a cruel, almost gloating, tone for a modern reader who lives in the growing shadow of nuclear winter. It is essential that we identify our reaction: sometimes we have felt nothing because we have escaped feeling by turning off. If this has been our reaction, then probably we do not even hear what follows in the second and third verses, namely, God's loving voice, speaking apparently about us the survivors after the doom is past: "I will leave a people humble and lowly." The anger has past by and we have been spared. We are living in God's protection and love. And God describes us as humble, trusting, innocent, simple, comfortable and unafraid! At the very end there is the image of a flock of sheep, pasturing and resting in tranquility.

Just what is this liturgical text? It is not an exhortation addressed to us: Zephaniah spoke the first verse, and then the second and third verses in two separate exhortations, at different times, to Jews in the reign of Josiah, six hundred years before Christ. He was not describing us. The editors of Zephaniah after the Exile, a hundred years or more later, may have wanted to read it as a description of Jewish communities of that era. But for us in the liturgy it is a literary construct in which we overhear and react to a drama of long ago. It is now, not two, but one oracle, to be understood as a literary unity.

If it is a literary unity, we must reflect on it as such.[2] We must see how it is a unity, feeling and imagining and understanding our way through it as we would any literary text. We must attend to all the data of the text, and to all the nuances of our response as reader. In this case, it is clear that the image of a flock of sheep carries the meaning of the central theme of "humility," and it should control the text. If the liturgical writer has brought this image in only at the end, then the homilist must correct for this artistic failure, perhaps by introducing the image before reading the text. If we now reread the text within that image, imagining ourselves as sheep and hearing God's voice as shepherd from the beginning, the whole feeling and meaning of the text changes. In particular the clause "perhaps you may be hidden on the day of the wrath of the Lord" is experienced with gratitude, as by those who in fact know they have been spared.

We may or may not be, in fact, humble and trusting and simple and so forth. However, it is a stance which we can understand, and which we can adopt for the moment, participating in the artistic structure of the liturgy. It is, in fact, an attitude in prayer. It is the attitude which is implicit in the text, and which the text evokes in us if we do not resist and reject it.

This will be the first, and only essential, task of the homily: to allow the text to work its literary effect on the hearers in the congregation. This is called *interpretation* in Lonergan's scheme of operations. In order to succeed in doing it effectively for a given congregation, the homilist may have to work very hard and very skillfully: a great many shifts may be required in the attitudes and feeling states of the hearers, in their perceptions of meanings, and in their *foundations*. There should result a congregation sharing in a stance before God, a stance of expectancy about God's intervention in life, a stance from which one can easily move to common prayer, or to commonly motivated decisions about activities related to God. The move from a specific shared stance before God to a specific application in life must be done with sensitivity. Trusting sheep at peace with their shepherd will feel urged to virtues and activities only within a specific range. For example, on the basis of this text one would not move easily to an exhortation about contributing to the support of the pastor, or to an exhortation to political activism.

The Nature of Literature

The text, then, is literature. We must ask about the relationship of literature to truth, if we are to understand how to move from text to sermon by passing through the complex apparatus of truth and meaning, as argued above. Northrop Frye has produced a wonderful little book called *The Educated Imagination* in which he collects his most helpful insights and presents them in simple form.[3] In it he shows that literature is radically different from descriptive or scientific writing in that the latter begins with real things and turns them into words, whereas the former begins with imaginative constructs, metaphors, literary forms, and turns these toward real things. To understand literature, then, one has to begin, not with the realities written about, but rather with the images and relationships in the writing.[4] Thus for the Zephaniah text one has to begin not with the historical experience of the Jews originally addressed by Zephaniah, but rather with the images and feelings and ideas which his text grouped together in order to address them. More precisely, we must begin with the images and feelings and ideas which this composite liturgical text has grouped together in order to address us. One must begin in the imagination. Any other approach will fail. This approach begins with the data of the text, data which both the homilist and the congregation have before them and can study together. Any other approach effectively bypasses the text, and requires its own presentation of data. This approach presupposes all the scholarship, now available in every library, which is required to establish the meaning of these words and their original application and feel. But it begins with the words as understood by the imagination, as literary.

A literary author, who writes poetry, or stories, or sermons, is not primarily asserting facts. For example, if "Star Trek IV" states that the spaceship lands in San Francisco in a specific year, and that there are two whales in captivity, one of them pregnant, this contains some implied affirmations about the reality of that city, and about the possibility of whales being captive, and about the threat to their survival, and so forth. A sensitive reader, now or at some future date, will be able to discern quite accurately what is historically real and what is fanciful in the text, and all the degrees of reality in between. However, the primary affirmation of the text is not an affirmation of these realities. If a reader, two hundred years from now, fastens on those realities, he or she will be reading the text, not primarily for its meaning, but rather for the evidence it *unintentionally* contains about life in late nineteenth-century San Francisco.

Now this is true for all literary texts. And it is important to state right away—without wanting to get into a lengthy discussion here about whether modern texts may be purely scientific and objective or purely literary and subjective—that all ancient texts are at least partially literary, and must be read with careful attention to that aspect of their meaning.[5]

The primary affirmation of a literary author, therefore, is not an affirmation about something objective. Rather, it is an affirmation of the author's way of being in the world as unified in the imagination. It is an affirmation of the author's expectancy about meaning, an affirmation that in combining fact, emotion, image, past, present and future in these specific ways, one finds something valuable. It is an affirmation, not only that this literary product is going to sell, but also that it is somehow true in that it embodies a way of looking, thinking and feeling which is human and real and rewarding. Literature expresses an author's way of loving, and it invites conversion on the part of the reader.

The subjective stance of expectancy of the author is never explicit in the text, never directly mentioned. It is implicit there. Because it is implicit, you can't easily argue with it. Rather, it tends to affect you without your fully realizing it. That is the power of a text, as it is the power of a person. That is why we like some texts, and some persons, without being able to give an adequate reason for it. It is not what the text or person says so much as the way they talk, the way they address reality, the hidden agendas, the implicit values, the shaping of love, the way they are. That is why politicians get elected due to their "personality" or "image," and issues are little more than a technique which sometimes forces them to reveal indirectly their inner stance. So literature is a performance in which the author affirms a specific inner stance of expectancy about God and the universe. That is the hidden power of texts and the real authority of the Bible. Biblical literature contains the basic range of foundational expectancies which have founded the Judeo-Christian tradition upon which we live toward the future. That is why it is normative.

It is commonplace, when speaking of literature, to point out that one can never assign its meaning by paraphrasing it.[6] The attempt to paraphrase a poem, or a novel, by saying that it means this or that is simply destructive of literature. It implies that the poem or novel is descriptive writing, rather than literary writing. It implies that if Shakespeare had just been a little smarter, he needn't have written *King Lear* just to say that love cannot be manipulated; or that if the author of Exodus had just been a little more sophisticated he could have described political liberation in a paragraph or two. The fact is that, if literature is not primarily interested in affirming physical facts, it is equally not primarily interested in affirming moral values. Literature cannot be resumed, or simplified, or summed up in a lesson. It is an artistic cry, containing its author in all his or her depth. If Marshall McLuhan has taught us that the medium is the message, surely we have also understood that literature does not contain a message, but rather is a message. The message is the self-affirmation of the author as author. One first feels it, then distinguishes it from other messages, then reacts positively or negatively towards it, loving or hating it. Eventually, one may attempt to point it out to others. That is the role of interpretation. It is a role played by literature teachers. It is also the role of the liturgical preacher.

Liturgical Literature

It must first be said that biblical texts are written in ancient genres far removed from those of today. In particular, historical texts in the Bible are not written in a genre which is purely descriptive on the one hand, or purely literary on the other. And in understanding such texts, one has to begin by developing an accurate feel for the genre used by a given author. However, as we said above, no biblical text is purely descriptive. It follows that all biblical texts must be understood in a way which begins with a literary approach, and which searches for a truth which is not primarily factual or moral, but rather for the truth of a subjective stance, the affirmation of expectancy.

Secondly, it is true that many liturgical texts, like the Zephaniah text above, are composites. They affirm, then, not one authorial attitude, but two or more. As a composite, they are really the artistic creation of the compositor, who often has been a very poor artist indeed! Still, that is the liturgical text, and we have to work with it for the time being. The reading of that text, if well carried out, has affirmed a specific subjective attitude which was implicit in the text, and produced a definite reaction in the hearers. It has produced a reaction which can be influenced, and which can become a shared attitude toward God.

Biblical texts are accepted as the Word of God by the believing community. As a result, hearers who dislike the foundational space implied in them feel that they cannot simply reject the text. They must discuss it, worry about it, understand it differently, or change something fundamental in themselves. Biblical texts are always understood as imposing something central in our psychic life, something about our relationship with God. Hence, these liturgical texts are incredibly powerful tools in correcting, deepening and broadening the spirituality of those who hear them.

It happened that, while working on this paper, I participated in the liturgy for the feast of the Holy Family, at the end of December last year. The homily focused on the second reading, Colossians 3:12-21, and in particular on the exhortation that "you should be clothed in sincere compassion, in kindness, and humility, gentleness and patience . . . (and) put on love." The homilist focused immediately on a lesson found in these words. He expanded on it by going to his Webster's dictionary for definitions of the various virtues enumerated in the text, distinguishing them carefully one from the other, and suggesting concrete examples of each in family life. My seventy-five-year-old mother-in-law loved it, finding it "down do earth." I strove to keep my head from drooping. My teenage children found reading material to occupy their minds! The preacher was charming and witty, but totally without passion. There was no mention of God in this discussion, and no evocation of a spirituality, or of a stance in prayer. He did not bore us by adducing the scholarship which could define the meaning of those words in Hellenistic society two millenia ago. Instead he adduced the irrelevant scholarship of Webster's linguistic research in the last century, finding in it a convenient bridge from Paul's words to my mother-in-law, who was delighted. But he found no bridge from those words to contemporary understanding of human relations as explored passionately month in and month out by novelists, film writers, or T.V. writers. He found no bridge to my children, or even to myself. And yet his text from the Epistle to the Colossians is a marvelous discussion of the Mystical Body of Christ, and of how we must feel united to Christ, with his very own love flowing through our hearts, and of how we must relate to others out of this experience.

If the homilist had not thought to look for a lesson, but rather to feel his way to the God-feeling of the author, he could not have given such a poor sermon. The text is full of passion and power. If the homilist had not immediately conceptualized lessons, but had allowed the text to play with his imagination and feelings, the spontaneous flow of his own thoughts would inevitably have contained more passion, more vitality, more spirituality, than the witty word game which he actually presented. If the homilist had allowed himself to adopt the posture in prayer which is implicit in the text, his thoughts would have spontaneously selected doctrines, images and practices, each of which has its own history and Christian validity, but all of which would have been compatible with the stance of the liturgical text, and appropriate to developing a sermon from it.

Conclusion

We react to people for what they are, for their unthematized attitudes towards ourselves, others, the universe, before reacting to what they actually say. That is the secret of good advertising and selling technique. It begins by striking the right attitude (and industry spends billions of dollars on researching that one thing), before going on to the actual choice of data for the message. Similarly, participants in the liturgy react to the author in a text before they react to the doctrine or lesson drawn from the text.

And they are right. The self-affirmation of the author is what is of value: it affirms a stance in the imagination; it is timeless; it invites to conversion.

Of course, a good sermon goes on to a further step. After establishing a common attitude in prayer, it looks at the world around us in order to express that attitude, and reinforce it, by concrete decisions and practical acts. In response to the Zephaniah text, if we stand as a remnant of simple trusting people around our Shepherd, we might feel drawn, or obliged, to resist and reject all the messages of despair, or cynicism, carried by the media which never leave us alone. We might declare war on the desperate escapism which our civilization urges on us in the face of nuclear danger. We might determine to impose a period of calm on our day, to listen to the news only once a day, to fight advertising for children, to introduce family prayer, and so on and so forth. The possibilities are clearly limitless. Zephaniah would never have thought of things which we would find useful today. But we are merely overhearing Zephaniah in the past in order to become ourselves today before God. And we express that new self in ways which fit our own needs.

Notes

1. Cf. Bernard Lonergan, *Method in Theology* (London: Darton, Longman and Todd, 1972). The interpretation theory which justifies the approach I have taken in this essay is worked out primarily in chapters 1–5 (The Affirmation of Truth in the Bible) in this volume, pp. 7–73.

2. Many homilists feel that they must preach on all three of the appointed texts, finding a common theme. This is invariably ill-advised. The three texts are not a unity, and the effort to make them into one is an artificial intervention which comes between the sermon and the Word-of-God authority of Scripture. Usually, unity is achieved by virtue of some bloodless thematic abstraction, or else some overly clever accommodation of meanings. This approach serves to begin the sermon on a trick of logic, rather than on the religious passion of a biblical author.

3. Cf. Northrop Frye, *The Educated Imagination* (Bloomington: Indiana University Press, 1964).

4. Cf. Northrop Frye, *The Great Code: The Bible and Literature* (Toronto: Academic Press, 1982). In this book, Frye develops a concept of reading the Bible as totally "centripetal," that is, unrelated to reality beyond the imagination. This concept denies the constant intent of the biblical text to refer to reality, even if it begins in imagination. His position here is unacceptable, not only to the preacher, but even to the literary scholar, since it imposes unjustifiably a modern category on an ancient text, namely, the category of pure literature. For an excellent, brief, discussion on the relation between biblical literature and truth, or external referant, cf. Ben. F. Meyer, "Did Paul's View of the Resurrection of the Dead Undergo Developments," *Theological Studies* 47 (1986) 363–387, especially 382–387.

5. This point is well discussed in Northrop Frye, *The Great Code*, 5–30.

6. A compelling demonstration of this point is provided by Cleanth Brooks, *The Well Wrought Urn: Studies in the Structure of Poetry* (New York: Harcourt Brace Jovanovich, 1947).

Chapter 14

Uses and Abuses of the Bible in the Liturgy and Preaching

Introduction

The word "hermeneutics" means simply "theory of interpretation." It can make us nervous because it is radical, and it suggests that maybe we have never quite known what we are talking about. Still we need to think about interpretation both in the Catholic churches and in the Protestant churches.

In the Protestant churches the problem is due mostly to scholarship. Over the last two hundred years, the brilliant contribution of scholarship toward an accurate understanding of the Bible has made biblical texts ever more meaningful to the ancient contexts in which they were written, but ever less applicable to our contemporary spiritual needs. Suddenly the Bible can seem a burden, a wearisome set of problems and uncertainties, rather than a liberating Word of God.

Even the scholars are not happy. Several Protestant Scripture scholars have told me that, for example, they experience the scholarly "documentary hypothesis" concerning the Pentateuch as an oppressive constriction. They are delighted with recent methods of reading Scripture which enable them to break free from those bonds! For others, the ancient meaning of biblical texts represents a conservative authority, an oppressive denial of contemporary knowledge, to the point where they are obliged to read the Bible one way in the university and in an entirely different way in the church. This is deadly for those for whom the Bible is the only Word of God.

In the Roman Church, the problem arises in connection with the liturgy. The Second Vatican Council decided that the liturgy should be in the vernacular, and that meant that the ritual words changed their function from being a sacred sound to being a communication of meaning. Moreover, the council introduced the practice of reading a considerable quantity of biblical texts in the liturgy, texts with which many Catholics had not been very familiar. Since that time, the liturgy, for many, ceased being a prayerful encounter with God, and became rather a failed communication and an aesthetic disappointment.

This problem is crucial. Human beings need liturgy, as much as they need friendship. If the Church does not provide a satisfactory symbolic enactment of our union with God, then people will go elsewhere for it!

Liturgy is essentially an aesthetic act, composed of literary texts, musical compositions, and dramatic activities. In the Roman Mass, we are taught that Christ is truly present in the appearances of bread and wine, and is not present if the bread and wine do not appear to be bread and wine. If the symbol of the Last Supper and of the death of Christ is not artistically present there, if the aesthetic act does not succeed, then the Mass is not valid. Since the Second Vatican Council, the task is more demanding, because now this symbol must be framed within a context of meanings expressed in prayers said in our own language, in readings of Scripture texts, and in a homily. Neither the average parish priest, nor the average Catholic parishioner, is certain about how spiritual truth can be drawn from ancient texts. The readings and the homily often do not provide us with a spiritual meaning. In fact, they sometimes depress us and close off our minds and hearts. Thus, the symbol enacting our union with God is threatened, if not destroyed. The experience of these problems has driven scholars to create a jungle of hermeneutics, in an intense desire to clarify issues of meaning and interpretation, so that Protestants and Catholics may once again find the Bible to be, not a burden, but rather a liberation, a release into the sunlight.

One important step toward a solution will consist in understanding the nature of literature, and the relation between literature and truth, literature and moral judgment, literature and spirituality. The Bible consists of literary texts, written in various literary genres. The Bible does not contain theological texts. The Bible is not written as scientific statement, as factual history, as philosophical thesis, or as logical controversy. All of these are literary conventions unknown to ancient writers. No text of the Bible is written that way. Everybody knows this. But our uncertainty about literature, about the seriousness of literature, and about moving from a literary text to encounter with ultimate Reality, along with our failure to deal with these uncertainties, may have led us, both Catholics and Protestants, into the problems outlined above.[1]

It will be helpful to move to a concrete example, despite the limitations of any example, rather than continue with abstractions and generalities.

An example

Last December I happened to go to Sunday Mass at a parish in New Orleans. It was the feast of the Holy Family, and the liturgy called for reading the following texts : Sirach 3:2-6, 12-14(17); Colossians 3:12-21; Matthew 2:13-15, 19-23.

The sermon was upbeat. It consisted of two developments. The first argued that, despite daily reports of divorce and child abuse in North American families, one must be encouraged by the evidence of significant moral progress through treating wives as truly equal to their husbands, and through respecting the rights and liberty of children. The second reflected on the idea that, although the Scriptures tell us little about the family relations within the Holy Family, still it is evident that each member of that family played an important role in the history of salvation, and each role was diverse from the others and respected by the others. The sermon was, then, a moral exhortation to mutual respect.

Refined as this exhortation was, it must be noted that I can remember no effective invocation of Church, or Eucharist, or mystery, or Trinity, as the basis for our practice of respect. So the sermon was weak. Moreover, no attempt was made to relate the message to specific texts of the Bible, and certainly not to any of the texts we had just read. As a result, the reading of three scriptural texts was made irrelevant. These were not easy texts. Their reading had set in motion a set of images and a series of questions in my mind, an involvement with the Spirit and a beginning of prayer, which were simply broken off by the sermon. It was as though an orchestra played the overture to a symphony, and suddenly broke off and played a sonata written by another composer. In effect, the rest of the Mass then followed after the sermon as though the Scripture had never been read, so great was the *caesura*, the artistic gap, introduced between the texts and the sermon.

That admirable New Orleans homilist, whose liturgical style was otherwise prayerful and elegant and graceful, had all but cut off my experience of union with God. Now the fault was not primarily his. It was the liturgical authority which, in assigning readings, led him astray.

If we start with the Sirach text, we have first to notice that the text assigned had excluded verses 7-11. Verses 15-16 were also excluded. Verse 17 was placed in brackets, with the foreseeable effect that the reader did not read verse 17 at all. In fact the leaflet published by the Oregon Catholic Press, and distributed at the door of the church, did not print verse 17. There results a text which begins, "The Lord sets a father in honor over his children; a mother's authority he confirms over her sons," and which ends, "For kindness to a father will not be forgotten, it will serve as a sin offering—it will take lasting root." The reduced text reads easily, and seems to present a very simple idea. In fact, the reader should see for him/herself that it is difficult to move beyond the unidimensional idea that children must honor and obey their father (and also their mother), first because God orders this, and second because God will reward compliance. That is a pretty thin idea! Can one blame the priest for not trying to build a sermon on it? Especially when there were virtually no children present at the Mass!

But how about the omitted verses? This is after all a literary text. And the very first, and only really rigid, rule in literary theory is that texts must be read from beginning to end, as the meaning of each word is not determined by definition (as it is in scientific and theoretic writing) but only by the relations of all elements of the whole text to all others. Of course, parts of texts may have some independent integrity, but certainly within any part of a text, you simply denature the meaning when you cut out words and sentences.

Moreover, I would contend that no literary text, and no biblical text, expresses such a linear and unidimensional thought as was suggested above as the meaning of the reduced text. Scientific and theoretical writing may want to define concepts and secure logics in such a way as to achieve a single univocal meaning. But literary writing has an entirely different aim. It aims to communicate the experience of the author to the reader, and to communicate that experience in a unified form which is shaped in such a way that the reader can be expected to reach the preconceptual insight which the author has arrived at. Thus, for example, a national anthem will evoke images and feelings and ideas and historical moments all at once, so as to convey a unified attitude and understanding about one's country. This attitude and understanding could, perhaps, be broken down into psychological components, factual components, political components which could be expressed conceptually in psychological jargon, historical summary, political theory. But the national anthem does not do this. Rather, it expresses a whole human way of being in the world, a composite of awareness which is wonderfully bound into a single artistic experience, a single preconceptual insight.

Now chapter 3 of Sirach is not the most powerful passage in the Bible, but still it is literary in nature, and thus far richer than the reduced text might lead one to perceive. Moreover, like all biblical (literary) texts, it includes a perception of God's presence and activity within its way of being in the world. One has to read it as one reads all literature, that is, patiently and repeatedly, with a readiness to glimpse a hitherto unknown dimension. A reader has simply not understood a biblical literary text until he or she has come to share the author's experience of God in the world, and to share the artistic insight which unifies it. The prerequisite here is, sometimes the scholarship which is easily found in commentaries, and always a depth of faith which can reach towards the faith of the author.

In this perspective, we should attempt to read Sirach 3:2-16(17). Not that the shortened text contained only a trivial idea, but only that the shortened text easily led to a trivial idea.

Sirach 3:2-16(17)

Verse 17 is properly placed in brackets, for it is the first verse in the unity which follows (vv. 17-24). Still, a following text is always linked to what precedes, and in this case verse 17 can even be read as a suggestive conclusion: "My son, perform your tasks in meekness; then you will be loved by those whom God accepts." The virtue desired here is "meekness," and meekness is a natural companion to "respect," the virtue extolled in verses 2-16. The fruit of meekness will be that you "will be loved" by those who are "accepted" by God, that is, the chosen ones, the elect. This is not in the next life, but rather the elect in this life. The movement of thought here is in the area of a sacred community: meekness enhances one's status in a community of love.

The preceding chapters (i.e., 1–2) consist of an analysis of, and exhortation to, the "fear of God." In Sirach "fear" is a word which denotes the central experience of religion, the experience for which Luther used the word "faith," the medieval theologians use the word "sanctifying grace," and which the mystics treated dynamically in terms of "way of union."

Our text, then, at the beginning of chapter 3, is a first application of this fear of God, relating it to status in the community. It develops the idea of honoring father and mother. Verse 7 will say: "Whoever fears the Lord will honor his father; he will serve his parents as his masters." And in the other verses of our text the notion of honoring is progressively related to many other family interactions: obedience, praise, not dishonoring, blessing, respect, helping, not grieving, kindness, not forsaking, not angering, and in verse 17 meekness and love. There is built up an image, not just of one-to-one obedience, but of the complex mutuality of a whole family over generations, and the strength of such assured mutual support. This social structure is presented as the place of grace, the place which God blesses, the place where one's love for God flourishes. The causal links are not simple, such as the idea that obedience causes divine rewards. Rather, they are complex and reversible. Verse 6, then, is not a failure of parallel logic, perhaps needing emendation, but rather is an apt crossing of ideas: "Whoever glorifies his father will have long life; and whoever obeys the Lord will refresh his mother."

In fact, verse 6 would be an excellent place to begin one's sermon, once one has understood what experience of God Sirach was trying to embody and communicate in this text. On the face of it, the opening clause is patently false: "whoever glorifies his father will have long life!" And the second clause seems almost offensive, as it might seem to suggest that one should obey God in order to please one's mom. This is the kind of line which, in reading literature, one stumbles over, and then stops to puzzle over. One recognizes that it is a key to opening a door: either this author is a fool, or else I am still reading this text without the correct initial insight. Probably the author is no fool. So when I understand this line, the key will fit, and my eyes will be open.

When one understands that glorifying one's father is understood in Sirach 3:2-16 as an extension of one's love of God or fear of God, and as part of a whole network of family strengths, then one can well understand that glorifying one's father will normally result in long life, and even in eternal life. Similarly, obeying God, where the ancient word for "obey" is the same word as "hear," is clearly not something one does in order to please one's mother! It is a gift from God. The psychic spin-off, if I may speak in those terms, of "hearing God" will quite naturally find expression in a positive relationship with one's mother. One feels this is true, and the Bible authorizes one to affirm that it is true.

At that point, one might ask why this is so. This would be a specifically theological question, since classically theology is defined as "faith in search of understanding." And the answer can, in fact, be found in theological studies of the act of faith, which analyse its content and its effects. The sermon could go into that kind of material, or it could stop short of theology, and turn to the simple purpose of the text itself, namely, to urge the cultivation of family respect and love as experience of union with God.

Thus, the sermon which the pastor in New Orleans gave was on the right topic. Unfortunately, the shortened and denatured text, which doubtless led him to this topic, did not easily lead him to the reflection demanded by a complete literary text. And, apart from Sirach, there was nothing else to help him find a spiritual dimension, a divine presence, within the ethical discussion of respect between family members. His sermon was stuck at the level of good advice, without finding a way to a level of prayer or theology, and without conscious scriptural reference.

Sirach 3 is pretty blatantly an exhortatory text, leading directly to exhortatory preaching. But, as we have seen, biblical texts are always literary. They always have a fuller dimension, as they present, not a simple message, but an author's experience of God. I would suggest that literature is always serious, and always reveals some depths of experience. That is why it is so surprisingly hard to write literature, as only those who have tried can realize. Literature is not just a clever form. It is always also, at least to some degree, an objectification of the self. And the self is inevitably some kind of message, some kind of demand, upon others. Scriptural literature must not be read for theological doctrines, or for laws of conduct. It must be respected as literature, and read for mystery, for presence of God to the writer, for total way of being in the world.

Matthew 2:13-23

We turn now to the third text assigned for this liturgy. I must first point out that the same liturgical authority denatured (or "deliteratured") this text as well, by excluding verses in the middle. Whoever made this decision, excluded the reference to the slaughter of the innocents, and doubtless thought thereby to focus better on the theme of the feast of the Holy Family. There is no need to repeat here the points made above about literary texts, beyond noting that the effort to focus on the Holy Family apparently prevented the New Orleans pastor from finding any meaning in this text which he could use in his sermon! This well-intentioned liturgical authority denatured the text by disguising its literary character, and thereby rendered it relatively useless.

We must first discover God in this text. What experience of God does the text embody? What authorial self-before-God, self-as-experiencing-God, is presented in this text? Only when we have answered this question should we proceed to the writing of a sermon.

It is clear that the text has three parts, each one of which ends with a citation from the Old Testament. First, after recounting the flight to Egypt, verse 15 cites the last half of Hosea 11:1, the whole of which reads : "When Israel was a child I loved him, and out of Egypt I have called my son." In the second part, after telling the story of the slaughter of the innocents, Matthew cites Jeremiah 31:15: "A voice was heard in Ramah, wailing and loud lamentation, Rachel weeping for her children; she refused to be consoled, because they were no more." And finally, in a third section, after the return to Nazareth, we have a reference to Isaiah 11:1, which plays on words to connect the name Nazareth to Isaiah's prophecy of a Savior to be born in the family of David. Matthew made use of these stories, with whatever degree of factuality they embody, in order to be able to cite the Old Testament texts and refer them to Jesus the infant. Matthew's meditation is about the infant, not as a cute little tyke, not as a helpless and endangered child, but precisely as embodying major themes of the history of Israel.

First, just as Israel became Yahweh's people by being freed from slavery in Egypt (and continued as Yahweh's people by being returned from exile), so Jesus is to be understood as one who had to be exiled to Egypt in order to be freed by his Father. And second, just as Israel's great mystery and ongoing meditation, was the problem of evil as experienced in disaster at the hands of Assyrians and Babylonians, so this infant's life was to be marked by lamentation. And third (as Micah had foretold that the Messiah would be born in Bethlehem and Jesus was born in Bethlehem, so), Isaiah had referred to salvation from Nazareth and Jesus was brought up in Nazareth.

Well, all of that is clever enough, but so what? What spiritual message can I get out of that fancy footwork? Does it strengthen my faith? No wonder the New Orleans pastor skipped this text when he thought of writing a sermon. Even in its longer form, it does not seem to have a message. . . . Clearly, we have not yet got to God in the text. We are not experiencing what Isaiah experienced when he wrote it, nor are we in possession of the insight he wanted to communicate. We have traced some lines of logic in this text. But what world of meaning, what self-in-God's world is Matthew evoking here?

If we read the text again, looking for the key which gives meaning to it, we can sense that Matthew seems to be dwelling on the presence of God in Israel's history: God who is revealed in the Exodus experience which the Jews recover every year in their paschal liturgy; God who is revealed in the anguish over the Exile, which is the subject of so many of the Old Testament books; God who was gloriously manifest in the magical time of David. All of this rich awareness of God's presence in history is evoked, and is applied to Jesus at his very humble birth. This is a colossal act of faith. One either believes it or one does not. (Or one does not quite admit one way or another . . . .) An infant with these dimensions . . .! My whole sense of wonder, mystery, suffering, terror, hope is to be discovered in this single male baby! "What is man that thou art so mindful of him, and a son of man that thou dost so care for him!", to paraphrase Psalm 8. This is the experience of Matthew, and his preconceptual insight, which he tries to express in a literary form.

Such a shaped experience, if we share it, makes a lot of diverse demands upon us. In the context of the feast of the Holy Family, one might be drawn to consider the respect we must have for each child, and for each individual member of the family. Each one, my mother, my father, my sister, my brother, my daughter, my son, each one has been given dimensions of meaning in Christ which makes each life valuable beyond my imagination. What respect should I show! What care could be too much in assuring supportive relations, in reconciling differences, in forgiving failings! And so forth.

Once again we have fallen into line with the sermon given by the pastor in New Orleans. But once again we have got there with spiritual dimensions still attached, and in direct reference to the biblical text. It is only by taking the time, by accepting to reread and reread this text as literature, that we have managed to link the liturgical text both to our concrete life today and to a symbol of our union with God.

Conclusion

The point of all this is that biblical texts must be read as literature, and the homily must begin as would a good class about a piece of literature, so that the being-with-God expressed by the author is shared in the congregation. Any other way of reading Scripture is abusive in itself, and useless to liturgy.

In the Roman Church a reform is needed. We must review the lists of texts assigned to the various days, and restore their literary character. It will probably be necessary to reduce the number of texts each day: far better one longer text, or at most two texts which really do speak to each other.

Once one begins to treat the texts as literary texts, then the scholarship of the past two centuries ceases to be a problem. Rather, it becomes a precious contribution. If the preacher begins by puzzling over the spiritual world of a given text, certain precise questions will arise. These will be questions for which the homilist will have a personal curiosity. Usually, such questions will be precisely the ones which previous readers and scholars have looked into. At that point, recourse to the excellent commentaries now available will be a delight.

Note

1. There is a wonderful short history of some of this hermeneutical confusion in Edgar V. McKnight, *Post-Modern use of the Bible: The Emergence of Reader-Oriented Criticism* (Nashville: Abingdon Press, 1988) chapter 1. McKnight's phrase is "making sense of" the biblical text, and what follows in this article is an attempt to define more precisely the kind of "sense" we can legitimately make of biblical texts. The basic source of this presentation lies in the work of Bernard Lonergan, *Method in Theology* (London: Darton, Longman and Todd, 1972), especially chapters 3 and 7. A fuller presentation of the theoretical basis for my position may be found in S. McEvenue, *Interpreting the Pentateuch* (Collegeville: The Liturgical Press, 1990).

Author Index

Ackroyd, P.R., 121, 122
Alonso-Schokel, L., 22
Alter, R., 22
Aquinas, T., 61, 108, 109
Augustine, 9, 25, 105–106, 112, 119

Barr, J., 139
Baum, G., 62
Beardsley, M. C., 111
Begrich, J., 60
Bellarmine, R., 119, 122
Blake, W., 19, 85, 94
Blenkinsopp, J., 30–31, 38, 139
Blum, E., 111
Bonino, J. M., 122
Borklund, E., 36
Bovon, F., 141
Broderick, J., 122
Brooks, C., 22, 38, 49–50, 51–52, 63, 111, 167
Brown, R. E., 62

Campbell, A., 156
Cazelles, H., 139
Chardin, T. de, 21
Chesterton, G. K., 123
Childs, B. S., 25, 37, 38, 62, 63, 111, 121, 123, 139, 157
Clements, R. E., 63
Clifford, R. J., 39
Clines, D. J. A., 52–55, 63
Coats, G. W., 111
Croce, B., 88

Cross, F. M., Jr., 34, 38, 39, 122
Crowe, F. E., 62
Crüseman, F., 63
Culler, J., 26, 37, 38, 80, 84
Curie, M., 44

Davies, J. G., 122
Davis, C., 81, 83, 84
De la Mare, W., 50–51
Denzinger, H., 112
Derrida, J., 16, 22, 29, 40, 80, 96, 111
Dickens, C., 13, 81, 82, 158
Donne, J., 49
Duhaime, J., 139
Durkheim, E., 22

Eagleton, T., 22
Eichrodt, W., 48, 62
Eissfeldt, O., 117
Eliot, G., 82
Eliot, T. S., 50, 74, 77–79
Elliger, K., 111
Euclid, 15

Fahey, M., 62
Fallon, T., 5
Flanagan, J. W., 156, 157
Flannery, E. H., 64
Fohrer, G., 63, 121
Foucault, M., 80
Fowles, J., 81
Frei, H., 37

Freud, S., 26, 115, 122
Frick, F., 118
Frye, N., 9–10, 22, 25, 37, 38, 85–94,
  110, 138–139, 163, 167

Gagné, J., 5
Gadamer, H.-G., 29, 36, 111, 138
Galileo, 91
Gelin, A., 63
Gibbon, E., 87
Gottwald, N. K., 117, 122
Greeley, A. W., 80
Grindel, J., 124
Guillet, J., 63
Gunkel, H., 22, 58–60, 139, 140
Gunn, D., 121, 122, 157
Gutiérrez, G., 122

Hartman, G., 38
Haspecker, J., 139
Hefling, C. C., 64
Hemingway, E., 78, 79
Hirsch, E. D., 36
Homer, 74–76, 79, 80
Horace, 80
Horgan, M. P., 37

Jeremias, J., 63
Jung, C., 76, 115, 122
Jüngling, H.-W., 140

Keats, J., 80
Keesh-ke-mun, 76–77, 79, 80
Kelsey, D., 37
Kermode, F., 22, 81, 82, 83, 84
Kilian, R., 63, 140
Kittel, B., 139
Klauck, H. J., 112
Koch, K., 140
Krauss, H.-J., 62

Lamb, M., 5
Landes, G. M., 139
Leavis, F. R., 9, 36, 110, 138
Lentricchia, F., 36, 139
Lessing, D., 38

Lodge, D., 84
Lohfink, N., 111, 112, 122, 139, 157
Lonergan, B., 5, 8, 22, 30, 37, 38,
  46–49, 51, 52, 55, 57, 58, 60,
  61–62, 63, 64, 80, 83, 112, 113,
  121, 139, 159–160, 162, 167, 176
Longinus, C., 74–76, 80
Loyola, I., 35
Luther, M., 72, 172

Machiavelli, N., 119
Malinowski, B., 22
Mallory, T., 82, 109
Marx, K., 16
Massie, R. K., 122
Matarasso, P. M., 112
McEvenue, S., 37, 46, 63, 64, 73,
  110, 111, 112, 139, 140, 157, 176
McKnight, E. V., 73, 176
McLuhan, M., 164
McShane, P., 121
Metz, J. B., 122
Meyer, B. F., 5, 81, 84, 86, 94, 112,
  167
Miller, D. J., 141
Miller, H., 139
Mills, J. S., 80
Milton, J., 19, 23
Murphy, R. E., 139

Nadeau, J. G., 6
Noth, M., 63, 121, 122

Outler, A., 5

Perlitt, L., 63
Pitt-Rivers, J., 22
Plato, 36, 80, 119, 153
Polzin, R., 38
Pope, A., 80
Poulet, G., 36, 139

Quesnell, Q., 64

Rad, G. von, 48, 63, 114, 121, 122,
  139

Rahner, K., 112, 120
Ratzinger, J., 62
Rendtorff, R., 123
Rettig, J. W., 112
Riley, P., 5
Robert, A., 111
Rost, L., 143, 156
Rouiller, G., 141
Ruprecht, E., 111
Ryan, J. J., 122

Sand, G., 9
Sandburg, C., 10–11, 17
Sartre, J. P., 83
Schleiermacher, F., 64
Schmitt, H.-C., 73
Shakespeare, W., 23, 164
Sheppard, G. T., 37
Smend, R., 139
Smith, M., 62
Sparks, M., 82
Sternberg, M., 22
Stevens, W., 94
Suarez, F. de, 119
Sutton, V., 80
Sutton, W., 80
Swetman, J., 141

Tennyson, A., 109
Tolkien, J. R. R., 72
Tompkins, J. P., 46, 112
Tucker, G. M., 64

Untermeyer, L., 50–51, 63

Valaskakis, G., 80
van Imschoot, P., 48, 62
Van Seters, J., 123
Vaux, R. de, 117, 122
Vawter, B., 139
Voegelin, E., 122

Warren, W., 80, 110
Weber, M., 120
Weimar, P., 123
Wellek, R., 110, 138
Wellhausen, J., 117, 123
Westermann, C., 38, 58–61, 64, 139, 140, 141
Wilson, R. R., 39
Wimsatt, W. K., 111
Wohlmuth, J., 112
Wolffe, H. W., 55–57, 60, 63, 122, 139, 140
Wordsworth, W., 19, 103, 112
Wright, T. R., 110
Whybray, R. N., 156

Yeats, W. B., 49

Zenger, E., 73
Zimmerli, W., 63, 111

Biblical Index

Genesis	19, 22, 87, 136, 139	16	96, 97, 125, 126, 129, 135
1:1–2:4a	93	16:2-6	125
1	21, 22, 25	16:9-10	135
1:3	29	16:14	68
2–11	70, 136	18:17-18	56
2	68	18:22b-23	56
2:2-3	102	20–22	124, 129, 135
2:4a	55	20	71, 124, 125, 126, 127, 129, 130, 132, 133, 135, 139
2:4b-3	69		
3	68		
4	69	20:1-8	124
6–9	87	20:1-2a	125
6:5-8	56	20:1	128, 133
8:21-22	56	20:2	128, 135
11	53, 69	20:2a	133, 139
12:1–13:4	65, 70	20:2b	125, 134
12	70, 125, 126, 135	20:3-17	128
12:1-3	63, 70, 136	20:3	125, 128, 132, 134
12:1-4a	55, 56, 57	20:4-5	128, 134
12:3	71	20:6-7	128, 134
12:3b	56	20:6	125, 132, 135
12:4-7	70	20:7	125, 132, 140
12:8-9	70	20:8	127, 128, 134
12:10–13:2	70	20:9-10	128, 134
12:10	71	20:9	134
12:10ff.	135, 140	20:10	134
12:11	71	20:10a	134
12:14	71	20:11-13	128, 131, 134
12:15	71	20:11	128
12:17	71	20:13	125, 126, 133
13:3-4	70	20:14-16	128, 134
14:22	69	20:15-16	132
15	136		

20:16	133
20:17-18	134–135
20:17	125, 128, 140
20:17a	129
20:18	125, 128, 135
21	126, 127, 128, 130, 135
21:1-7	124
21:8-21	124, 128, 131, 139
21:8	131
21:9-10	125
21:9	131
21:9a	128
21:9b	139
21:10	131
21:11	125, 127
21:12-13	132
21:12	125, 127
21:13	133
21:14	125, 128, 132
21:14a	127
21:15-16	132
21:16	125, 127
21:17-18	132
21:17	132
21:17a	127
21:19-20	125
21:20	132
21:22-34	129
21:22ff.	129
21:27	129
21:31	68
21:33	69
22	37, 125, 126, 127, 128, 130, 134, 135 136, 137, 139, 140
22:1-13	124
22:1-19	139
22:1	127, 130, 134
22:1a	130
22:1b	130
22:1b-2	130
22:2	125
22:3-6	130
22:3	125, 128, 130, 131
22:5	130

22:6-8	127
22:7-8	130
22:8	140
22:9-10	125, 131
22:11-13	125
22:11	131
22:12	127
22:14	140–141
22:15-18	37, 136
22:19	124
23:16-18	88
26	126
26:1-16	71
26:1	135
26:8	125
32:30	68
32:32	69
47:13ff.	63
Exodus	35, 71, 84, 105, 164
12:32	56
15	33, 36
15:1-12	34
15:1-21	34
15:1	34
15:3	34
15:5	34
15:8	34
15:12	34
15:13	60
15:13-18	34
15:16	34
15:17-18	34
15:17	60
15:19-21	34
16:1–17:1	97
16	98, 102, 103, 104, 105, 106, 107, 108, 109, 110, 111
16:1	97
16:1-2	98
16:2-3	98, 105, 111
16:2-8	97, 98
16:2	99
16:2a	100
16:4-5	98, 99

16:4	98, 104, 111, 112
16:4a	98
16:4b	98
16:5	98
16:6-7	98, 99, 111
16:6-15	98
16:6a	100
16:6b	100, 111
16:7a	99, 100
16:8	99
16:9-15	97, 99
16:9a	100
16:10a	100
16:10b	99, 100
16:12	99
16:13	99
16:13-14	102
16:15	99
16:15a	100
16:16-19	99
16:16-21	97, 99
16:16	98, 111
16:19	99
16:20	99
16:20b	98, 102
16:21	99
16:22-26	100
16:22-31	97, 100
16:23	98, 102, 111
16:23b	100
16:27	100
16:28-29	100
16:28a	98
16:28b	102
16:30-31	100
16:31	102
16:32-34	97, 100
16:32	111
16:32a	100
16:32b	100
16:33a	100
16:33b	100
16:34b	100
16:35-36	97
17:1	97
22:25ff.	63

24ff.	102
32–34	69
37–50	73

Leviticus
1–9	102
8	122
19:1-2	158
19:17-18	158

Numbers	56
11	98, 102, 103, 111
11:6	103
11:7-9	102
13–14	37
14	97, 111
14:1-5	97
14:1a	111
14:1b	111
14:2	111
14:3-4	111
14:5	111
20	111
24:9b	56
25:5	55

Deuteronomy
	106, 112, 115, 116
1:19-46	37
3:11	88
4:2	25, 42
4:5-8	104
4:10-24	37
4:32-40	104
8	103, 104, 109
8:2-3	107
8:3	104
8:14-16	107
17:14-20	152
17:14ff.	115–116
17:16-17	116

Joshua
5	103, 104, 109
5:12	104

Judges
5   34, 35
19   133, 140
19:1-30a   140
19:3-10   133
19:20b-28   130
19:21   140
19:22-26   133
19:29   133

1 Samuel   117, 121, 157
6:17-18   88
7–12   152
7:3-4   152
8   119
8:4-22   116
8:6-20a   152
10:18-19   152
12:6-25   152
14:47-52   121
15–2.8   157
15   121
16   121
16–2.8   113
16:1-3   118
16:1-13   114, 117
16:14-23   114
17:12-15   114
17:42   114
17:55-58   114
18:1-4   121
20:13-17   121
20:30-31   121
21:10-15   114
24   114, 121
24:1-7   121
26   114, 121
26:1-12   121
27:1-7   114
29   121
31   121

2 Samuel   117, 121, 157
1   121
2:4   121
2:31-39   121

4   121
5:3   121
6–7   121
7   118
7:11b-16   116
8:15-18   121
9–15   145
9–20   115, 121, 142, 156
9   143, 146, 148
9:1   144, 148
9:3   148
9:4   142
9:5   142
9:9-10   148
9:9-13   115
9:11   148
9:12   143
9:13   148
10–12   149
10   146, 147, 149, 151
10:1-2   144
10:12-14   144
10:12   150, 154
10:17   149
10:18   144
11–12   144
11   115, 146
11:4   146
11:6   146
11:8   147
11:10   146
11:11   146
11:12   146
11:18-21   149
11:18-24   147
11:26   146
11:27   146, 151
12   144, 147, 149, 151
12:1-4   147
12:10-14   151
12:11   150
12:15   151
12:18-23   147
12:22   151
12:24-25   143, 152
12:24   146

12:25	150		18:2-4	149
12:27-28	147		18:2	143
12:27-30	149		18:5	143, 144
13–18	144		18:12	143
13	147		18:19-33	147
13:3	145		18:19	152
13:12-13	145, 147		18:28	152
13:19	147		18:31	152
13:20-36	147		18:33	144
13:20	147		19–20	144, 147, 151
13:39	115		19	148
14–18	151		19:1-8	115, 149
14	147, 148		19:11-15	149
14:1-3	149		19:18-20	144
14:11	151		19:22	144, 152
14:17	146, 151		19:24-29	115
15	147		19:29	143, 148
15:1-6	147		19:31-40	143
15:7-12	147		20	149
15:9-22	143		20:6	149
15:24-28	147		20:16	145
15:25-26	150, 154		21:19	114
15:31	151			
15:32-37	147		**1 Kings**	117, 157
16	147, 150		1–2	115, 121, 142, 144,
16:1-4	115			147, 156, 157
16:4	143, 148		1	115, 118, 147, 150,
16:5-14	149			156
16:8	144		1:6	115
16:11-12	144		1:11-31	149
16:12	144, 150		1:12	146
16:15-19	147		1:22-23	150
16:20-23	147		2	147, 152, 156
16:21-23	151		2:1-4	149
16:23	146		2:5-9	115, 150
17	147		2:5	149
17:7	146		2:6	145
17:11	146		2:9	145
17:14	146, 152		2:15	152
17:15	146		2:27	151
17:21	146		2:32-33	151
17:23	146		2:33	152
17:27-29	143		2:39-40	143
17:27	142		2:42-46	151
18–19	149		2:46	143
18	147		3–11	91, 115

3	156
4:29-34	91
2 Kings	117, 157
18:22	115, 116
25:27-30	116
1 & 2 Chronicles	37, 119
Ezra	
1:7-11	112
9	129
10	129
Job	67–68, 131
28:14	90
28:23-27	90-91
Psalms	41, 42, 58
2	114
8	25, 175
8:4-6	25
47	63
77:25	109
78	102
78:24-25	102
Proverbs	41, 68
1:6	68
16:1	154
16:3	154
16:9	154
16:10	155
24:21-22	155
25:1	155
25:3	155
29:26	155
Song of Songs	20, 21
Isaiah	20, 42, 60, 89, 158
6	60
6:3	59
11:1	174

19:23-25	63
58:7-10	158
Jeremiah	37, 42, 89, 116
1:5	114
4:1-2	63
31:15	174
44:15-19	116
Ezekiel	
33:31-32	23
Hosea	
11:1	174
Amos	44
Jonah	
4:11	100
Micah	175
Zephaniah	161, 163, 165, 167
1:1	161
2:3	160
3:12-13	160
Zechariah	
8:13	63
8:23	63
Wisdom of Solomon	45, 105
1:13-15	105
16:20-21	97
19:10	105
19:21	97
Sirach	139, 172
1–2	172
3	171, 172, 173
3:2-6	170, 172
3:2-16	172, 173
3:2-16(17)	172–174
3:6	172
3:7-11	170

3:7   172
3:12-14   170
3:15-16   170
3:17-24   172
3:17   170, 172
44–50   37
50   122

Matthew
1:18-25   140
2:13-15   170
2:13-23   174–176
2:15   174
2:19-23   170
5:18   25, 89

Luke   42, 88
1–2   140
12:22-32   111
16:16-17   25

John   62
6   105, 109
6:25-34   105
6:25-59   106
6:26-27   106
6:26   105
6:29   105
6:30-31   106
6:32-33   106
6:47-49   106
6:51-59   107

6:57-58   106
16:7   112
18:33-38   122
20   88–89
20:29   87

Acts   88

Romans
5:5   113

1 Corinthians
10:16-17   108
11:24-25   111
11:29   106

Galatians
3:8   63
4:29   140

Colossians   165
3:12-21   165, 170

Hebrews   141
1:1   31
2:6-9   25
11   37

**Revelation/
Apocalypse**   67, 68, 84
21:1   93
22:18-19   25, 42

DATE DUE

JUN 3 0 1999			
MAY 24 '00			